RAIN MAKER

NEIL PLUMRIDGE | ROBERT NASON

RAIN MAKER

How the Best Consultants Think, Act, and Win in an AI-Accelerated World

WILEY

Published by John Wiley & Sons, Inc., Hoboken, New Jersey.

For general information on our other products and services or for technical support, please contact our Customer Care Department within the United States at (800) 762-2974, outside the United States at (317) 572-3993 or fax (317) 572-4002.

Wiley also publishes its books in a variety of electronic formats. Some content that appears in print may not be available in electronic formats. For more information about Wiley products, visit our web site at www.wiley.com.

Library of Congress Cataloging-in-Publication Data:

ISBN 9781394440672 (Cloth)
ISBN 9781394440689 (ePub)
ISBN 9781394440696 (ePDF)

Cover Design: Wiley
Cover Image: Lidia Shapoval/Getty Images
Author Photos: Courtesy of the Authors

SKY10163843_072926

AI Disclosure

In writing this book, we made considered use of a range of AI-enabled research and writing tools, including but not limited to OpenAI's ChatGPT, Anthropic's Claude, Grammarly, Google Gemini, Perplexity AI, and other AI-powered assistants. These tools supported us in tasks such as language refinement, structural editing, grammar review, summarizing complex material, and accelerating research synthesis.

At every stage, final interpretations, conclusions, and the creative expression of ideas remain entirely our own. The authors retain full responsibility for the accuracy, integrity, and originality of all content. The use of these technologies was guided by professional judgment, ethical intent, and a commitment to enhancing clarity and reader value, never as a substitute for human thought, expertise, or experience.

To a century of problem solvers who made their clients better.
And to the next generation, who will be called to do
the same, only more so and in a more complex world.

A rainmaker is a top-tier performer who possesses a rare ability to cultivate and leverage strategic relationships, consistently originating significant new business and material opportunities. In an era where clients are more informed and choice is abundant, rainmakers differentiate themselves through relevance, teamwork, judgment, and their ability to shape the right opportunities early. They typically deliver five to ten times the results of the average performer and are often decisive in winning their firm's most important deals.

Contents

Introduction

There was a moment in my consulting career when something didn't quite add up.

On paper, things were going well. The numbers were strong. The work was solid. Clients were satisfied. By most measures, I was progressing exactly as a consultant should.

And yet, before certain meetings, I felt an unease I couldn't quite explain.

It wasn't fear exactly. It was something quieter. A small question sitting at the back of my mind: *Do I really belong in this room?*

Consulting has a way of placing people in situations like that. You find yourself sitting across from executives responsible for decisions worth billions of dollars. Their industries are shifting quickly. Their boards expect answers. Their careers are often on the line.

And you're there to help.

Early in your career the tension is obvious. You wonder whether you're experienced enough, credible enough, ready for responsibilities that seem slightly ahead of you.

Later the feeling changes shape but rarely disappears. The stakes grow. The conversations become less scripted. Clients care less about polished analysis and more about whether they can rely on your judgment.

At some point most consultants discover that expertise alone isn't enough.

Understanding that difference is part of becoming truly effective in this profession.

I began to see it clearly during a client visit to Mumbai.

■ ■ ■

The motorbike cut through the traffic with far more confidence than I felt.

Mumbai surrounded us on every side. The noise was constant—horns, engines, voices, music drifting through the heat. Rickshaws slipped between cars. Buses advanced with determination rather than precision. The air carried the dense mixture of diesel, dust, spices, and street food.

I held onto the back of the seat and tried not to think too much about the fact that I had no helmet.

This was not how most consulting engagements begin.

The man driving the bike was my client, the chief operating officer of a fast-growing telecommunications company. He seemed entirely comfortable navigating the city's traffic, dressed in a crisp white shirt and dark jacket that suggested he had somewhere more formal to be later in the day.

Our morning had started in a familiar setting: a modern office tower, good coffee, a structured discussion about market growth and competitive positioning.

Then he stood up, checked his watch, and said, "If you want to understand this business properly, come with me."

Ten minutes later we were weaving through the streets.

Eventually he pulled into a narrow alley far from the glass towers of the financial district.

The place was crowded with small stalls selling mobile phones and accessories.

Screens flickered from every direction. Vendors called out to customers while negotiating loudly with one another. Music played from small speakers balanced on plastic tables.

The COO stepped off the bike and glanced around.

"This," he said quietly, "is where the real business happens."

For the next hour I followed him through the market.

He greeted people by name. He asked questions. Sometimes he negotiated directly; other times he simply listened. Conversations moved quickly but never felt rushed. Deals were made in minutes.

There were no slides, no spreadsheets, no prepared talking points.

Just conversations.

Just relationships.

Just connection.

Watching him work felt like observing a different language of business.

Until then most of my consulting training had centered on analysis. Break the problem down. Structure it carefully. Gather the evidence. Present the conclusions clearly.

All of that matters. It still does.

But in that alley it wasn't the most important thing happening.

The COO wasn't explaining strategy. He was strengthening relationships.

Each conversation reinforced something larger than the immediate transaction. People spoke to him with the ease that comes only from familiarity built over time.

Influence, I realized, was not coming from expertise alone.

It was rooted in accumulated trust.

That trust had been built gradually, through hundreds of conversations, through decisions made together, through the quiet reliability that develops when people observe how you behave over time.

You cannot manufacture that with a presentation.

You cannot accelerate it with a clever framework.

You have to earn it.

Standing there, surrounded by the noise and heat of the market, I began to understand something that would reshape how I thought about consulting.

The best consultants are not simply analysts.

They are trusted participants in important decisions.

That trust changes everything. It determines which conversations you are invited into. It shapes how openly clients share what is really happening inside their organizations. It influences whether your ideas are debated, adopted, or quietly set aside.

And it takes time to build.

The professionals who do it consistently at an elite level are often known inside firms by a particular label.

Rainmakers.

The term can sound slightly theatrical, but in practice it describes something very real. These are the consultants who create opportunity where others see only problems. Clients seek them out. Colleagues want to work with them. Important work finds its way in their direction.

From the outside their success can appear effortless.

In reality it rarely is.

Rainmakers combine several capabilities that do not always develop together. They understand complex industries. They recognize patterns others miss. They build relationships that last years, sometimes decades. And when the moment arrives, they know how to translate insight into action.

Just as importantly, they know how to build connection under pressure.

That ability has become more valuable with each passing year.

The consulting environment today looks very different from the one many firms were built for.

Clients have access to more information than ever before. Technology is reshaping how organizations operate and how advice is delivered. Artificial intelligence (AI) is accelerating everything—analysis, research, modeling, even parts of the consulting workflow that once required teams of analysts working late into the night.

At the same time, the problems clients face have grown larger and more complex. Global supply chains shift overnight. Regulation tightens. Technology cycles shorten. Entire industries are being reconfigured. Many of the decisions leaders now confront carry consequences measured not in quarters but in years.

The consulting engagements that support those decisions have grown in scale as well. Major assignments increasingly combine strategy, technology platforms, data capabilities, and sometimes ongoing managed services that extend long after the initial advisory work is complete.

Procurement teams now run highly structured processes for selecting advisers. Internal teams are stronger and better informed. Specialist boutiques compete alongside global firms. And much of the analytical work that once defined consulting like data gathering, modeling, and benchmarking, has become faster, cheaper, and in many cases commoditized.

Generic consulting has quietly disappeared.

In this environment, expertise alone is easier to replace.

Trust is not.

But trust by itself is no longer enough either. Clients want advisers they believe in and advisers who bring the depth of capability to stand alongside that trust when the work becomes difficult. And some of that capability comes from outside the local firms through global delivery models, alliance partners, and specialist organizations located in other parts of the world.

Clients still hire consultants because they need help navigating decisions that matter. But they choose carefully. They look for people who understand their context, who listen well, who bring perspective without arrogance, and who have the experience and capability to help turn difficult decisions into real outcomes.

In other words, people they trust.

For much of the profession's history, lessons like this were passed down informally. Consultants learned through stories, shared after difficult client meetings, discussed during late-night project reviews, or quietly unpacked by experienced partners over coffee.

Those stories mattered. They carried the practical wisdom that rarely appears in training manuals.

But something has shifted.

Consulting now moves faster. Teams are more dispersed. Much of the work happens through screens. Consultants often move from call to call, project to project, with little time to reflect on what they are learning.

In the process, something subtle has been lost.

Many consultants feel deployed rather than developed.

The field lessons, the quiet judgment calls, the signals experienced advisers learn to read: Too often they disappear between video calls and deadlines.

That is one reason this book exists.

Because if you are a consultant today, you have probably felt the pressure: to sound certain before the facts are clear, to move quickly while still thinking carefully, to remain billable while still building your opportunity pipeline.

You want to do great work.

But you also want to feel steady doing it.

This book is about how that steadiness is built.

It draws on the experiences of consultants who have spent years earning the kind of trust that allows them to shape important decisions. Their stories are different, but the patterns behind them are surprisingly consistent.

Over time those patterns become habits. Habits become routines. And routines shape careers.

The day in Mumbai did not teach me all of that at once.

But it showed me where to start looking.

And once you see the difference between impressing a client and truly understanding them, it becomes difficult to approach the profession in quite the same way.

Neil Plumridge

Who This Book Is For

Rainmakers are the professionals who consistently stand out in consulting firms. Not just because they win large clients or prestigious assignments but because they secure the opportunities that genuinely move organizations forward.

They don't just sell work. They help clients achieve outcomes others struggle to deliver. Over time they create value that endures.

Rainmakers are high performers, and they can come from any level in a consulting firm, not just the partners. They see possibilities where others see none. They earn trust that opens doors others cannot. They build confidence not through flash or volume but through presence, substance, and a deep understanding of people and situations.

They read the room. They sense the moment. And when the stakes are high, they act with clarity.

Rainmaking is not luck, charisma, or a gift reserved for a few personalities. It is a craft, built through habits, judgment, and disciplined ways of working.

Yet most consulting professionals do not begin their careers operating in that space, and that is entirely normal. Successful firms need a wide spectrum of strengths: people who anchor culture, those who deliver exceptional work, and those who nurture long-term client relationships. Each contributes something essential.

But the most effective firms share one additional characteristic: They develop more rainmakers over time.

The encouraging truth is that rainmaking is not an exclusive club. The principles and disciplines that define the top performers can be learned, practiced, and embedded across a firm. When that happens, collaboration strengthens, client confidence deepens, and the entire firm grows more resilient.

This book is not only for the small percentage who already operate at that level.

It is for consultants who want to move closer to it.

If you are still building your reputation, rainmakers offer patterns worth studying rather than mysteries to envy. If you are already delivering strong results, the gap to rainmaker-level impact is often less about capability and more about confidence, structure, and mindset. And for those already operating at rainmaker level, the ideas in this book provide language, frameworks, and stories that can be shared with teams and colleagues, helping to develop the next generation of rainmakers within their firms.

The aim is not to become someone else.

It is to become more effective and more trusted under pressure.

Between us we have spent decades working in consulting around the world: across more than 30 countries, from New York and Singapore to Jakarta, Mumbai, and São Paulo. We have worked with global corporations, government institutions, and fast-growing organizations navigating profound change.

We have also sat on both sides of the table, as partners earning the trust of chief executives and boards and as a client commissioning hundreds of millions of dollars in consulting work from many of the world's leading firms.

Across those experiences, certain patterns became impossible to ignore. Some consultants consistently earn deeper trust. They shape more important decisions. And when critical opportunities arise, clients turn to them first.

This book explores what they do differently.

You won't find neat case studies or theoretical models presented at a distance. The stories here are real, sometimes messy, occasionally uncomfortable, and often revealing. Names have been changed where needed, but the situations and lessons are drawn from lived experience.

Our aim is simple: to give you practical ways to strengthen the judgment, relationships, and habits that define the very best consultants.

How This Book Is Structured

We've built this book around a simple metaphor: the rainmaker's ecosystem. Because in today's consulting environment, sustained success rarely comes from a single strength; it comes from how multiple capabilities work together under pressure. Like a thriving tree, it comes from the interconnection of many parts like deep roots, strong structure, adaptive strategies, and the ability to renew and grow with the seasons.

Nothing stands still. Growth isn't linear. And what's visible on the surface—the wins, the trust, the reputation—is just the canopy. The real work happens below, where few are looking. If your consulting life currently feels fragmented—strong delivery here, stalled momentum there, confidence high one month and tested the next—this structure is designed to help you see the whole ecosystem in which you work and decide where to focus next. Again.

Here's how the book unfolds—not as a linear journey but as a system you can return to at different points in your career and your pipeline. You may not need all of this at once, but at different moments, under different pressures, you'll need different parts of the system to hold.

The Soil

Before anything grows, you must understand the ground you're standing on. Today's consulting world isn't what it used to be. The soil has shifted—shaken by economic shocks, the rise of AI, growing client skepticism, and more complex expectations.

We explore four key layers, each revealing a different set of opportunities for those who know how to read them:

1. The enduring principles that form the foundation of the profession
2. The shake-up reshaping the supply side of consulting

3. The shifts in demand redefining what clients value today
4. The immediate issues and realities facing clients today

Rainmakers don't ignore these forces; they study them. They stay curious, they adapt, and they draw the insight needed to position themselves and their firms where the best opportunities emerge.

The Roots

At the core of every rainmaker is something deeper—an internal foundation built on self-awareness, purpose, resilience, and responsibility. These are the qualities that nourish everything else.

Like roots, they're mostly unseen. But they matter more than most realize. And just like roots must adjust to changing soil, these inner drivers of rainmakers must evolve too. When they do, they anchor performance and shape the way Rainmakers show up.

The Trunk

The trunk is the backbone—where strength and structure live. The core attributes that define a rainmaker are in four categories:

1. Character and Connection
2. Clarity and Presence
3. Action and Impact
4. Growth and Vision

These attributes help rainmakers stay grounded while still moving forward. They bring focus, form, and the flexibility to adapt—without snapping under pressure.

The Branches

The branches are the strategies rainmakers use to find and win the work that matters. They're not isolated tools and they reinforce each other:

- **Hunting with precision:** It's not about chasing everything. It's about knowing where the value is and going after it with clarity and intent.
- **Creating unmatched value:** Rainmakers deliver more than deliverables. They bring insight, solve problems others can't, and create outcomes clients didn't see coming.
- **Forging unshakable trust:** This isn't the kind of trust you build with a polished proposal. It comes from presence, empathy, and follow-through.
- **Mastering the routine of success:** High performance isn't a fluke. It's the result of systems, habits, and discipline that compound over time.

The Canopy and Fruit

The canopy and fruit are what show up on the outside—the outcomes, the impact, the visible signs of success. But they aren't the final chapter. In any healthy ecosystem, the canopy supports renewal. The fruit feeds future growth.

Rainmakers don't just celebrate wins. They reinvest them. They plant again.

Thoughts on the Consulting Industry

Consulting, done well, is a force for good. It brings clarity to chaos, focus to complexity, and momentum to stalled organizations. At its best, consulting is a profession built on insight, empathy, and impact. Good ideas, breakthroughs, and effective practices spread fast across borders. Clients benefit from global knowledge and experience without seeing the machinery behind it.

Of course, not every engagement delivers. And not every consultant earns the right to be there. Some failures of values, ethics, or delivery have rightly drawn criticism. But those moments don't define the profession; they challenge it to do better.

Consulting spans a broad range—from strategy to tech, brand to risk, transformation to regulation. And it's expanding. Legal firms now offer strategy advice. Technology providers deliver end-to-end consulting. Even infrastructure companies bundle in advisory services. The lines are blurring. But the goal is the same: Create value for the client.

Rainmakers understand their role. They don't seek the spotlight. They support. They partner. They know that the client owns the decision and the risk. Consultants advise. Clients lead. That distinction matters. It is only within the consulting industry that rainmakers are known.

In this book, we celebrate the best of what consulting can be and offer a roadmap for those who want to raise the bar.

A Note on Artificial Intelligence

AI is no longer on the edge of consulting. It's at the center. The question isn't whether AI will change the game. It already has. The question is: How will *you* respond?

Leading firms are embedding AI in everything from delivery to client service. Clients expect it. Competitors use it. Platforms like McKinsey's Lilli,[1] BCG's AI offerings,[2] and Goldman Sachs' in-house assistants are moving fast.[3] They're not waiting.

Across industries, AI is collapsing the time it takes to move from insight to action. Decisions that once required weeks of analysis can now be informed in minutes. Massive datasets are scanned continuously, giving leaders real-time visibility into markets, competitors, and customer sentiment. At the same time, the cost of expertise has dropped sharply. Tasks once limited to highly trained specialists, like legal research, financial modeling, market analysis, even software development, can now be accelerated or partly automated by intelligent systems.

The implications extend well beyond efficiency. AI is compressing the traditional constraints of time, cost, and scale. Product development cycles are shortening as companies generate concepts, simulate designs, and test market responses faster than ever before. Organizations can personalize millions of customer interactions simultaneously, expand into new markets with fewer barriers, and automate large portions of knowledge work from customer support to contract analysis and reporting. In this environment, entire businesses are being built AI first, with operating models designed around these capabilities from day one.

Rainmakers are already using AI to:

- Spot opportunities before others do.
- Customize solutions with speed and precision.
- Free up time for honest client conversations.
- Promote ethical, responsible use of data and automation.

AI won't replace rainmakers. It will amplify them. As the routine gets automated, what's left is the human edge—judgment, creativity, and connection. The traits that truly build trust.

This book doesn't focus on AI; others do that well. But we don't ignore it either. Because in the world of high-value consulting, AI is already part of the ecosystem.

The ground has shifted. The nutrients are different. It's time to adapt.

Final Thoughts Before We Start

In today's world, consulting isn't just about what you know. It's about the way you show up, how you carry yourself, how you connect with people, and what kind of presence you bring into the room. And if that feels harder than it used to, you're not imagining it. The margin for error is thinner. The pace is faster. And the space to pause, reflect, and recalibrate is smaller than ever. This book is written for those moments—when you're expected to lead, decide, and reassure others while still working things out yourself.

That's what this book is here for.

Not just to help you land more business—though that will be a by-product. This book aims to help you make better decisions when the stakes are high and the information is incomplete. To help you become the kind of consultant who moves the needle. The kind people trust, remember, and call when it matters.

Let's get started.

PART

I

The Soil

Understanding the Rainmaker's World

CHAPTER

1

The Ground We Stand On

Why Rainmakers Identify More and Larger Opportunities than Most of Their Peers

Every great tree begins with the ground it grows in. Its strength, resilience, and potential don't come just from what's visible above; they come from what lies beneath. The depth, richness, and stability of the soil determine whether growth is possible and how far it can go.

The same is true for rainmakers.

Before we dig into the mindsets, attributes, strategies, and routines that define high-performing consultants, we need to look down and into the ground for the source of all opportunities for consulting projects to improve organizations.

The world of consulting is in the middle of a profound transformation. The old model of the trusted advisor, sitting atop the value chain, is no longer the norm. The profession has splintered. Boutique firms are thriving. In-house consulting teams have matured. AI is redrawing the

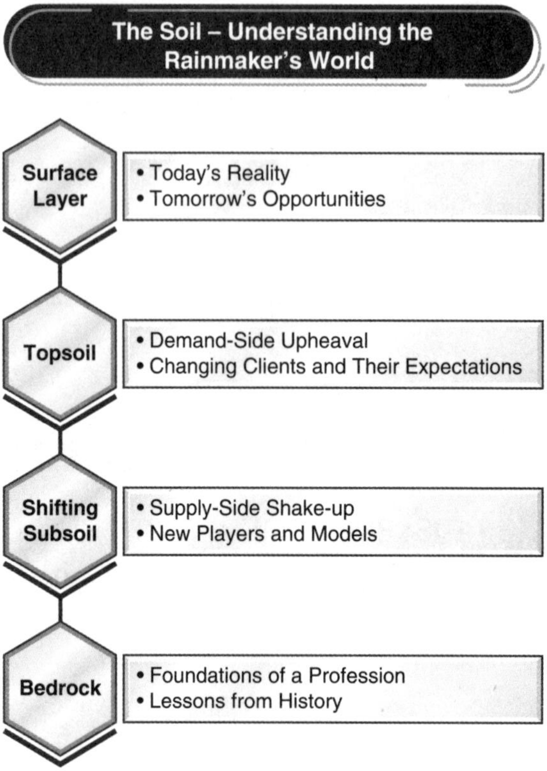

FIGURE 1.1 Understanding the rainmaker's world.

boundaries of insight and delivery. Clients expect more, trust less, and move faster. The climate, in every sense of the word, has changed.

To thrive in this environment, it takes more than just skill; it takes awareness. Rainmakers read the ground they're standing on better than others in their field. They find more opportunities, they find bigger and bolder projects, and they develop elite insights that open doors to the C-suite, create meaningful conversations with clients, and deliver strong results. Rainmakers know where the profession started, how it's changed, and what's driving it now. The ground beneath them isn't steady; it's layered, uneven, and constantly shifting, shaped as much by people and culture as by markets and money.

In this chapter, we explain the consulting terrain through a rainmaker's lens—four layers of soil that reveal something essential about the world in which rainmakers operate. (See Figure 1.1.)

Bedrock: Foundations of a Profession

Soil begins when rock and soil break down over time due to pressure, wind, sun, and water. Consulting emerged in much the same way, not as a sudden invention but as a natural response to shifting industrial forces.

As industrial growth and expansion accelerated through the late 19th and early 20th centuries, economies and organizations became more complex. A new need arose, not just for management but for independent, structured insight. People like Arthur D. Little and James O. McKinsey recognized this. They didn't offer easy answers; they brought practical thinking, rigorous analysis, and an external perspective to help businesses adapt, evolve, and perform.[1]

Their early work laid down principles that still hold firm beneath the profession today: clarity over chaos, method over guesswork, insight over instinct. Though the surface of consulting has changed, shaped by technology, globalization, and shifting client demands, the bedrock principles remain. Modern rainmakers recognize these enduring values and use them to see opportunities in their markets and clients that others can't. They don't simply react to change; they anticipate it, drawing from the foundational lessons of the past to spot what others overlook, turning uncertainty into strategic advantage.

Just as soil draws its strength from the rock beneath, today's rainmakers continue to draw on the enduring bedrock of their industry's origins, using it to build future success.

Shifting Subsoil: Supply-Side Shake-Up

As bedrock breaks down, new layers form. The first layer is the subsoil—nutrient-rich yet unsettled and always shifting. Consulting has evolved in much the same way. Boutiques rose to prominence, in-house strategy groups gained ground, and technology-driven platforms unsettled traditional firms. Fresh opportunities appeared, but so too did uncertainty and volatility.

For rainmakers, this is the zone of adaptive strategy. The terrain is competitive, specialized, and crowded. Clients now test their advisors regularly, weighing value against emerging alternatives. Consultants now pitch their own ideas, not just respond to client briefs. Agility matters, but so does awareness of competitor offerings, specialist capabilities, and your own firm's evolving strengths.

Rainmakers stay rooted in insight, although the time from insight to execution is compressing fast. They study the moves of rivals not to mimic but to anticipate. They scan thought leadership, dissect case studies, and seek feedback from clients on where others fall short. They know that winning the first project on a new issue can unlock long-term positioning and that deep knowledge of their firm's global reach, resources, and track record creates a potent edge.

In this layer, no one stands still. Networks must extend beyond firm boundaries to access niche expertise. Collaboration becomes currency. Delivering results through implementation, with often AI-enabled models from within or outside your firm, becomes table stakes. Knowing where to go and whom to call matters as much as what you know yourself.

The subsoil is dynamic, rich, and unpredictable. But for those who learn to move through it with balance and focus, it becomes not just a challenge but a source of strategic strength.

Topsoil: Demand-Side Upheaval

Topsoil is where things grow, but only if the conditions are right. It's rich, responsive, and alive with potential. This is the first client layer. And for rainmakers, it's where deep client insight is rewarded.

Today's client environment is anything but uniform. Boards, CEOs, procurement leads, and delivery executives, each with their own metrics, pressures, and agendas. It's a layered terrain shaped by regulation, competition, capital markets, and internal politics. What takes root here depends not on credentials but on context.

Rainmakers know this. They don't just speak about industries; they know them intimately. They track their clients' earnings calls, read investor presentations, and decode organizational charts like maps. They study and decipher plans, budgets, and vision statements. They identify patterns across clients in the same industries as well as aspects that others may overlook. They're students of their clients' worlds: their strategies, yes, but also their cultures, ambitions, anxieties, and blind spots.

From this insight, they identify opportunities. Not just more of them, but bigger, more strategic, and better-timed ones. They arrive in moments that matter, not by accident but through deliberate attention: observing, questioning, connecting patterns others miss. Engaging earlier, formulating projects, building connection.

To the average consultant, demand looks like a meeting or a brief. To the rainmaker, it seems like a landscape, and they know how to read the soil. They follow emerging issues. They track stories. They build and maintain a living list of opportunities and conversation points. Here, relevance isn't earned just once; it's earned continuously.

Topsoil shifts with weather, season, and use. But for those who cultivate it with discipline and insight, it yields growth others never see.

Surface Layer: Today's Reality, Tomorrow's Opportunities

At the surface, everything is in motion. This is the top layer of the soil, exposed to the elements, shaped daily by sun, wind, and sudden storms. In consulting, this is where change hits first. Shocks to the system, from technological disruption and regulatory shifts to market turbulence and cultural fatigue, land here before they settle anywhere else.

For rainmakers, the surface layer is not just noise; it's a signal. It's where today's realities collide with tomorrow's possibilities. It's where firms win or lose their footing.

Rainmakers learn to read the surface with precision and have the information, confidence, and instinct to act faster than the average consultant. They observe how organizations evolve, not just structurally but also culturally. They understand rhythms: planning cycles, budgeting windows, board meetings, investor days, and off-sites. They track market intelligence in real time, leadership changes, policy shifts, and moments of strain, because opportunity often arrives disguised as a leadership reshuffle, a sudden budget realignment, a cultural reset.

In these moments, responsiveness isn't optional; it's expected. Clients don't always ask twice. When they signal need, rainmakers are already ready: attuned to the context, prepared with ideas, positioned to act.

They walk the halls, physically or virtually, listening, anticipating, sensing where things might crack open. They understand that in an unstable environment, timing can be more important than tenure, and agility can outweigh legacy.

Yes, the surface is volatile. But it's also fertile. For those who pay attention, who stay close, and who move quickly with relevance and intent, it's a layer rich with growth if you know where and when to plant.

Reading the Soil

This is the current soil of consulting: layered, alive, and evolving. It holds history, pressure, and possibility all at once. Above all, it represents the population of options to serve clients, making meaningful change and delivering results. The next four chapters go deeper into each layer to help you understand how rainmakers operate inside it today.

Rainmakers don't wait for clarity. They read the soil around them. They research, examine, and regularly inspect it. The soil is where opportunities are identified and insights are developed. Rainmakers recognize this as a skill that differentiates them. They ground themselves in the truth of the moment.

Let's begin.

CHAPTER

2

Bedrock: Foundations of a Profession

How History Shapes Client Expectations and the Opportunities Available to You

When we began writing this book, we were struck by the fact that all the rainmakers we had met were students of consulting history—both their firms' and their industries' history.

We reflected on our own interest in consulting history, which went back farther than most would expect. Not just to early firms or management theories but to something older, to the original rainmakers. The ones who didn't write reports but read the skies. Who didn't sell frameworks but brought change when it mattered most.

The Ancient Rainmaker: Reading the Skies Before the Storm

In many African societies, the rainmaker was a respected figure who played an important part in community life. According to John S. Mbiti, rainmakers were closely connected with traditional religious practices and were believed to possess special knowledge or power to influence rain, which was vital for agricultural success.[1] Their role highlighted the deep relationship among people, nature, and the spiritual world in African religious thought.

During drought, the village would turn to them. They'd climb to a high point in the area, watch the clouds, feel the wind, and move with purpose. Their rituals weren't just tradition; they carried knowledge passed down over generations.

When the rain finally came, villagers spoke of power. But the rainmaker would quietly say, "It's not magic. It's knowledge."

Their true gift, as described by Mbiti, was their deep understanding of nature, presence, and humility. That disciplined, intuitive approach resonates in the best consultants today; they too read signals others miss and act confidently even in uncertainty.

Business Rainmakers Step onto the Stage

By the 19th century, rainmakers were of a different kind. They were stepping onto the business stage and reshaping the world around them.

These early business pioneers didn't cast spells or read clouds. But they did share something essential with their spiritual predecessors: They could see what others couldn't. They recognized patterns before they were apparent. They saw opportunity in complexity. And they had the courage and the influence to act.

In the United States, J. P. Morgan and Andrew Carnegie reshaped finance and steel, laying the infrastructure for America's industrial dominance. In the United Kingdom, Nathan Mayer Rothschild became a central figure in European banking, financing everything from railways to revolutions. Japan had Shibusawa Eiichi, who helped modernize the country's economy during the Meiji Restoration, founding over 500 companies along the way, all guided by a belief that ethics and enterprise could coexist.

In British India, Jamsetji Tata was building what would become one of the country's most respected business empires, not just in steel but in energy, education, and science. And in Brazil, Irineu Evangelista de Sousa pushed railroads, shipyards, and telegraphs into reality despite political resistance.

These weren't just wealthy men. They were systems thinkers. Builders. Visionaries. They didn't merely grow businesses; they shifted the conditions under which growth could happen. Like the rainmakers of old, they didn't wait for change. They made it happen.

Rainmakers study the business leaders of today and yesterday. They identify rainmaker traits and how industries evolved under visionary leadership.

Arthur D. Little and the Birth of Consulting

Jump ahead to 1886.

Arthur D. Little, a chemist with a sharp eye for opportunity, founded what's widely seen as the world's first management consulting firm. But he didn't just show up with advice. He came with ideas, often spotting a client's need before they did.[2]

Little understood something many still miss: Consulting isn't about giving clever answers. It's about framing better questions. It's about helping leaders see new possibilities, not just refining existing ones.

Little was a true rainmaker. He didn't wait for briefs. He showed up early with insight. He didn't sell output, he sold outcomes. He helped clients move forward when the path wasn't clear.

And he wasn't just a strategist. He was a builder. He pushed the boundaries of consulting, pioneering analytical methods, launching research and development labs, and guiding national resource strategies.

He once helped launch one of the first research labs in the automotive sector, a move that changed how innovation was approached in industry. In another project, he and his team were asked to map a country's natural resources, work that would shape the trajectory of that nation's economy.

What made Little stand out wasn't just foresight. It was his consistency. His curiosity. His ability to stay relevant by adapting without losing his core.

Rainmaking isn't a one-time feat. It's earned over time through insight, trust, and the ability to stay ahead. Arthur D. Little gave the profession its legs and a model still worth studying.

From McKinsey to Follett: A Profession Takes Shape

Then came structure.

James O. McKinsey brought order to the emerging profession. A man of precision, he earned trust not with charisma but with discipline, sharp analysis, thoughtful questioning, and a strong sense of personal accountability. He helped translate big ambition into practical execution, creating systems and standards where there had been none.

McKinsey's first partner was Andrew Thomas (Tom) Kearney, who helped the firm expand into operations consulting during its early years. The firm was then known as McKinsey, Kearney & Company. After the death of founder James O. McKinsey, the two offices split, Chicago under Kearney and New York under Marvin Bower, becoming the two independent firms we know today: McKinsey & Company and Kearney.

Another influential voice that shaped the character of management consulting and more broadly business was Mary Parker Follett. Often overlooked in traditional consulting histories, Follett saw organizations not as machines but as living systems.[3] Her call for "power with" rather than "power over" was radical at the time and still resonates today.[4]

Follett brought heart to what was then a very mechanical view of leadership and collaboration. Her ideas were decades ahead of their time, offering a human-centered vision of how people could work together with purpose and dignity. And while she didn't run a consulting firm, her fingerprints are all over modern organizational thinking.

Together, McKinsey and Follett brought shape and depth to the profession, one through structure, the other through humanity. Their work still underpins much of what great consultants do: Apply sharp thinking to human problems, with empathy and clarity.

Marvin Bower and the Moral Spine of Consulting

If McKinsey gave the profession its frame, Marvin Bower gave it its soul.

At McKinsey & Company, Bower championed the view that consulting should be a true profession, one built not just on expertise but on ethics. He believed consultants should hold themselves to standards as high as those in law or medicine.

Integrity. Confidentiality. Long-term commitment. These weren't just values to Bower, they were nonnegotiables. He believed a consultant's advice had to come from principle, not profit.

He didn't invent the profession. But he gave it its moral spine. And many of today's expectations around discretion, client loyalty, and partnership trace directly back to him.

The Intellectual Foundations: Theory Meets Practice

Behind these consulting pioneers stood a different kind of influence, the theorists. Frederick Taylor, Henri Fayol, and Lyndall Urwick were thinkers who laid the groundwork for how we understand organizations, productivity, and decision making. They didn't call themselves consultants, but their ideas shaped the tools and language we still use today.

From Taylor's scientific management to Fayol's administrative principles, their work formed the playbook of early consulting engagements. Many rainmakers still pull from these early learnings, sometimes without even knowing it.

Consulting by the Decade: Evolving with the Times

We believe that for more than 60 years, consulting has moved in step with the shifting priorities of organizations—adapting as new challenges emerged and as each wave of change reshaped the landscape.

- In the 1960s, strategic planning took center stage. Firms like Boston Consulting Group introduced foundational concepts such as the experience curve, demonstrating how learning drives efficiency and proving that strategy could be driven by data rather than by instinct.
- In the 1970s, as management theory matured, consultants turned their attention to organizational design. Models like McKinsey's 7S Framework provided consultants with new tools to analyze and improve client performance.
- During the 1980s, there was a considerable rise in mergers and acquisitions and corporate balance sheet restructuring, allowing consultants to play key roles as navigators through complex and often high-stakes deals. At the same time, Bain & Company's partners went on to form Bain Capital, and Andersen split into two companies, Arthur Andersen & Company (accounting services) and Andersen Consulting (consulting services).
- By the 1990s, the rapid rise of global supply chains, outsourcing, offshoring, and technology advancement brought a wave of business process reengineering. Consulting firms began moving beyond offering strategic advice to helping companies implement new systems and technologies actively, and Kearney (formerly A.T. Kearney) spearheaded a new approach to strategic procurement. The likes of IBM, EDS, Capgemini, and BearingPoint (formerly KPMG Consulting) grew by acquiring consulting divisions from

firms such as Price Waterhouse, Ernst & Young, KPMG, and Kearney, signaling the growing importance of IT consulting and systems integration.

- The 2000s ushered in an era of globalization and digitalization. Consulting became increasingly borderless as e-commerce and big data emerged as game-changers. Firms didn't just advise on strategy but also on how to scale it and automate operations. Clients demanded new offerings, such as customer relationship management, data and analytics, productivity, and change management. Many consulting firms also globally adapted and distributed methods and approaches developed by others, including Lean Six Sigma, a continuous improvement methodology invented by Motorola and made famous by General Electric. One of the oldest consulting firms in the world, Booz Allen Hamilton, decided to split into two firms, creating Booz Allen and Booz & Co.
- In the 2010s, traditional strategy consulting began to shift. With many large organizations building their in-house strategy teams, the consulting edge increasingly came from operational expertise, agile methodologies, and the ability to execute on a global scale. The role of consultants became more focused on delivering value through implementation rather than merely advising on abstract strategy.
- Then the 2020s hit. The COVID-19 pandemic didn't just disrupt; it rewired entire economies. Remote work took hold almost overnight. Digital transformation, once a slow build, sped up fast. Supply chains, business models, even client expectations were shaken. Consulting had to shift with it. Firms leaned hard into technology, delivering work virtually and adapting at a pace the industry hadn't seen before. Firms began expanding into sustainability, where environmental, social, and governance goals are no longer a checkbox but a core driver of profitability and long-term success. Private equity saw massive growth, and emerging markets, particularly China, took on a greater role in the global economy. As disruption continued and AI took off, the stakes for consultants grew even higher.

At every turn, rainmakers adapted. But the core foundations—objectivity, relevance, trust, and insight—remained.

A Profession Shaped by Scrutiny

We recognize and do not shy away from the hard truth: The road has not been smooth. Consulting, like many influential professions, has had to reckon with its past. And rightly so.

Over the past six decades, the world has witnessed some of the most damaging corporate failures in history: Enron. WorldCom. The opioid crisis. Lehman Brothers. Volkswagen Dieselgate. At the heart of these events were systemic governance breakdowns, corrosive internal cultures, misaligned incentives, and unchecked ambition. In several of these cases, consultants were not bystanders; they were part of the picture. That reality is uncomfortable but essential to confront.

More recently, new challenges have arisen to test the profession. At one major firm, partners came under intense scrutiny for their involvement in supporting an aid organization operating in Gaza, an engagement marred by flawed information, questionable due diligence, and apparent lapses in internal oversight. These incidents don't just raise eyebrows; they raise serious questions about judgment, accountability, and the ethical foundation on which trusted advisory work must rest.

And yet, from that scrutiny, real change has emerged.

We believe the profession, led by some of the world's most respected and influential organizations, has grown significantly more mature, more accountable, and more ethical. Firms have invested profoundly in governance, compliance, and conflict management. A renewed focus on long-term, sustainable value is helping to challenge short termism. Senior consultants now more fully recognize their role not simply as advisors but as active shapers of direction, tone, and consequence.

But with that influence comes greater responsibility.

In our view, the bar for trusted senior client relationships must now be set even higher, not just institutionally but personally.

Rainmakers today operate in environments where trust cannot be assumed; it must be earned repeatedly through a deep commitment to integrity, transparency, and sound judgment.

This is not simply a professional expectation; it is an ethical imperative.

We explore this imperative further in Chapter 10, "Root Cap: Ethics and Responsibilities," and again in Chapter 19, "Forging Unshakeable Trust," where we examine the evolving standards rainmakers must embody to lead with credibility in a world that watches and remembers.

Conclusion: Bedrock

Rainmakers stand not only on the strength of their own expertise but on the foundations laid by those who came before. By learning the history of the profession and their firm, they gain insight, build credibility, and carry forward a legacy. To lead at the highest level, rainmakers must first understand what they are standing on.

Next: Shifting Subsoil—New Players, Models, and Competitors

Now that we've walked through the bedrock, the origins, the pioneers, and the principles that shaped the profession, we turn to the next layer: the dynamic, fast-changing subsoil.

Because the ground is no longer stable, new players keep entering. Business models are multiplying. And the definition of a "consultant" is changing by the day.

Let's dig into what these changes mean for the modern rainmaker and how to stay sure-footed when the terrain keeps shifting.

Let's begin.

CHAPTER

3

Shifting Subsoil: Supply-Side Shake-Up

Why Waiting for the Phone to Ring Means You Have Already Lost

In fertile soil, life multiplies. And with life comes complexity.

Consulting is no longer a neat profession where a few elite firms advise CEOs and dominate the market. Today the supply side has exploded into a tangled, fast-moving ecosystem. Boutique firms, AI-driven disruptors, in-house teams, engineering groups, and global tech giants now compete for the same client budgets. It's a richer, more dynamic environment than ever, but it's also one of constant change and heightened competition.

For rainmakers, this isn't a threat; it's an invitation. The consultants who thrive in this environment are those who see patterns others miss, anticipate competitive moves, and create opportunities where others see chaos. Doing that requires more than delivering excellent work; it demands constant scanning of the landscape, precision positioning, and a clear understanding of your own firm's unique capabilities.

A profound shift over the last 10 to 15 years has seen this category become the predominant source of large, high-value projects. Rainmakers pitch great ideas, approaches, concepts, and strategic actions born out of deep research and insight. Executives welcome this contribution and reward the consultants who bring the right opportunities forward. Consultants who wait for clients to ask for advice rapidly lose relevance in today's world.

Global Scale, Fierce Competition, and the Rainmaker's Edge

Consulting has become a truly global, hypercompetitive marketplace. The industry surpassed $1 trillion in global revenue in 2024, driven by vast scale players with Accenture, Deloitte, PwC, and others employing hundreds of thousands of professionals, alongside thousands of niche boutiques, regional specialists, and nontraditional entrants such as law firms and advisory groups backed by private equity firms.[1]

For clients, this crowded field can feel like a blur of sameness. Almost every firm claims expertise in "digital transformation," "AI," or "cyber," yet few demonstrate real depth or originality. For rainmakers, this represents both risk and opportunity. They know that clients will periodically benchmark relationships, issue requests for proposals (RFPs), or invite new players into their boardrooms. No relationship is guaranteed.

Rainmakers treat competitive intelligence as a discipline, not a sideline. They scan competitor offerings, download and dissect thought leadership papers, review media coverage, and, most important, ask their clients for candid feedback on other providers. They do this not out of paranoia but to sharpen their positioning and anticipate competitive threats.

Key Insight: In this intensely globalized market, being chosen is never about who you are; it's about how relevant you are at the moment a client is deciding.

Offensive and Defensive Strategies: Playing Both Sides of the Field

Rainmakers think like strategists; they defend their most valuable relationships by investing in them deeply, bringing proactive insights, anticipating procurement cycles, and being present before a need is formally articulated. They also prepare for offensive opportunities, identifying accounts where competitors are vulnerable or where a client's needs are shifting.

Defensive strategies include:

- Staying close to decision makers and influencers.
- Continuously demonstrating value with small, high-impact contributions between major projects.
- Anticipating competitor moves and shaping the narrative before rivals arrive.

Offensive strategies often involve recognizing patterns others miss. A leadership change, regulatory shift, or strategic pivot can create an opportunity to reposition. Rainmakers know when to step forward, when to wait, and when to bring in a specialist to tip the balance.

This dual lens—attack and defense—is essential in today's environment. Waiting for RFPs is a recipe for irrelevance. Rainmakers are in the game long before a brief is written.

First-Mover Advantage: Winning Before the Market Catches Up

First-mover advantage in consulting doesn't always come from developing something entirely new; it often comes from identifying an idea, solution, or challenge early and acting more quickly than competitors.

Rainmakers are natural scouts. They track regulatory changes, geopolitical risks, and competitor moves in other industries or markets. They take lessons from one geography and quickly apply them in another. They look for signals that a client is about to face a challenge and show up with answers before anyone else.

Some of the most influential consulting innovations came from firms that moved early:

- **McKinsey and Stellantis:** When tariffs threatened European automakers in 2025, McKinsey's early analysis of Alfa Romeo and Maserati's exposure positioned them as Stellantis's trusted partner, earning a cascade of follow-on work in other clients and industries.
- **Accenture and Telstra:** In January 2025, Accenture partnered with Telstra to rebuild its AI and data architecture. This wasn't innovation for show; it was a scalable, compliant system that gave Accenture a template for other telcos worldwide.
- **Deloitte's platform leadership:** Deloitte's early alliances with SAP, Oracle, and Microsoft made them indispensable digital transformation partners while rivals were still framing themselves as "advisors."
- **Kearney's strategic sourcing:** Kearney's now-famous seven-step sourcing methodology wasn't a marketing exercise; it was born from necessity and stuck because it worked, cementing their reputation globally.

Rainmakers understand these lessons: They don't just follow trends; they turn early insight into lasting influence.

Knowing Your Own Firm's Power: Global Capability and Collaboration

Many consultants underuse one of the most valuable assets they have: the scale and expertise of their own firm. Global consulting organizations hold immense intellectual capital: successful project playbooks, proprietary tools, sector-specific insights, and long-standing client relationships. Much of these assets remain untapped, but rainmakers know how to draw on them to create powerful import and export opportunities.

Rainmakers who rise to the top are masters of internal navigation. They know who leads major client relationships in other markets, which partners have developed breakthrough methodologies, and where the firm's true strengths lie. They bridge internal silos with purpose, connecting offices, practices, and people who might otherwise never collaborate.

This capability goes far beyond internal networking; it is a competitive weapon. By assembling a cross-border team or introducing a client to a lesser-known internal expert, rainmakers demonstrate that their clients have access to the full depth and reach of the firm. In a fragmented market, this is one of the clearest ways to stand apart.

Rainmakers also recognize export potential in their own work. When they create new insights on an industry issue or deliver exceptional results for a client, they know how to craft and share that story responsibly, protecting confidentiality while enabling colleagues to replicate success in other markets.

In today's consulting environment, this approach has driven a quiet but important shift: Many new projects now emerge through proactive pitches and cross-firm collaboration rather than through formal client requests or RFPs.

Extending Networks Beyond the Firm

A single firm rarely solves today's client problems; clients need multidisciplinary, multi-organization solutions. For rainmakers, this means cultivating a network that extends beyond their firm's walls, including alliances with boutique experts, academic institutions, industry associations, executive advisors, executive search firms, private equity firms, legal firms, and technology platform providers.

This external ecosystem is not just a safety net; it's a source of competitive strength. Rainmakers who can call the right person, whether a cyber expert in a boutique firm, a tech innovator at Amazon Web Services (AWS), or a regulatory advisor in another jurisdiction, become indispensable.

Ecosystems like Salesforce, AWS, and ServiceNow are now marketplaces of talent and solutions. Rainmakers don't just sell within these ecosystems; they orchestrate them. Their value lies in knowing how to integrate talent, tools, and partners into a seamless client experience.

Clients as Competitors: The Rise of In-House Consulting

An often-overlooked shift in the supply side is the rise of sophisticated in-house consulting teams. Amazon, Unilever, and major government departments have established internal teams capable of leading strategy and transformation work, often staffed by former consultants who possess both in-depth business knowledge and the playbook of external firms.

These teams operate with speed, carry deep organizational knowledge, and often deliver with less friction than outside advisors. These teams don't bring in consultants to validate their thinking; they bring them in to fill capability gaps or deliver scale.

Rainmakers understand this dynamic. They don't see internal teams as competition to outmaneuver but as partners to collaborate with. They listen carefully, respect the expertise these teams bring, and step in where they can add unique value.

Key Insight: By supporting internal teams, not overshadowing them, rainmakers earn a different kind of trust: the trust of being seen as an enabler rather than a threat.

This significant mindset shift is critical. The future of consulting is increasingly collaborative, with external advisors working shoulder to shoulder with client teams. Rainmakers who navigate this well deepen relationships and position themselves as long-term strategic allies.

Research as the Enabler

The key to identifying opportunities within the supply side, the subsoil of the rainmaker's ecosystem, is research. Not just of competitors, but of your own firm, your industry, your practice specialty, and the projects that have delivered genuine impact.

In the past, this work was painstaking and time-consuming. It always produced insight and occasionally revealed a golden opportunity, something that could differentiate your approach and capture a client's attention. Today, artificial intelligence has transformed that process. It has made research faster and broader, but it has also raised the bar. The tools may be easier to use, yet they demand sharper diligence, curiosity, and discernment, and they have lifted expectations inside firms and out.

AI now extends far beyond the back office. It is shaping how consulting work is delivered, how opportunities are found, how relationships begin, and even how trust is earned. Leading firms are investing heavily in proprietary AI systems trained on their intellectual property, project archives, and sector insights. These platforms are fast becoming competitive weapons, capable of spotting patterns, surfacing opportunities, and equipping rainmakers to enter client conversations with a depth of context that once was unimaginable.

For many clients, AI has become a leveler. With large language models and digital copilots, in-house teams can model scenarios, test strategies, and benchmark performance without calling in external help. This makes the first conversation with a client even more important. By the time you walk into the room, they may already have a plan.

Rainmakers don't resist this shift; they harness it. They use AI as a force multiplier to work smarter, faster, and with greater precision. They:

- Analyze client sentiment, boardroom dynamics, and public disclosures to anticipate priorities.
- Map decision-making networks and identify hidden influencers.
- Draft tailored proposals and thought pieces in hours, not days.
- Track competitor activity globally to help clients see what's next, not just what's known.
- Build prototypes, data visualizations, and diagnostics before a formal brief is even issued.

Inside firms, AI knowledge hubs are transforming access to insight, consolidating decades of data, case studies, and intellectual property into searchable, intelligent systems that rainmakers can draw from instantly. Externally, firms are embedding AI into client solutions, codeveloping models for everything from supply chain optimization to ESG performance.

Key Insight: AI is no longer just a tool for delivery efficiency; it's a capability that can *win the work itself*. Rainmakers who master AI-driven insight enter meetings 10 steps ahead, already understanding the client's market, challenges, and options before the first question is asked.

Yet AI is also a competitor. Clients can now generate draft strategies or run diagnostics internally at almost no cost. What sets rainmakers apart is their judgment and ability to interpret, simplify, and apply insight with narrative clarity and emotional intelligence. That is the last mile of value, and it remains distinctly human. The future belongs to those who know when to trust the machine, when to challenge it, and how to integrate it into the story they tell.

A Closing Challenge: Creating Your Own Weather

The consulting market is no longer a tidy pyramid of firms; it's an ever-shifting network of players, partnerships, and capabilities. Rainmakers who succeed are those who embrace this complexity and turn it to their advantage:

- They study competitors relentlessly, not to imitate but to anticipate their moves.
- They balance offensive plays with defensive vigilance, guarding relationships while seeking new ones.
- They act early, leveraging a first-mover advantage to establish thought leadership and a strong market position.
- They deeply understand their own firm's strengths and unlock its global potential.
- They cultivate networks that extend beyond their badge, giving clients confidence that they can solve any problem.
- They treat client-side consulting teams as allies, not adversaries, building trust and earning a seat at the table.
- They research continuously, utilizing AI to amplify their impact, combining machine intelligence with human judgment.

This is not about chasing trends. It's about identifying opportunities and crafting solutions and stories that can be brought to clients that demonstrate your value as a trusted advisor.

Next: Topsoil—Changing Clients and Their Expectations

Now we move upward, into the organizations themselves. Where decision makers are stretched thin, expectations are rising, and the bar for value has never been higher. Rainmakers who succeed here know how to listen, align, and land real impact.

Let's keep going.

CHAPTER

4

Topsoil: Demand-Side Prospects

Everyone Knows the Client Situation. But How Do You Convert That Knowledge into Programs That You Can Win?

The topsoil in our ecosystem is where client demand for consulting services initially takes shape. It is not a flat surface but a living layer, full of signals, announcements, and public information. Rainmakers know that to grow extensive, high-impact work, they must first read and deeply understand this soil because without it, nothing takes root.

To understand how demand emerges, we need to examine three layers:

1. The *global forces* shaping entire markets

2. The pressures and shifts within *specific industries*
3. The *client's own specific strategies* to address its local market

Each of these layers feeds into the next. A geopolitical tremor can unsettle a sector overnight. A regulatory shift in one country can have a ripple effect across competitors. A leadership change can trigger bold new priorities or stall existing initiatives. For rainmakers, this interconnectedness is the point: They don't treat these pressures as isolated fragments but as a system of influences that shape where opportunities lie.

This is why the topsoil matters so much. It is the traditional area of focus of all consulting firms. Knowing a client, their industry, and the issues that matter to them is not a luxury; rainmakers see it is the key to being taken seriously at senior levels. Rainmakers don't arrive at a meeting simply with credentials; they come with context. They bring observations that connect global shifts to local realities or insights that reframe a client's challenge in light of what's happening across their sector. When done well, rainmakers earn entry into conversations that matter: boardroom discussions, off-agenda questions, and the moments when leaders are weighing their next move.

What sets rainmakers apart is not just that they do this work but *how* they do it. They don't skim the headlines or settle for secondhand commentary. They read competitor announcements, listen to investor briefings, study cultural change programs, and track signals others miss. Some rainmakers, for instance, choose a handful of industry peers to shadow closely, dissecting quarterly earnings calls, comparing leadership language across time, or monitoring regulatory submissions to see where the currents are shifting. Others keep live lists of emerging issues and potential discussion points, so they never arrive unprepared.

Today, AI has supercharged this discipline. What once required weeks of manual analysis, sifting through reports, transcripts, and market data, can now be done in minutes or a couple of hours. A rainmaker can walk into a client meeting with a sharper, deeper grasp of context than ever before, armed with perspectives drawn from thousands of pages of material that AI has distilled, connected, and highlighted. This information doesn't replace judgment, but it provides rainmakers with more raw material, insight, and precision than their peers.

This is the work beneath the surface—the difference between waiting for a brief and cultivating opportunity. Rainmakers always start here, in the soil. Next we share an experience at a major client that illustrates this. This is Neil's story.

The Alley: A Story from the Soil

It was the late 1990s and a time when workplace norms bore little resemblance to those of today. I was new to management consulting, still learning how to read a room, how to influence without authority, and when to speak and when to remain quiet. I was there to listen and learn. Robert, by contrast, was an established partner—sharp thinker, respected leader, trusted by clients. He had earned the kind of access that gets you invited into the conversations that matter most.

I was fortunate to be part of the meeting.

The client was under pressure from every direction. Share price sliding. Analysts circling. Media sniffing for weakness. Customers drifting. Service levels slipping. Internally, the culture was fraying at the edges. The CEO hadn't become the story yet, but you could feel it coming.

Everyone could see the symptoms. But Robert read the soil differently.

- At the **global level,** he recognized why analysts were discounting the company's share price: Compared with international peers, its operating margins were falling behind. Investors were losing confidence that it could keep pace in productivity and performance, and that pressure was only going to grow.
- At the **industry level,** he saw new competition emerging in the form of fast, lean startups that were operating more efficiently,

cost-effectively, and intelligently. Established players were starting to shift, but the company hadn't yet confronted the potential disruptiveness of those entrants.

- At the **client level,** he noticed something few others had. The leadership agenda was full—dozens of initiatives, many of them worthwhile—but none addressed the core challenge of productivity in a structured and meaningful way. And that was the very issue that would soon determine whether the company could compete, survive, or be left behind.

And then there was the human dimension. Robert sensed the influence of one particular executive, two levels below the CEO, a strong supply chain leader nearing retirement, but still with enough weight, energy, and credibility to move the organization if he chose. Here was someone with a legacy mostly intact but perhaps open to a bold final act.

That morning, in a grimy alley behind the client's building, Robert turned those insights into action. We leaned against a brick wall, coffees in hand, waiting for the executive. He arrived, cigarette in one hand, jacket slung over his shoulder, sharp eyes betraying both fatigue and curiosity. After the usual small talk about horses and politics, Robert asked the question that shifted everything:

"Would you be up for something bigger?"

The man looked sideways. "Bigger than supply chain? This should be good."

"It's not about scale," Robert said. "It's about impact. There's a structural productivity problem at the heart of the business. Everyone knows it, but no one's facing it. You could. If you're willing."

A drag on the cigarette. A pause. Then: "Come by my office tomorrow. I want to hear the whole thing."

What followed was rare air. We weren't treated as vendors but as insiders. Whiteboards. Late nights. Drafts. Debates. His team leaned in too. Robert guided with calm clarity; I found my way to contribute by listening more attentively and reading the undercurrents. Together, we built not just a strategy but a story—one that was coherent, compelling, politically risky, yet bold enough to matter.

When the time came, our client took it to the CEO himself, not as a gamble but as a belief. He owned it, delivered it with pride, and won the credibility he sought. We secured a seminal cost transformation assignment that reverberated through the global industry. The company got a credible path forward. The market reacted favorably.

And me? That alley moment taught me something foundational.

Key Insight: Fundamental transformation doesn't begin with a slide deck. It starts with soil reading—understanding the global forces, the industry dynamics, and the client's inner terrain. It begins with presence, timing, and the courage to ask a simple yet bold question before the moment is lost.

Reading the Global Topsoil

Global forces—geopolitics, climate, macroeconomics, and disruptive technology—form the outer layer of pressure for every client. These aren't abstract forces; they shape strategy, unsettle markets, and create moments of opportunity. Rainmakers know this. They don't just read the headlines; they interrogate what these forces mean for *their* client, right now, and where the real openings lie.

Past Shifts Provide the Proof

When the 2008 global financial crisis triggered liquidity shocks across markets, average consultants reacted to cost-cutting briefs. Rainmakers, however, reframed the conversation. They anticipated the shift to regulatory scrutiny and capital adequacy, helping banks rethink risk management, compliance infrastructure, and trust restoration at the board level. Similarly, when the Paris Climate Agreement was signed in 2015, most firms issued sustainability reports. Rainmakers went deeper: They showed clients how to reposition supply chains, investment priorities, and innovation agendas to align with the coming wave of ESG expectations, winning multiyear transformation mandates in the process.

Brexit was another defining moment. While many professional services advisors produced generic scenario analyses, rainmakers delved into the details of specific client exposures. For one global logistics client, that meant rethinking hub locations and contingency routes, a mandate that evolved into a multiyear transformation of the client's European operations.

Current Shifts Are Reshaping Demand in Real Time

The rapid adoption of AI is a perfect example. Many consultants are offering "AI readiness" workshops; rainmakers go further. They connect AI to their clients' unique operating models, surfacing risks such as bias in decision making or opportunities like hyperpersonalized customer engagement. The same applies to today's geopolitical realignments: supply chain "friend shoring," energy volatility, and inflationary pressures.

COVID-19 supply chain shocks demonstrated this difference starkly. Average consultants focused on firefighting, finding emergency sourcing options, and managing shortages. Rainmakers recognized the deeper story: the fragility of global just-in-time models. They positioned clients to redesign for resilience, building dual sourcing, regional hubs, and digital visibility platforms. Those who seized the moment turned survival into a strategic advantage.

Future Shifts Are the Richest Soil of All

Rainmakers don't pretend to predict the future, but they keep their eyes on the horizon. They ask questions like: *What happens when quantum computing breaks today's encryption models? How will synthetic biology or lab-grown food reshape global supply chains?* or *What political realignments could redefine market access in Asia, Africa, or Latin America?* These questions aren't speculative for their own sake; they're conversation openers, designed to position clients ahead of the curve and show them a path to act before their competitors.

This is what sets rainmakers apart. They don't stop at *what* is happening; they dig into *what it means here, now, for this client.* They notice when a global trend connects to a client's exposure, capital structure, or cultural reality. And increasingly, they use AI to do the heavy lifting, scanning hundreds of reports, investor briefings, and risk scenarios to highlight the two or three insights that really matter.

The result? Rainmakers walk into conversations armed with perspective, not platitudes. They arrive with a point of view that connects the global soil to the client's site, and that's why the most significant projects often begin with them.

Reading the Industry Topsoil

If global forces set the broad climate, industry dynamics shape the immediate terrain where consulting clients operate. Regulation, disruption, consolidation, and competitor behavior don't unfold overnight, but they often shift faster than companies can adapt. Rainmakers excel here because they read these shifts early, connect them to client realities, and use them to frame bold conversations.

Past Industry Shifts Show the Pattern

When deregulation swept through telecommunications in the 1990s, most consultants focused on functional cost reduction programs and incremental efficiencies. Rainmakers, by contrast, helped telcos reimagine their business models, shifting from monopolies to competitive service providers and creating entirely new revenue streams in mobile, broadband, and digital services. The same was true during the rise of e-commerce: While many advisors analyzed "online channels" as a bolt-on, rainmakers showed retailers how to rethink logistics, data strategy, and customer experience—conversations that led to multi-year reinventions of their operating models.

Current Shifts Are Rewriting Industry Rules

In the financial services sector, fintech startups are eroding profitable niches from payments to wealth management. Average consultants write reports about "the threat of disruption." Rainmakers ask sharper questions: *Which parts of your value chain are already under attack, and which ones could you spin out or defend with partnerships?* In the energy sector, the global shift to renewables is forcing incumbents to confront stranded assets, new regulatory regimes, and rising investor activism. Rainmakers don't stop at the compliance conversation; they work with boards to reposition portfolios, accelerate divestments, and capture first-mover advantage in emerging markets.

Healthcare during the COVID-19 pandemic provides another good example of where rainmakers differentiated themselves. Just as many advisors responded with crisis management and operational continuity, rainmakers saw the acceleration of telehealth and digital platforms as a long-term structural change. They worked with healthcare providers to rethink patient engagement models, funding structures, and workforce allocation. That foresight enabled some healthcare organizations not only to survive the pandemic but to thrive in its aftermath.

Future Shifts Are the Frontier

Rainmakers constantly scan for the next wave of industry transformation. In the automotive industry, we are seeing electrification and autonomous vehicles no longer being speculative; instead, the competitive battle-ground is shifting to battery supply chains, charging infrastructure, and software ecosystems, and rainmakers from different firms are positioning themselves for transformational plays. In professional services, AI is beginning to rewire delivery models, pricing, and talent strategies; rainmakers are already asking clients how to stay ahead in a world where knowledge work itself is being reshaped. And in agriculture, synthetic proteins and lab-grown food could disrupt value chains that have stood for centuries. These aren't certainties, but they are scenarios rainmakers prepare their clients to test against.

AI in Action

The power of AI is evident at the industry level. A rainmaker preparing for a client meeting in pharmaceuticals can now ask a Large Language Model to synthesize the last 100 FDA announcements, cross-reference competitor trial data, and highlight regulatory bottlenecks. Instead of arriving with generic "market updates," they come with a sharp point of view: *We see a 12- to 18-month window before regulators tighten on X; how are you positioning for that shift?* That depth builds credibility and creates openings for serious work.

This is the rainmaker's edge. Average consultants stop at commentary: *Here's what's happening in your industry*. Rainmakers translate shifts into impact: *Here's what it means for you, and here's where you can get ahead.* They combine industry pattern recognition with client-specific context and, increasingly, with AI-enabled preparation that makes their perspective both broader and deeper than that of anyone else in the room.

Reading the Client's Topsoil

Within a client's topsoil lie opportunities that stem directly from its business strategy. These opportunities are often hidden in plain sight, buried within corporate plans, budgets, business unit targets, and internal communications.

Rainmakers have a unique ability to translate those corporate strategies into discrete project opportunities. They dissect investor day presentations, media releases, results announcements, analyst reports, and planning documents to identify where targeted support can add value. They also make themselves available during the client's planning and budgeting cycle, helping business unit leaders prepare stronger, more relevant submissions.

In today's corporate and government worlds, the competition for scarce resources is intense. A well-crafted business case or budget submission can be the difference between securing funding or watching it go elsewhere.

AI in Action

Rainmakers now use AI-powered tools to surface client-specific insights that others might miss, subtle shifts in executive tone across quarterly briefings, patterns in board memberships that reveal influence lines, or employee feedback that hints at cultural pressure points. They use this intelligence to frame conversations that feel uncomfortably precise, the kind that makes a client pause and ask, "How did you know that?"

Average consultants wait for the brief. Rainmakers sense the undercurrents before they are voiced. They test the ground with thoughtful questions that expose hidden tensions, competing priorities, or unspoken opportunities. They know that real demand rarely sits in the stated problem. It lives in the politics, the culture, and the leadership pressures that shape decisions.

Reading the client's soil is not just analysis; it's presence. Rainmakers earn the right to be in the room when it matters because they've done the work that others won't. They listen more closely, observe more carefully, and connect the dots more quickly. That is how they move from being a vendor to becoming a voice that leaders trust.

Bringing the Topsoil Together

Global, industry, and client topsoil don't exist in isolation. They interact, overlap, and compound. An international regulatory shift cascades into industry upheaval; an industry disruption amplifies client-level tensions; a change in leadership reframes how global and industry forces are prioritized. Rainmakers thrive in this complexity because they see the linkages others miss.

Average consultants might enter a meeting prepared to discuss a global trend, an industry disruption, or a client initiative. Rainmakers arrive with the connections already drawn: *This regulatory move will hit your sector in 18 months. Here's how your competitors are preparing. And here's where you, given your culture and capital position, can get ahead.* That integration is what earns them a seat at the table, not as observers but as trusted advisors.

The pattern is consistent:

- From the **global topsoil**, rainmakers bring perspective, showing how broad forces create both risk and tailwind.
- From the **industry topsoil**, they bring relevance, translating disruption into competitive advantage or exposure.
- From the **client topsoil**, they bring precision, naming the unspoken tensions and opportunities that define whether action is possible.

AI is accelerating this ability. Where once the synthesis required weeks of fragmented research, rainmakers now harness AI to compress the cycle, connecting hundreds of signals across all three layers and developing the few insights that matter most. What remains uniquely human, and uniquely rainmaker, is the judgment to decide which connections are significant and the courage to voice them at the right moment.

This is why rainmakers consistently uncover bigger, more material opportunities than their peers. They don't treat the soils as background noise. They cultivate the soils globally in their industry and with their clients into fertile ground for bold, high-value work.

Next: Surface Layer—Today's Realities, Tomorrow's Opportunities

We're almost at the final layer of this soil journey, the world of consulting as it is today. It's messy. Fast. Unpredictable. Pressure is everywhere. But so is potential.

Let's keep going.

CHAPTER

5

Surface Layer: Today's Realities, Tomorrow's Opportunities

From Unexpected Events, Great Opportunities Emerge. . .If You're Not Asleep at the Wheel

The uppermost layer of soil is where the real weather hits. It's exposed. Unstable. Unforgiving. And it's changing faster than ever.

Whereas the topsoil opportunities are found in disclosed strategies, the surface layer opportunities arise from unforeseen events, changes in leadership, or urgent client needs.

This is the layer where rainmakers respond to fast-moving events: the unanticipated events, actions, pressures, and disruptions that create urgency for clients.

This chapter examines what it takes to thrive in the day-to-day world of modern organizations, a world marketed by turbulence, acceleration, and profound change. We look at the shocks that shape a senior client's world (many visible, many hidden), the human side of those clients who bring their emotions, fears, and ambitions to the table, and the seven underlying reasons they turn to consultants for help. Together, these threads demonstrate not only how rainmakers thrive in this exposed layer but also how they capitalize on the opportunities it presents.

Shocks That Shape a Senior Client's World

For senior clients, the surface layer is shaped by shocks that arrive without warning, some visible and systemic, others hidden and deeply personal, each capable of shifting priorities, disrupting momentum, or redefining what matters most. At the outer edge, the shock might be a sudden regulatory change or new government policy that forces an organization-wide response. It could be the unexpected approval or rejection of a budget or out-of-cycle funding request that alters the trajectory of strategic initiatives overnight. Sometimes it's the discovery of a compliance breach or legal issue that threatens reputation and consumes leadership attention for months.

Competitive pressure never really lets up. A rival might launch a headline-grabbing product, announce a surprise partnership, or make a move that puts years of careful planning in jeopardy. Larger economic shifts, rising inflation, changing interest rates, or supply-chain disruption can also throw off the assumptions leadership teams rely on. Analysts and investors can add heat through downgrades, activist campaigns, or pointed questions that accelerate decisions faster than leaders would like.

And then there are the leadership shocks, the moments that change everything inside the client's walls. A new CEO, chair, or key executive often arrives with a fresh agenda that resets priorities and rewrites the playbook almost overnight.

Or when another senior executive departs, whether through promotion, a restructure, retirement, or abrupt exit, the shock ripples widely.

Major programs lose their sponsor, internal teams lose direction, and consulting partners can suddenly find months of alignment work undone overnight. For clients, uncertainty rises; for consultants, access and momentum often stall. The best advisors don't panic or push harder. They steady the relationship. They reconnect with the incoming leader's priorities, reaffirm the value already created, and help the client organization maintain continuity while preparing for transition. Rainmakers recognize these moments as tests of trust; when others retreat, they step forward with calm, context, and clarity, seeing not a pitch opportunity but a chance to help reposition the organization for what comes next.

Following the global financial crisis, for example, several major banks appointed new CEOs. Rainmakers didn't just propose cost-cutting programs; they reframed the conversation around transformation: culture, governance, and customer trust. These weren't short-term fixes; they became multiyear programs that reshaped markets. Similarly, after large merger and acquisition deals, rainmakers who tuned into the politics between legacy leadership teams uncovered opportunities in integration support, cultural alignment, and portfolio rationalization that others missed.

Executive tenures have become shorter, and leaders now face immense pressure to deliver visible results fast. A cautious consultant might back away from that intensity; rainmakers lean in. They ask sharper questions: *Where can we create a 100-day win that builds credibility for your broader agenda?* In government settings, where leadership changes can stall reforms, rainmakers know when to pause and when to reframe, aligning their work to new priorities rather than clinging to the old.

COVID-19 revealed this distinction clearly. While many consultants offered operational continuity playbooks, rainmakers looked deeper. They saw cultural fractures, leadership fatigue, and the chance to redesign ways of working. One rainmaker-led program inside a global technology company reframed remote work not as a stopgap but as a long-term strategic advantage helping leadership retain critical talent while competitors struggled with attrition.

Rising generational turnover is now bringing new leadership styles, values, and risk appetites. Boards are becoming more activist, demanding faster change and greater transparency. Rainmakers are already reading these signals in the soil, asking: *What happens when the next generation of leaders pushes harder on ESG? When activist investors judge culture and governance alongside earnings? When AI-driven decision systems reshape how executives allocate capital or measure performance?*

These questions aren't distant hypotheticals. They are visible shifts, already forming the surface layer of a client's world, the part that rainmakers learn to read first.

Rainmakers don't just watch that exposed layer; they harness its volatility. Where others see disruption, they see signals. Where many are caught off guard, they anticipate, prepare, and position themselves so that when the storm breaks, they're already at the client's side. They stand out by reading the culture of a client's organization with absolute precision. In every conversation, they pick up on how decisions are really made, who holds influence, and what the company values most.

They also invest in understanding the rhythms of the business, when budgets are set, when strategic reviews occur, and when off-cycle requests are likely to land. By aligning their ideas with those key moments, they avoid pushing against the flow. Their proposals appear right on time as if they were the missing piece the client was already looking for.

Another defining habit is building a broad internal network within the client organization. Rainmakers don't just focus on top decision makers; they engage chiefs of staff, deputies, and emerging leaders. These relationships act as an early radar, signaling shifts in priorities or leadership moves long before they reach the surface. This network also makes rainmakers less dependent on any single sponsor and more deeply embedded across the client's ecosystem.

Consistency is just as important as insight. The most effective advisors maintain regular contact with senior leaders, staying visible by offering insight and value even when no immediate project exists. They build their internal calendars around the client's world, tracking board meetings, investor briefings, strategy offsites, and leadership changes. Increasingly, they use AI to sharpen that awareness, scanning for regulatory updates, competitive signals, or early indicators of organizational stress.

There's nothing flashy about these habits. They're quiet, deliberate, and deeply human. But together, they turn volatility into opportunity and ensure that rainmakers aren't just reacting to change; they're helping shape what comes next.

The Human Side of Clients

Behind every strategy document and project brief is a real person, someone dealing with ambition, pressure, hopes, and doubts. The best advisors never forget that. Rainmakers understand that a client's world isn't shaped just by business goals but by people—executives, managers, future leaders, and veterans—each with their own story, and each more than just a title on an organizational chart. They are individuals with reputations to protect, legacies to build, risks to weigh, and aspirations they may never voice aloud.

This is the human terrain of consulting. Miss it, and you miss the moment. In high-stakes work, content and context matters. But neither alone will get consultants to the "big dance." What bridges the two is connection. Progress begins not with a pitch but with presence. Rainmakers connect before they propose. They earn the right to advise by being trusted as thinking partners, not just technical experts. That trust is earned slowly through consistency, empathy, and perceived integrity, and contemporary research shows it also depends on communication, rapport, and sustained relationships.[1]

In our story in Chapter 4 of a career-defining transformation project, the strategy itself was strong. But what landed was not the slide pack, it was Robert's ability to deeply read the soil and emotional weight carried by the CEO. He didn't advise from a distance. He stepped into the frame, quietly, thoughtfully, and with the courage to help shape a better future. That is the work that distinguishes rainmakers.

And it is not just anecdote; it is behavioral science. Daniel Kahneman and Amos Tversky's Prospect Theory showed that people are wired to avoid losses more than they pursue gains, and those insights remain just as relevant today.[2] In consulting, this evidence changes everything. Even bold executives often are more focused on what could go wrong than on what might go right.[3] Protecting reputation, preserving cohesion, avoiding regret—these motivations shape decisions as much as the promise of transformation. Rainmakers understand this deeply. They don't just sell upside; they neutralize risk. They show that a great idea can also be a safe idea.

That's why they break big ambitions into manageable steps. They ask, "What if this succeeds?" but also face the question: "What if it doesn't?" They earn trust by showing how risks can be controlled. Take a digital transformation; it's not sold as a giant leap but as a careful, flexible approach that delivers early wins and keeps options open. The way they talk matters: "We're not here to shake things up for no reason. We want to build on what's already working." Or: "If we don't see progress by Month 3, we adjust course. You're never stuck on just one path."

Rainmakers also bring hidden concerns to light. They sense unspoken worries, like political risks and internal tensions, and deal with them before they slow things down. They might say, "I've seen similar efforts stall when all the risk fell on one leader. Let's set up a governance structure that shares responsibility and builds trust across the team." By doing this, they ease the fear that saying yes could backfire, making it safer to pursue bold goals.

They also recognize that clients are never singular. They work in matrixed teams, under shifting political winds, inside cultures that prize caution as much as creativity. A bold idea that ignores human dynamics will never take root. So, rainmakers test the soil. They watch body language. They ask second-level questions. They listen more than they speak.

And they use storytelling, not spin. Their narrative is grounded in the client's world, framing the arc from pressure to progress. Research shows that storytelling reduces cognitive strain and increases perceived truthfulness, especially in complex decision-making situations. A well-told story clears fog, creates belief, and gives clients something they can champion.

Key Insight: Rainmakers don't romanticize clients; they humanize them. They bring logic and warmth. They know every deal is more than a transaction. It is a leap of trust, taken by someone with much to lose and, perhaps, something even greater to gain.

Seven Reasons Why Clients Ask for Help

Need is the third dimension of the surface layer. If the first was about shocks that reshape a client's world and the second about the human side of the executives themselves, this section turns to the practical: why clients bring in consultants at all and why rainmakers, in particular, are called for the biggest moments.

Landing insight at the right place and time is only half the equation. A client also has to want help, to feel the moment is big enough, complex enough, or risky enough to call in trusted advisers. Robert, drawing on his own executive experience, has seen these choices up close. Executives don't invite consultants in lightly. They weigh the decision as carefully as they would a new board appointment. Increasingly, the selection of a consulting advisor is treated as a fundamental driver of performance, not unlike the selection of executive team members themselves.[4]

Clients engage rainmakers for seven practical reasons:

1. **Specialized expertise:** To inject deep, hard-earned expertise developed across industries and transformations that would take internal teams years to accumulate.

2. **Speed of execution:** To accelerate progress by mobilizing experienced teams quickly, applying proven approaches, and maintaining momentum when internal capacity or alignment slows action.
3. **Source of ideas:** To bring fresh thinking from diverse client situations, translating emerging practices, technologies, and strategies into practical ideas tailored to a client's context.
4. **Risk and scenario planning:** To help leaders test assumptions, explore scenarios, and evaluate risks, providing structured analysis that strengthens decisions in uncertain and high-stakes environments.
5. **Objectivity and independence:** To offer independent judgment, unencumbered by internal politics or legacy positions, enabling leaders to challenge assumptions and address difficult truths.
6. **Global perspective:** To allow leaders to compare performance, spot emerging trends, and anticipate shifts earlier from consultants working across geographies.
7. **Scalable capacity and methodology for complex initiatives:** To provide disciplined methodologies and experienced teams that scale rapidly, enabling organizations to deliver complex, multistakeholder transformations with structure and pace.

Other consultants may bring some of these capabilities. Rainmakers bring all of them and know how to use them in the moment. In meetings, pitches, and proposals, they don't just run through a list of points; they bring these ideas into the conversation, showing how they matter right then and there. That's where most consultants fall short.

Rainmakers don't just say they offer a global perspective; they bring in top experts from around the world. They don't just promise quick results; they time their plan to fit the client's key moments and explain how they'll manage risks every step of the way. (See Figure 5.1.)

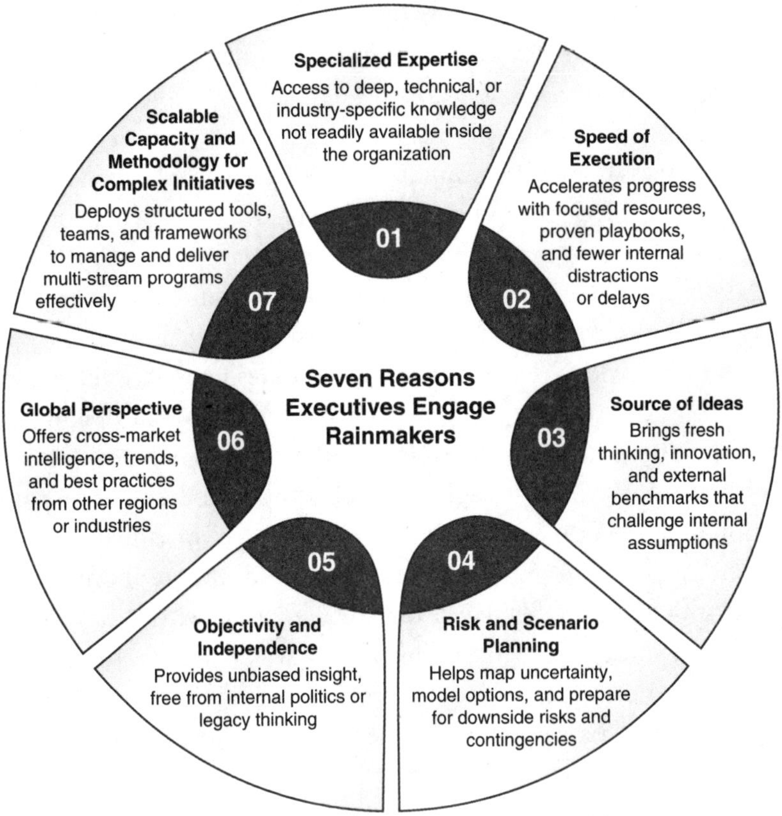

FIGURE 5.1 Why executives engage with rainmakers.

Speed to Get to Market First

Consider the story from Robert's time as CEO of Malaysia's number one mobile telecommunications company, Maxis.

I was sitting in my apartment in Kuala Lumpur at 2 a.m. on the morning of May 10, 2018, at a dramatic moment in Malaysia's history. The opposition parties had just won an election victory over the coalition government, the first change of government since Malaysia achieved independence in 1957.

While opposition supporters celebrated, I experienced a stressful night fielding urgent conference calls with the industry regulator and the CEOs of other telecom companies. As the major provider of mobile phone services in the country, we were operating under emergency directions to ensure security across Malaysia.

I resolved to do an all-nighter to ensure that the country had uninterrupted access to mobile communications. Still, while I watched events unfold on the television and in the streets below, I recalled a conversation I'd had with our consulting advisor weeks earlier regarding opportunities that might arise for us under a new government. The prospects for the opposition's success had been considered small by most commentators, but one of the potential opportunities interested me greatly.

During the campaign, the opposition had proposed opening the fixed broadband market to competition by enforcing new network access provisions recently legislated. The opposition had gone to the election with a "double the speed at half the price" broadband policy.

The prospect of gaining a first-mover advantage loomed if we moved quickly. So, the day after the election, while the country enjoyed an unexpected public holiday, I was deep in conversation with my executive team and our consulting partner. To capitalize effectively on this opportunity, we need to work smart and fast. There was significant execution risk and potential damage to our brand if the launch of a broadband business fell over. Our team was up for the challenge and put together a business case that got the green light from the board. We concluded that we could handle the regulatory approval and marketing requirements in-house. At the same time, consultants could mobilize to support us with sales and service procedures, equipment sourcing, customer targeting, and negotiating access.

Within weeks, we launched Fibernation—our new broadband product offering double the speed at half the price. Within three months, we captured 15% market share from the existing fixed-service provider, with no other new competitors entering the market. The wonderful people of Maxis and our consulting partner harnessed the euphoria of the election to capture new customers and fundamentally change our company to become a full-service fixed and mobile carrier.

Our success validated the government's strategy of opening markets to competition. It provided the people of Malaysia with a faster and cheaper broadband service, generating millions of dollars in value for our company.

As I reflected on the success we delivered in that period, I concluded that no other company in the market could have pulled it off. We had the team capability and consulting support to make us unbeatable. And importantly, to help me weigh the downside risk just as heavily as the upside opportunity.[5]

When Only the Best Will Do

In another corporate role, I was tasked with a cross-company customer service transformation. A reading of the soil would have identified that:

- This strategy was the single most significant public objective of the company and the driving force of the CEO.
- 40% of executive compensation was riding on the outcome.
- The many past attempts at improvement had failed due to the organizational complexity.

We were presented with a proposal to move our customer service and management to a Net Promoter Score system and a complete reframing of our approach to customer service to create advocates and eliminate detractors. The consulting firm rainmaker, leading the discussion, recognized the need for success and did not offer up himself or his local team. He organized the authors of the leading book on the subject, who were on the other side of the world, to personally invest their time in guiding the implementation of the system.

That's why executives hire the best consultants, particularly in the moments of significant impact and big decisions when they need results fast. They want the global A team, not the B team, and rainmakers know this.

The Rainmaker Difference

So, what sets rainmakers apart?

- They decode the unspoken. They listen between the lines. They tune into pressure, politics, and posture.
- They reframe the problem. They elevate conversations. They challenge assumptions.
- They focus on outcomes. Reports are fine. Results are better.
- They earn influence.[6] Steady presence. Quiet confidence. Trusted voice.
- They use AI to move faster, with more impact.[7]

Their approach aligns with what Richard H. Thaler and Cass R. Sunstein call *choice architecture*. Rainmakers don't dictate. They guide and structure conversations in a natural way.[8]

In my executive career, the best consultants helped me make faster and better decisions. They gave me confidence, not by making the hard call for me, but by walking alongside me until I could make the call.

That's the real magic of the rainmaker: clarity and courage, delivered quietly.

Conclusion: Thriving in the Surface Layer

Rainmakers deeply understand and are present at the surface level, where disruption first hits for a client. It's also where the human side of every role, agenda, and decision quietly but strongly influences what happens next. And it is where clients finally decide whether to invite outside help, weighing the seven reasons that drive them to bring in advisors when the stakes are highest.

Average consultants see turbulence and wait to be called. Rainmakers see signals. They anticipate shocks, prepare for volatility, and remain calm and clear-headed when others are rattled. Average consultants treat clients as functions and processes. Rainmakers treat them as people, with fears, ambitions, reputations, and risks that must be navigated with empathy as much as with analysis. Average consultants pitch their capabilities. Rainmakers embody the seven reasons for engagement, using each not as a slide in a deck but as a lever in conversation, a way to unlock trust and move action forward.

A mindset of discipline and awareness is what it takes to thrive in today's exposed, unforgiving layer of the consulting world. Rainmakers don't just survive here. They adapt, translate, and shape opportunities from volatility. They are as adept at understanding human dynamics as they are at developing effective strategies. They are as ready for shocks as they are for the long game. And they never forget that every deal, every transformation, every bold step forward depends on one fragile but powerful thing: trust.

To thrive in this layer is to accept that the weather will never be calm. The storms will come, the soil will shift, the pressure will intensify. But for rainmakers, that is not a threat. It is the environment in which they grow.

PART

I

SUMMARY

The Soil: Understanding the Rainmaker's World

Up to this point, we've looked at how rainmakers have emerged and the changing environment they face. From this, four key truths become clear:

1. **Bedrock: foundations of a profession.** Consulting didn't just appear overnight; it grew out of the challenges businesses faced, much like soil forming from rock. The early leaders in the 19th and 20th centuries set down principles of clarity, method, and perspective that still form the foundation of the profession today. The industry has evolved with the growth and sophistication of organizations, and modern consulting has earned a respected position as a change initiator and ideas generator. Rainmakers are students of this history. They have a deep understanding of the profession and their firm's place in it. They admire and follow leaders who make a difference and position themselves as ambassadors for their firm and the profession.

2. **Shifting subsoil: supply-side shake-up.** Beneath the surface, consulting's supply side is changing at a rapid pace and in a profound way. Boutique firms, internal teams, platforms, and specialists continually shift the ground. Rainmakers thrive here by studying their rivals, extending their networks into related organizations and deeply researching, assessing, and evaluating their own firm's successful projects and capabilities.
3. **Topsoil: demand-side upheaval.** Topsoil is the first segment of the client layer. It is relatively predictable and has been the traditional hunting ground for all consulting firms. All modern organizations adopt strategic planning and budgeting processes that reveal objectives, strategies, targets, and plans. Rainmakers focus on getting in at the budget and planning submission stage assisting business units win resource allocations. The secret to success here is hard work, presence, the accurate interpretation of plans and statements made by executives, and deep analytical understanding of global and industry-level developments and potential actions required of organizations.
4. **Surface layer: today's reality, tomorrow's opportunities.** The surface is full of sudden shifts and surprises. But for rainmakers, the turbulence is not just noise. They spot patterns, pick up on early signs of change, and act when the moment is right. They stay close to their clients and adjust quickly. They are first in the door when there is an executive change, when a crisis emerges, and when there is a major unplanned shift in the environment. Responsiveness and deep insight earn the rewards here.

Review Questions for Potential Rainmakers

1. Do my client conversations utilize foundational principles, such as clarity, insight, and perspective? Do I have interesting topics to raise with my clients?
2. How well do I anticipate change in my market rather than simply reacting to it?

3. Which enduring lessons from the origins of consulting and my firm could I apply today to strengthen my positioning with clients?
4. Do I truly understand how my clients view the alternatives to me, such as rivals, boutiques, platforms, and internal teams?
5. Do I have response plans ready to act to anticipated competitor moves at my clients?
6. Where am I building collaborations and networks beyond my firm that give me a distinct competitive advantage?
7. Am I reading my clients' world deeply enough—for example, their earnings calls, strategies, politics, and anxieties—to spot opportunities before they ask?
8. How often do I create and show up in moments that matter rather than waiting for briefs to land?
9. Do I treat demand as a living landscape or as a series of transactions?
10. Am I close enough to my clients to sense leadership shifts, budget realignments, and cultural cracks as they emerge?
11. Do I act with speed and relevance when opportunity appears, or do I risk hesitating until it passes?
12. How well do I convert turbulence, disruption, and volatility into opportunity?
13. How much time do I spend researching my competitors, my firm's successful projects and capabilities, and my industry?

Looking Ahead: Into the Roots of a Rainmaker

But great consulting doesn't start with strategy. It starts from within.

In the next part of the book, we dig beneath the surface, into the roots, where purpose, drive, and ethics take hold.

Because without deep roots, even the tallest tree will fall in the storm.

Let's explore what truly sustains the best consultants and how you can cultivate it for yourself.

PART

II

The Roots

Inner Life of a Rainmaker

CHAPTER 6

Beneath the Surface

You're Smart and Hardworking. So Is Everyone Else. Your Brand Is Built on What You Stand For

Before rainmakers grow upward, they must first grow downward.

Every towering consulting career is built on something far less visible, an inner system of roots that anchors identity, absorbs strength, and adapts to change. These are not soft skills. They're not optional.

At the center of this root system are four essentials: self-awareness, purpose, resilience, and ethical responsibility. These aren't just abstract ideals; they form the inner framework that everything else depends on. Self-awareness anchors who you are. Purpose stretches you toward something bigger. Resilience keeps you moving when things get tough. And ethics? They hold the line when it really matters. (See Figure 6.1.)

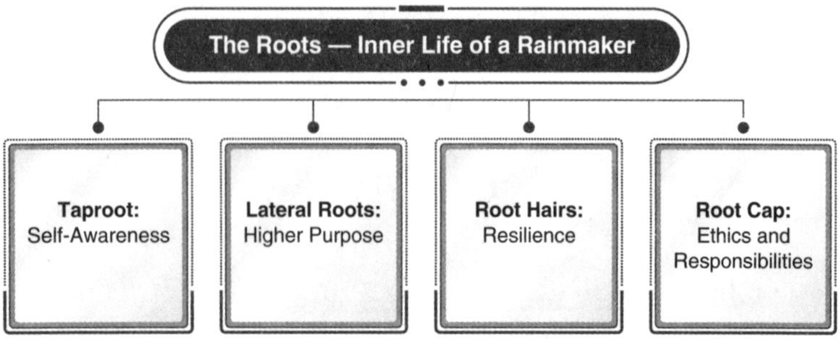

FIGURE 6.1 The inner life of a rainmaker.

When the surface world is chaotic—volatile markets, shifting client needs, new technologies, internal pressure—rainmakers who know who they are, why they're here, how to recover, and where they draw the line don't just survive. They grow stronger.

Like a tree's roots, these traits must evolve. The soil around you will change. Trust may erode. Expectations may rise. But the deeper and healthier your roots, the more capacity you'll have to respond, realign, and rise again.

In the next four chapters, we explore each of these elements in turn. But first, a closer look at what makes them so essential:

- **Taproot: self-awareness:** The taproot is the firm, central root that grows straight down and stabilizes the tree. In a rainmaker, this is self-awareness—the deep, honest understanding of your identity, emotions, patterns, and motivations. Without it, you drift. With it, you gain clarity, consistency, and confidence. Self-awareness allows you to reflect without ego, receive feedback without fear, and adapt without losing your center. Like a taproot reaching deep into the soil, self-awareness draws the nutrients that support every other part of your growth.
- **Lateral roots: higher purpose:** Lateral roots stretch outward from the taproot, increasing reach and resilience. A rainmaker's higher purpose works the same way, connecting you to something beyond yourself. Purpose is what gives your effort meaning day after day; it's the "why" that keeps you going long after the initial

spark fades. Maybe it's reshaping an industry, guiding the next generation, or tackling tough public challenges. Whatever it is, purpose expands your reach and fuels your resilience. Like lateral roots spreading wide to anchor a tree, purpose gives you stability, grounding your work in something bigger: impact, legacy, and service.

- **Root hairs: resilience:** Tiny but powerful, root hairs increase surface area and extract nutrients from even the most depleted soil. That's resilience. In a rainmaker's life, pressure is constant: deadlines, rejections, restructures, and reversals. But like root hairs, resilience doesn't just survive stress; it adapts to it. Root hairs absorbs strength from small wins, learns from setbacks, and continues to grow even when the soil turns dry. This quiet persistence, often invisible to others, is what keeps you moving when others stop.
- **Root cap: ethics and responsibility:** At the very tip of the root, there is a protective mechanism—it's the root cap. Ethics play the same role in a rainmaker's world. They guide decisions, shield reputation, and ensure that progress doesn't come at the cost of principle. Your ethical compass is what keeps you aligned in moments of pressure, temptation, or moral ambiguity. Like a root cap, it allows you to move forward, not recklessly but with integrity and direction.

Next: Look Inward

We begin where all growth must: at the center, the taproot. In the next chapter, we dig deep into self-awareness, the trait that anchors rainmakers through uncertainty, empowers reflection, and provides the clarity needed to lead others. Without it, nothing holds. With it, everything starts to grow.

Let's begin.

CHAPTER

7

Taproot: Self-Awareness

The Search for Success Starts with You

Say "self-awareness" in a consulting room, and you'll often get a polite nod, followed by a quick pivot to something that sounds more commercial: pipelines, deal velocity, or industry insight. But here's the truth: Self-awareness isn't soft. It's structural. It's the taproot of rainmaker performance, that central, anchoring force beneath the surface that sustains growth above it.

And not just personal growth. Commercial performance. Client impact. Market relevance.

Recent McKinsey research highlights that executives who demonstrate strong self-awareness are more likely to lead high-performing business units, especially in volatile and rapidly changing environments.[1] Why? Because self-awareness sharpens decision making, reduces misalignment, and strengthens trust, all of which correlate strongly with win rates in complex sales and consulting contexts. In big-ticket pursuits, perception isn't peripheral; it's decisive.

Without a deep, healthy taproot, even the strongest tree struggles in shifting soil. In consulting, the ground shifts often, with demanding clients, tight timelines, sudden leadership transitions, and relentless performance pressure. The rainmakers who thrive in that terrain aren't just technically brilliant. They're anchored. Self-aware. Able to absorb feedback, course-correct, and stay true to purpose even under stress.

In this chapter, we dig deep, literally and metaphorically. We refine the definition of self-awareness, demonstrate how it drives rainmaker-level performance, and examine the research findings. Because while most firms skim the surface, the science runs deep. And when we've seen rainmakers nurture this root system intentionally, everything above the ground—their influence, followership, revenue, and impact—flourishes.

But we've also seen the opposite. Competent, driven professionals delivering solid results while quietly limiting their potential—missing client cues, eroding trust, leaving revenue and relationships on the table—all because no one ever helped them tend their root system. No structured feedback. No high-trust coaching. No mirror. Just hustle, instinct, and an invisible ceiling.

And the toll isn't just personal; it also impacts commercially, culturally, and strategically.

Let me share a story to bring this to life.

The Cost of Shallow Roots: Eric's Story

Eric was a senior partner—technically sharp, publicly visible, and commercially strong. His name carried weight in the market. Clients knew him, his practice hit its numbers, and his profile seemed to rise every year. On the surface, everything looked healthy. Yet beneath that surface, something was off.

In many ways, Eric had the potential to be a rainmaker. He had senior relationships in major accounts, a commanding presence with executives, and, in his early years, he'd led one or two transformative projects that changed the trajectory of his clients' businesses. For a while, it felt like he was on the path, the kind of partner others watched closely, assuming bigger things would follow. But they never did. What started as promise gradually plateaued.

Inside the firm, collaboration was fading. Pursuits that once drew energy from across the partnership began to lose momentum. Deals that should have been ours slipped away, not for lack of capability but because people simply didn't want to team with him. Colleagues found him difficult to read. Teams described a kind of invisible barrier, meetings that left them drained rather than inspired. The work got done, but the spark was gone.

We tried to help. Coaching was offered, feedback was given, but it rarely landed. He listened politely, then rationalized it away. "That's just how I am," he'd say. Or "It's working, isn't it?" And for a time, it was. But only in the narrowest sense.

Eric measured success by visible markers, billings, media mentions, client lunches. What he couldn't see was the widening gap between what he thought he was creating and what others were actually experiencing. His self-assessment was rooted in outputs, not outcomes; in activity, not impact. The deeper work of reflection, understanding how his behavior shaped energy, trust, and collective performance, never took hold.

As the market evolved, his approach began to date. Clients wanted transparency and partnership, not just advice from a podium. Teams wanted collaboration and shared credit, not direction from above. But Eric kept doubling down on what had worked before. He was, in his own mind, still the hero of the story; he didn't realize that the story had moved on.

Eventually I had to make the call. Eric wasn't failing in the traditional sense—no scandal, no collapse, no missed revenue target. But he was quietly capping our growth. His presence created a subtle drag on trust and momentum. A firm can survive that for a while, but it can't grow through it. The decision to let him go was one of the hardest I've made, and one of the clearest.

When the roots stay shallow, the tree can look strong for years, until a change in weather exposes what's missing underneath.

Eric's taproot never deepened. And without that anchor of self-awareness, the discipline of honest reflection, even the tallest tree eventually falls.

What Is Self-Awareness?

Let's be clear. Self-awareness isn't "being nice" or "knowing your Myers-Briggs type." It's not about personality or positivity. And it's not optional.

It's the disciplined practice of understanding two things:

1. **What drives you internally:** Your patterns, motivations, values, and derailers
2. **How you're experienced externally:** Not your intent, but your real-world impact

Organizational psychologist Dr. Tasha Eurich, in her foundational work on the topic, draws a powerful distinction between internal and external self-awareness.[2] Her research indicates that the most effective leaders cultivate both. One without the other creates imbalance, like a tree with strong roots on one side and rot on the other.

Rainmakers who navigate this balance well are both steady and adaptable. They know their patterns: what triggers them, how they present themselves, and where they need to make adjustments. And they do change, not out of defensiveness but with intent and strategy.

That kind of presence changes the dynamic. It earns trust, yes, but more than that, it opens space. Space for clients to say what matters. Space for teams to step in and contribute. Space for more intelligent, more grounded decisions to take shape.

> **Key Insight:** Self-awareness isn't about being soft. It's about being sharp. Not polite for the sake of it, but deliberate and effective.

The Research Is Compelling

Too often, self-awareness is dismissed as soft science. That couldn't be further from the truth. The research is not just credible, it's conclusive.

Dr. Tasha Eurich's landmark study found that while 95% of people think they're self-aware, only 10 to 15% are. That means most professionals, including many partners and directors of consulting firms, are leading with a warped mirror.

And the cost is high.

A Korn Ferry study of 6,977 executives found that companies with more self-aware leaders consistently outperformed financially.[3] These leaders were rated higher in collaboration, empathy, and long-term thinking, all vital to consulting success. Their organizations had stronger employee engagement, faster decision making, and better retention of high-potential talent.

Other research from Harvard Business School and INSEAD suggest that self-aware leaders perform better when facing uncertainty and biases.[4] And neuroscience studies linked to the University of Toronto further suggest that self-reflection engages brain processes tied to empathy and perspective-taking, key traits for rainmakers.[5]

And furthermore, a 2021 study published in *The Leadership Quarterly* found that leaders perceived as self-aware were more likely to be endorsed by others, which fosters stronger leadership effectiveness and performance within organizations.[6] In today's consulting environment where collaboration, influence, and teaming across disciplines are more critical than ever, self-awareness isn't just a leadership trait. It's a performance multiplier for rainmakers and high-performing professionals alike.

In elite sport and the military, this is well understood. High-performing teams run after-action reviews not to assign blame, but to deepen insight. The All Blacks, a highly successful New Zealand national rugby team, have a legendary mantra: "Better people make better All Blacks." The mantra speaks directly to the fact that personal growth precedes peak performance.

And in our world of high-value consulting, the same holds: Rainmakers aren't just better at sales or delivery. They're better at seeing themselves clearly and growing from that clarity.

How Rainmakers Apply the Research

Rainmakers don't wait for the human resources department or an external body to run a 360-feedback survey or hope for feedback in a hallway. They build their own systems of insight and reflection and root-deep structures that nourish growth over time.

Two decades ago, self-awareness was largely episodic. Annual reviews, project postmortems, maybe a leadership offsite. Reflection came in bursts, often long after the moment had passed. Today, rainmakers treat awareness as a living system. They know that in a world moving at high velocity, with clients changing priorities weekly and teams shifting fluidly, static feedback models simply can't keep pace.

They operate through what we call the *rainmaker awareness loop*, a continuous cycle of sensing, reflecting, calibrating, and acting. (See Figure 7.1.) It's not about navel gazing; it's about maintaining the strategic edge that comes from alignment between intent and impact.

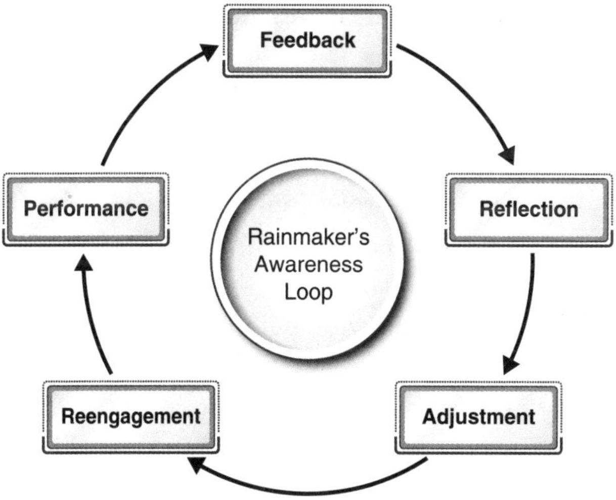

FIGURE 7.1 The rainmaker's awareness loop.

Here's what rainmakers do differently:

- They assume they're blind and stay curious. Their default is: *What am I not seeing?* This humility protects them from complacency.
- They invite structured feedback, often facilitated by a trusted coach or mentor, someone who interprets patterns, not just data.
- They run postmortems and playback loops after key meetings or client interactions, not to dwell on mistakes but to learn, reframe, and course-correct.
- They ask specific questions, such as "*How did I land in that room?*," "*What signals did I miss?*," or "*What would have made that better?*" These simple prompts open deeper insight.
- They build rituals around reflection: journaling, coaching check-ins, even client debriefs. These aren't administrative exercises; they're closing the loop between perception and performance.
- They make micro-adjustments in real time, pausing before replying, shifting tone, creating space for others, not from self-doubt but with strategic intent.
- They use AI as a feedback tool to test and improve their client communications and evaluate reactions received.

The difference today is that rainmakers use these loops continuously, often enhanced by real-time inputs from digital signals, AI summaries, meeting transcripts, or pulse surveys, turning self-awareness from a personal trait into a professional system. They blend intuition with analytics, emotion with evidence.

They also surround themselves with what we call *root sustainers*: truth tellers, challengers, and wise guides. These aren't cheerleaders; they're calibration points. They keep the taproot honest. And they understand that in fast-growth environments, not all roots are healthy. Ego, insecurity, and the need to be right can grow as fast as success itself.

But rainmakers prune constantly. They cultivate clarity, nourish humility, and deepen the habits that sustain real growth. They know that awareness—genuine, ongoing awareness—is not soft work. It's the hardest, most strategic work of all.

Conclusion

In consulting, the market eventually exposes what lies beneath the surface. Expertise may open doors, but self-awareness determines what happens once you are in the room. The rainmakers who endure are those willing to look inward as rigorously as they analyze clients. They listen, adjust, and grow. Over time, that quiet discipline deepens the taproot. And when the ground inevitably shifts, as it always does, that unseen strength is what keeps the tree standing.

Next: Find the Purpose

Self-awareness is the taproot. Nurture it, and everything above the surface grows stronger: resilience, empathy, influence, integrity, revenue. Ignore it, and even the best performers risk instability when their world changes.

Rainmakers know this. That's why they build root systems others can't see: quiet disciplines, deep practices, and honest reflection. Not to feel better. To lead better. To win better.

But self-awareness alone isn't enough. Even deep roots need a reason to grow. And the strongest roots aren't just driven by feedback; they're anchored by purpose.

And that's where we go next. Let's begin.

CHAPTER

8

Lateral Roots: Higher Purpose

No Passion, No World-Class Edge – So Why Should Clients Bother Meeting You?

We've been incredibly fortunate. Throughout our careers, we've worked alongside thousands of remarkable people in extraordinary cities around the world, from Dallas to Delhi, São Paulo to Singapore, London to Lisbon. Most of them aren't chasing the spotlight. They're not keynote speakers or LinkedIn influencers. But they are the engine room of the consulting profession: disciplined, thoughtful, and deeply committed.

And yet little is written about what anchors that commitment. Why do they do it? Why push through the long hours, the relentless expectations, the ambiguity, and the pressure that define consulting life? What gives rainmakers the energy not just to perform but to grow, stretch, and show up with such fierce intent, year after year?

As we explored this, a deeper pattern emerged.

If self-awareness is the taproot, the vertical force driving clarity and insight from within, then purpose is the system of lateral roots that stretches outward, quietly anchoring rainmakers in something larger than themselves. It doesn't always shout. But it stabilizes everything. It draws strength from different sources: personal values, professional mission, a sense of service, or legacy. And when purpose is well developed, it makes the whole system stronger, more resilient, and more expansive.

As part of writing this book, we set out to understand that root system more clearly. Through focused interviews, research, and hundreds of conversations, we listened to the rainmakers who consistently deliver the highest impact, not just commercially but culturally. And what we found wasn't always what we expected.

And then, in one of those unexpected moments, the kind that consulting life tends to deliver when you least anticipate it, the answer begins to take shape. Neil was on holiday in Florence when he stepped into the Galleria dell'Accademia. Let's let him tell the rest.

When Craft Becomes Legacy

I was entranced; the golden light filtered through high windows, casting a soft glow on the sculptures lining the halls. Yet nothing prepared me for what stood at the end of the gallery: Michelangelo's *David*.

The statue's scale—over 17 feet tall—was staggering. It was carved from a single block of marble, but you'd never know it as every muscle, every vein, every curve looked as if it had been shaped by life itself. The craftsmanship was extraordinary, but that's not what held me.

It was the eyes.

That gaze: steady, intense, locked onto something just beyond the edge of sight pulled me in. David didn't seem frozen. He seemed *to pause*. Like the breath right before a leap, the thought just before the strike.

Not a statue. A moment. Caught between stillness and movement, reflection and resolve.

Michelangelo began work on *David* when he was just 26 years old. He spent three years shaping what would become one of the most iconic representations of human potential ever created. As I stood in front of the statue, something clicked. The work wasn't about wealth or fame; it ran deeper than that and was about Michelangelo's vision and personal purpose. His legacy and the relentless drive he must have had to shape raw material into something that lasts. Something that matters.

And I found myself asking: What compels a person to give so much of themselves to create something so exceptional?

That question didn't leave me. It lingered, and, in many ways, it became the seed for this part of the book.

The Higher Purpose of a Rainmaker

Over the years, we've worked with and learned from hundreds of rainmakers and those aspiring to join their ranks. Different firms. Different markets. Different styles. Different times. For all the differences in style, background, or approach, one thing consistently rises to the surface: Rainmakers aren't in it just for the numbers, the titles, or the successive big wins. They're after something more profound.

In our experience, the truly great ones are driven by a higher purpose, a pull toward work that leaves a mark. A rainmaker's success isn't built on ambition; it's grounded in intention, and it starts at the person's roots.

Rainmakers are not just chasing deals or ticking off deliverables. They're stepping into the most complex, most high-stakes problems, the kind that reshape companies, industries, even whole systems. They're not looking to finish a project. They're looking to contribute to something that matters.

Take, for example, the deals in recent years, like the $12.7 billion acquisition of Sprint by T-Mobile, the $11.3 billion merger between LVMH and Tiffany, or the $10.7 billion acquisition of Grubhub by Just Eat Takeaway. These major deals didn't come together by luck. They took coordination across a web of players, navigating financial twists, regulatory minefields, and big-picture strategic bets. Pulling them off took a shared sense of purpose, the instinct to connect the right people, and the determination to shape something that would outlast the moment.

That kind of purpose doesn't always shout. More often it shows up quietly, in moments that speak volumes. It's the consultant who picks up the phone at midnight when a client's in trouble, not for credit but because doing so matters. It's the senior partner who pulls a struggling team member aside, not for praise but to keep the bar high. It's the team that goes the extra mile, even when no one's watching because they expect that of themselves.

In *Joy Works: Empowering Teams in the New Era of Work*, Alex Liu describes the goal as creating "apex moments," when what you care about and do well aligns perfectly with what the organization values and needs.[1] These are the moments you feel deeply connected, using your strengths on something that truly matters to you and to others.

According to psychologist William Damon, Purpose is a steady, guiding intention, something that matters deeply to you and also makes a real difference beyond you.[2]

Rainmakers embody this definition. While personal goals like advancement or wealth may fuel the early years, those who endure, those who rise, are driven by something more permanent: the belief that their work can change something for the better. They're grounded in something more profound than commercial targets. Like roots feeding a tree, a rainmaker's purpose is internal and unseen but is vital to everything above the surface.

It's what keeps them steady when things get tough. It's the quiet force behind the extra mile, the long hours, the thoughtful call.

Seeing the Bigger Vision

Michelangelo saw *David* in the marble before he picked up a chisel. That's what set him apart. He didn't just see a block of stone; he saw possibility. A symbol. A future.

Rainmakers do the same. They don't see projects; they see *transformation*. They envision what's possible for a client or organization, often before the client can fully articulate it.

Today, that vision is increasingly enhanced by technology. Rainmakers are using AI to draw out insights and plan their work with unprecedented precision.[3] But tools alone don't drive vision; it is the *purpose behind their use* that creates meaning in the work.

Rainmakers don't chase easy wins. They lean into ambiguity, complexity, and consequence. They are not just implementers; they are architects of change. Where others hesitate, they begin. Where others see barriers, they find momentum.

We've worked with rainmakers who helped government departments reimagine service delivery for millions of citizens. Others guided struggling companies back to purpose and profit. Others still stood beside CEOs in defining deeply personal moments, helping them lead with clarity and conviction.

These outcomes aren't luck; they are the product of people, often rainmakers, who can see a better future emerging from today's position.

The Legacy of a Rainmaker

Ask a rainmaker what they're most proud of, and it's rarely a pitch or a proposal.

That's not what sticks.

They talk about what came after, the impact, the ripple effect. The people they helped grow. The team that rose to the challenge. The path that shifted because of the work.

They remember the pressure, the trust it took to get there. The turning points that didn't just move the project forward but changed lives, careers, sometimes even whole communities. They remember what shifted.

Because rainmakers are building legacies.

They know their work will outlast them, in strategy, in culture, in the lives affected. That's why they challenge complacency. That's why they insist on quality. That's why they sometimes say the hard thing, even when silence would be safer.

A rainmaker from a global management consulting firm told us they helped the CEO of a healthcare provider navigate a significant restructuring. It was complex, technical, and politically sensitive. But what stayed with the rainmaker wasn't the operational model and the work that was done, it was a frontline worker who said, months later:

> *"Thank you. This made my work and my patients' lives better."*
> *That's legacy.*
> *That's the purpose, made real.*

Aligning Purpose with Passion and Skill

As we've written this book, one question has come up again and again:

> *Do rainmakers all do the same kind of work? The same practices? The same client industries? The same client topics? Do they use the same consulting?*

The answer is no. Not even close.

But what they do share, without exception, is total alignment. Rainmakers are unwavering in their alignment of purpose, passion, and skill. There is no compromise here. They are crystal clear about the work that matters to them, the impact they want to make, and the unique strengths they bring to the table. They don't dabble or chase opportunity for its own sake. They move toward the work that speaks to them and where they can deliver true excellence, and they do so with intention. Over time, this alignment doesn't just guide their work; it defines their reputation.

We've also found that to be a rainmaker, you must have a deep, visible passion for consulting as a profession, not just as a job or career but as a calling. This passion must be consistently demonstrated: in how you contribute within your firm, how you mentor others, how you articulate the value of your work, and how you present yourself in the market. Being good at consulting isn't enough, and even being great doesn't cut it on its own. You have to genuinely care about the work. Rainmakers bring that sense of commitment into every meeting, every conversation, every pitch. You can see their energy, and you can feel that they're fully in it. That kind of passion draws people in and it's what makes them stand out, both within their firms and with their clients.

We've observed that rainmakers tend to fall into two broad patterns, what we call *client anchors* and *topic flames*.

- **Client anchors** are masters of intimacy and influence. They are students of client psychology, organizational behavior, and leadership. They read sincerely, not just market reports, but books on trust, impact, and cultural change. They invest in self-awareness and coaching programs. They know how to build bridges across silos and navigate the undercurrents of power, history, and emotion within a client's world. They're the ones who can sense the tension before it surfaces and connect the dots others miss. Their relationships are not transactional; they're generational.
- **Topic flames** are brilliant domain thinkers. They're immersed in a specific field, be it digital identity, supply chain resilience, workforce strategy, or environmental, social, and governance (ESG) regulation. They publish. They speak. They're asked to join panels, advise CEOs, and brief boards. Their brand precedes them. But, and this cannot be overstated, they are not just thought leaders. They are *commercial.* They turn ideas into deals. Insight into action. Passion into performance. They are rainmakers, not lecturers.

To succeed at the highest level, you don't need to be both a client anchor and a topic flame. But you must be *world-class* in one. That clarity and the discipline to keep sharpening it are what turn a capable consultant into a rainmaker.

Let's look at three examples to bring this to life.

From Legacy to Leadership: A Topic Flame for a Greener Future

For this rainmaker, the project wasn't another average transformation project. Long before ESG became a boardroom priority, he had cultivated deep expertise in climate strategy and energy transition. He wasn't just following the trend; he was helping shape it. A lifelong believer in the power of business to accelerate climate action, he had spent years developing credibility in this space: writing, speaking, building internal capability, and advising clients across industries.

So, when the opportunity came to lead a significant program with a regional energy provider halfway around the world, pivoting them from fossil-heavy systems to a smart, green grid, he didn't hesitate. He brought together teams across continents and disciplines, leveraging AI, the Internet of Things, and advanced analytics to reimagine the customer experience and reduce emissions. It wasn't just about infrastructure; it was about reinvention of the whole company.

He helped the client navigate commercial trade-offs but reframed them as long-term value levers, aligning financial outcomes with environmental responsibility. This wasn't a side project. This was his domain. His voice carried weight, not because of his title but because of his fluency and passion.

Client feedback: *We chose him because he shared our passion. The capabilities of the firms were similar, but his belief, and his clarity, made the difference.*

Rainmakers like this are classic topic flames. They have deep, visible expertise. Credibility in a fast-evolving space. And critically, a commercial mindset that turns purpose into revenue. That's what makes them rainmakers, not just thinkers.

A Return with Purpose: When Commitment Becomes a Client Anchor

For the lead partner, this wasn't just another international deal. It was personal. A return to the region where he was born, a part of the world that shaped his early life and still held deep ties, including family.

He didn't just understand the commercial landscape. He knew the texture of the place, the politics, the customs, the conversations behind the conversation. He could read the room in ways others couldn't.

The risks were real. Many advised caution. Some suggested walking away altogether.

But he didn't flinch. He leaned in.

The client, a global player, was eyeing a complex acquisition in a politically sensitive environment. The deal was volatile. Unpredictable. The kind of deal that could easily collapse without the right leadership.

He didn't just manage the engagement; he led it. Not from behind a desk, but shoulder to shoulder with his team. He helped the client navigate murky regulations, steady shaky stakeholders, and uncover value others had missed. His leadership wasn't just execution; it was stewardship.

The consulting team did more than hit their numbers. They earned something harder to quantify: trust. And that trust came from more than technical expertise; it came from someone who knew the ground he was standing on and cared about getting it right.

The client later reflected: *We got a better result because of his commitment and knowledge. He brought a personal intensity we rarely see.*

That's what defines a true client anchor. It's not just about being effective; it's about being present, credible, and connected when it matters most.

This rainmaker didn't just understand the client's world.

He was part of it.

Protecting What Matters: When Purpose Runs Through the Roots

For another rainmaker, biosecurity wasn't just another policy brief. It hit close to home.

She grew up on a farm, where one outbreak could destroy an entire season, sometimes a family's future. That lived reality, the fragility of ecosystems, the quiet resilience of rural communities, never left her.

So, when a national agency faced a fast-moving threat to a critical import sector, she didn't see a project. She saw a line of defense worth fighting for.

She moved quickly, not just with frameworks and timelines but with heart. She rallied teams across departments, brought industry leaders into the room, and engaged with frontline personnel who knew what was really at stake. She helped integrate predictive tools, sharpen diagnostic systems, and tighten coordination fast.

What set her apart wasn't just her strategic thinking; it was how she spoke.

The advice didn't sound like it came from a textbook. It sounded like it came from experience.

She knew the beat of agricultural life. She understood how quickly things could unravel at a border checkpoint, what a delayed shipment really meant for a farmer, how one misstep could ripple across an entire season.

People listened because they recognized the advisor wasn't guessing, she was someone who genuinely understood their world.

As one client put it: *She had a deep, personal connection to the land, the farmers, and the industry. That made her advice more real and far easier to act on.*

That's client anchor territory. Not just expertise, resonance. A felt connection to the mission. The kind of advisor who doesn't just shape strategy but earns the right to help protect what matters most.

A Rainmaker's Higher Purpose

Like roots feeding the tree long before fruit appears, these rainmakers invested deeply before results showed up. Their work wasn't just smart; it was *worth doing*.

Psychologist Amy Wrzesniewski and her colleagues once described work viewed as a "calling" something people do not just for the outcome but for the meaning they draw from the doing itself.[4]

Rainmakers see their work as a calling too. They're not just professionals. They're stewards. Builders. Legacy makers.

Michelangelo didn't carve *David* for praise. He carved it because he believed in what it stood for.

Rainmakers operate the same way. They don't need the spotlight. Their work *is* the spotlight, long after they've left the room.

The Rainmaker's Higher Purpose framework captures what really drives top performers, not just the *what* but the *why* behind their work. (See Figure 8.1.)

At its core, it's built around three powerful, interlocking forces: *legacy*, *excellence*, and *impact*:

- **Legacy** is about lasting change, the belief that your work should mean something long after the project wraps.
- **Excellence** speaks to quiet discipline, the inner standard rainmakers hold themselves to, even when no one's watching.
- **Impact** is the visible result, the shift, the transformation, the proof that the effort mattered.

Each element holds weight on its own. But it's in the overlap that something more meaningful takes shape.

- **When legacy meets excellence,** it's not just quality; it's craftsmanship that endures, the kind of work people still talk about years later.
- **When excellence intersects with impact,** the result isn't just effective; it changes the game. Execution that lifts everything around it.
- **And when legacy connects with impact,** it becomes something larger, work that leaves a mark, shaping outcomes long after the engagement ends.

At the very center, where all three come together, is something rare: *the rainmaker's higher purpose*. This is the place where great work becomes lasting work, where intention, skill, and consequence align.

And here's what makes the interlinkages so powerful: A rainmaker's purpose isn't hidden. It's visible. You can feel it in how they speak,

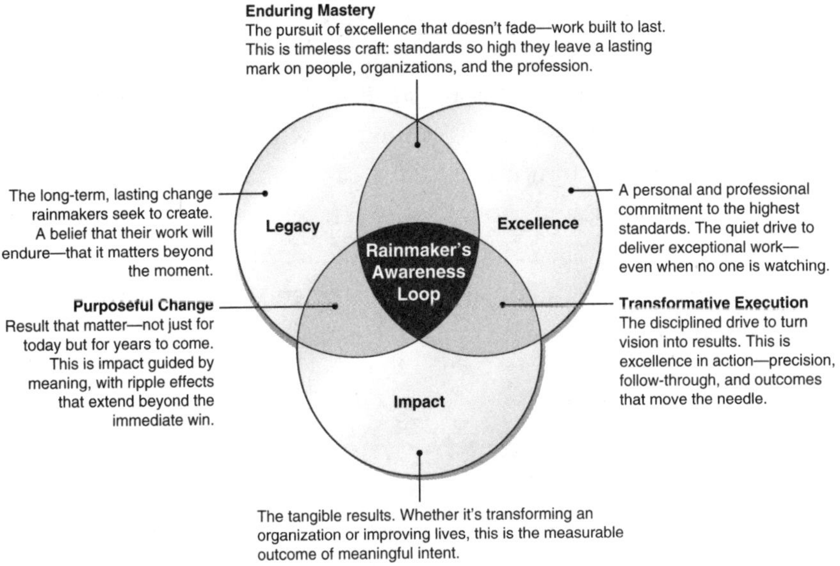

FIGURE 8.1 The rainmaker's higher purpose.

decide, and show up. Their clients and colleagues are drawn to it because it radiates energy and conviction. It demonstrates commitment, passion, and clarity, a sense that this person stands for something beyond the self. That authenticity becomes magnetic. It inspires trust and attracts opportunity.

When rainmakers operate from this deep alignment, something shifts. Doors begin to open to the C-suite. Executives recognize and respond to that level of purpose. They don't just see competence; they sense conviction. And in that moment, rainmakers stop being viewed as service providers and become what every senior executive seeks—strategic partners, trusted voices in the rooms that matter most.

Rainmakers reflect and refine their purpose as their careers progress, their reputation builds, and the world of their clients' change. A purpose statement relevant in 2015 is unlikely to be relevant now. A purpose relevant to your local market is unlikely to be relevant if your influence has become global. A purpose built on traditional business operations is unlikely to be relevant in a world driven by AI disruption. Rainmakers review, adapt, and keep their purpose relevant and contemporary.

Conclusion

Purpose widens a rainmaker's world. Like lateral roots pushing outward through the soil, it extends influence while strengthening resilience. Skill and ambition may ignite a career, but purpose sustains it when pressure builds and progress slows. It reminds you why the work matters and who it ultimately serves. Anchored in something larger than personal success, rainmakers gain the steadiness to endure setbacks and the reach to create impact that lasts well beyond them.

Next: Fuel for the Journey

Purpose is the anchor, the lateral roots that stretch outward and hold firm. But even with purpose, the rainmaker's path is demanding. The nights get long. The pressure builds. Setbacks come hard and often.

So, what sustains rainmakers?

In the next chapter, we turn to the finer roots, the root hairs of the system. Small, often invisible, but vital. They're what draw in the nutrients that fuel a rainmaker's strength over time.

This is where resilience lives, not as some dramatic surge of willpower but as something quieter. Steady. Daily. The ability to bounce back, keep going, and stay present when it counts.

Because deep roots do more than hold you in place.

They reach.

They adapt.

They find strength in the soil even when the ground is dry.

And in consulting, that's the real dividing line.

Not between the talented and the rest, but between those who burn out and those who break through.

CHAPTER

9

Root Hairs: Resilience

Celebrating Wins Is Easy. Showing Up When Things Don't Work Out Defines You

Resilience doesn't roar. Often it whispers and then gets back to work.

Think of Simone Biles at the Tokyo Olympics. Already the greatest gymnast of all time, she stunned the world not by winning but by withdrawing. Her body and mind, long tuned to perfection, were no longer in sync. She stepped away, citing mental health, and, in doing so, redefined what strength looks like at the elite level. Then she came back. And won again.

Or consider Sara Hector. Most have never heard her name. But in alpine skiing circles, she's known for something extraordinary. A promising young skier who suffered multiple injuries and years of frustrating results, Hector didn't fade. She rebuilt slowly and quietly. And after over a decade on the circuit, at age 29, she won Olympic gold in the giant slalom at Beijing 2022. Not because she had the flashiest technique. But because she endured.

Rainmakers in professional services live in the same world, just in a different arena.

You're surrounded by talent and trained in the best methods. Moving fast. Promoted quickly. But at the top, the rules change. You're up against the very best. Feedback is constant, brutal, and public. You win less than you lose. And a top-tier career? Maybe a decade. A little more.

Some crack. Others bend. A few—the rainmakers—deepen their roots. What keeps them going isn't brute strength. It's what we call the *root hairs*, small, consistent, sustaining habits of reflection, recovery, and discipline.

Because at the elite level, resilience isn't what you show.

It's what you *build* every day.

The Competitive Fire: Thriving on the Chase

Rainmakers are inherently competitive, but not in an ego-driven, win-at-all-costs way. Their competition is with complexity. With possibility. With themselves.

They're drawn to the highest-stakes challenges, not to win but to *transform*. Every opportunity is a chance to stretch beyond what's been done before. It's not about beating others. It's about realizing potential: their own, their clients', and their firm's.

The toughest competition rainmakers face isn't out there; it's within.

They don't coast on past wins. They raise their bar. Again and again.

After every pitch, every project, every conversation, they stop and ask themselves:

- Could that have gone better?
- What did I miss?
- What did I learn and what will I change next time?

It's not for show. It's just how they're wired. That constant loop of reflection and refinement doesn't just move them forward; it accelerates them.

Like roots pushing through rock, the growth is quiet and relentless.

Intrinsic Drive: Mastery, Autonomy, Purpose

At the heart of a rainmaker's performance is something that can't be seen or designed; it's called *intrinsic* motivation. It's not about applause or external rewards. It runs deeper than that.

Psychologists Edward L. Deci, Richard J. Vallerand, Louise G. Pelletier, and Richard M. Ryan, through their *self-determination theory*, pinpoint three core drivers: competence, autonomy, and relatedness. These foundational needs fuel ongoing growth and motivation, even when no one's watching and no one's asking[1]:

1. **Competence:** Rainmakers are obsessed with mastery. They read, rehearse, reflect, and refine. They raise the bar, not because they're told to but because excellence is their baseline. Increasingly, they use AI to deepen their insight, model scenarios, and accelerate their learning.
2. **Autonomy:** Rainmakers don't wait for permission. They shape opportunities, chart direction, and take initiative. They're trusted because they lead, not just execute.
3. **Relatedness:** They care deeply about the people they serve. Not transactionally, but relationally. They want their work to *matter*, improving lives, elevating teams, and leaving something better behind.

They also share generously. Rainmakers mentor, debrief, and coach without fanfare. Their impact isn't measured in applause but in contribution.

And for many rainmakers, that purpose doesn't end with retirement. Long after they've stepped back from formal roles, they're still contributing, still connecting people, offering fresh ideas, flagging opportunities, and guiding their firms toward impact. They remain embedded in the rhythm of the profession, not out of obligation but out of care.

Their purpose isn't swayed by trends. It's steady, a taproot anchored deep, holding strong no matter how uncertain things get.

Recognition and Reward: Fuel, Not Fire

Rainmakers operate in high-reward environments. The incentives and accolades are there, and, yes, they matter. But they're not the reason they do the work. In our experience, the rainmakers who thrive year after year aren't driven by money, even though they're often well paid. Money is expected, earned as part of the professional contract. It's the result, not the reason. It's not the fire in the belly.

Recognition is welcome, of course. Everyone appreciates being seen. But the truth is, for most rainmakers we've worked with or led, external recognition is fleeting. The real fuel comes from the work itself, the complexity, the challenge, the chance to shape something important. What matters is impact. Did the work change something? Did it shift a mindset, unlock a problem, or give a leader clarity they didn't have before?

Across global firms and national boutiques, in public partnerships and equity-backed firms alike, we've seen how organizations structure rewards: points systems, profit shares, equity stakes, deal bonuses, and client growth multipliers. We've sat in on thousands of performance reviews, often for partners at the very top of their game. And what strikes us most is this: The ones who rise and sustain are not necessarily the ones who receive the highest compensation. They're the ones who share, collaborate, and develop new partners and chase the most complex problem with the most meaningful outcomes.

We've also seen what happens when recognition becomes the only currency, when titles, bonuses, and "wins" replace purpose.

That kind of motivation can energize people for a moment, but it doesn't last. Short bursts of performance follow, not sustained leadership.

The rainmakers we admire are different. They know that the thrill of a closed deal fades quickly. But the satisfaction of solving a 10-year challenge on endures. Watching a client they've walked with succeed on a global stage? That sticks. Seeing that they helped redesign *work*? That's the reward.

Resilience: Setbacks as Fuel

Rainmakers lose. They get rejected. They fail.

But what sets them apart is how they *respond*.

They don't spiral. They reset. They recenter. They extract the learning and reengage better, sharper, stronger. They also ask themselves hard questions when they lose a major proposal or client:

- Did we rely too heavily on historical methodologies instead of adopting new technology to accelerate execution and decision making?
- Were there capability gaps we need to address?
- Did we build strong enough relationships to earn the client's trust?
- What can we learn to build a stronger proposition next time?
- How can we reconnect with the client and remain relevant?

According to Ann S. Masten and Mary-Gabrielle J. Reed, resilience isn't just about bouncing back; it's about growing through adversity.[2]

Let's look at these first two surface-layer issues a little more with a story from Robert's time as a senior corporate executive, which was a moment that revealed what it means to adapt with integrity.

Playing the Long Game When the Door Closes

I'd just come off an overnight international flight and walked straight into a high-stakes board meeting. My presentation lit a fuse. What followed was a two-hour debate that exposed deep cracks in customer service and financial performance. I had been brought in by the newly appointed CEO, not as a consultant but as an executive, to fix what was broken.

In my first weeks, my team assessed the scale of reform. That morning, I proposed a bold, centrally driven, company-wide transformation of costs and customer service. The board fully backed it: budget, resources, and delegated authority. But with one clear condition.

They had no interest in working with the incumbent consulting firm.

That firm had worked closely with the previous CEO. Their work hadn't failed, but the board was resolute. For the firm and especially their lead partner, Charles, it meant five years of investment in the relationship, reputation, and revenue gone in a moment.

Despite my jet lag, I asked Charles to meet me that afternoon. I told him plainly: The company would not be engaging his firm for the work ahead.

There was a pause.

Then Charles responded in a way I'll never forget. He didn't argue or deflect. He acknowledged the risk of being tied too closely to a CEO and stood behind the work delivered. Then, without hesitation or bitterness, he offered his and his team's time at no cost to brief me on what had been done, what was unfinished, and what still had potential.

Over the following days, Charles and his team delivered professional, generous, and thorough briefings. They shared insights I would not have uncovered on my own, accelerating my early impact. Charles described himself as "a student of corporate transformation" and spoke with pride about the years he had invested in the field. He asked only to check in occasionally and made himself available to clarify their previous work.

He never pushed. He never tried to reclaim ground. He stayed connected, curious, and constructive.

That's what stood out.

Charles embodied what a rainmaker is. They are not entitled to the work, not defensive about the loss, but committed to the long game. He understood the shocks that shaped a client's world: the turbulence of leadership change, the volatility of board demands, and the politics of trust. And he never forgot the human side: that beneath every strategy sat individuals with reputations to protect and risks to weigh. He responded not with fear but with presence, not with pressure but with perspective.

Eighteen months later, with my endorsement and the board's agreement, Charles's firm was invited back to conduct a component of the transformation.

That is rainmaking. Not because he won the contract, but because he stayed rooted in purpose, trusted the value of his contribution, and adapted without losing his principles.

Rainmakers know that setbacks vary, in scale and in their ability to influence them. We can understand them through two dimensions: *impact* and *control*. (See Figure 9.1.)

The next sections look at the four types of setbacks.

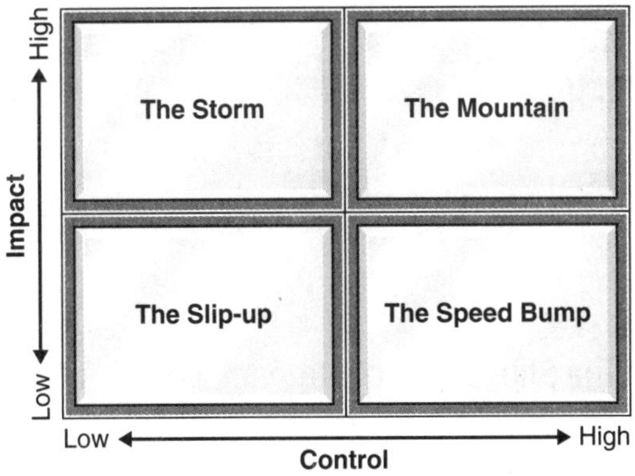

FIGURE 9.1 The rainmaker's setback framework.

The Storm—High Impact, Low Control

A significant deal falls apart. It might be due to market turbulence, a sudden leadership change, or internal politics on the client's side. Either way, it's out of your hands, or mostly so. Rainmakers don't disappear when this happens. They stay close to the client, helping them make sense of what unfolded, showing empathy, and quietly maintaining trust. But later they reflect. Could they have seen the warning signs earlier? Was there an overreliance on one sponsor? Were there political or emotional undercurrents they didn't fully read? Rainmakers use that reflection to refine how they map influence and risk in the future. They don't blame luck or circumstance. They extract insight and make sure the next storm finds them better anchored.

The Mountain—High Impact, High Control

This one's on you. The sales pitch that went flat. The relationship that broke down or was overestimated. The oversight that damaged trust. The instinctive move is to defend or deflect, but rainmakers do the opposite. They pause, take full accountability, and act quickly to repair what was broken. Then, when the dust settles, they look deeper. What drove the mistake: Fatigue? Ego? Overconfidence? A failure to research properly or to listen? They examine their decision patterns and stress points, often bringing in a mentor or coach to help see what they can't. It's not self-criticism; it's self-calibration. They know that climbing the same mountain twice means learning to watch their footing.

The Slip-Up—Low Impact, Low Control

The client meeting didn't land. The follow-up was late. The client didn't engage as expected. Small things, easy to brush off, but rainmakers don't let small things slide without reflection. They replay the moment, asking themselves: Did I prepare the room properly? Did my tone shift the energy? Was I distracted, rushed, or underestimating the interaction? Did I try to sell services when I should have asked questions? They note the signals, make a quiet adjustment, and move on without losing rhythm. Each slip-up becomes a data point, part of their internal playbook. Over time, that discipline compounds. The result is not perfection but awareness, an ability to recover so fast that others barely notice the stumble.

The Speed Bump—Low Impact, High Control

A clumsy email. A misread room. A poorly timed comment that changes the temperature of a conversation. Small moments but telling ones. Rainmakers catch them early and act fast to reset tone or intent. Afterward, they replay the moment with honesty: What triggered that reaction? Was I trying too hard to impress? Was I fully tuned into the emotional current of the room? They use these reflections to refine their intuition that invisible art of timing and presence. They know that momentum in consulting isn't about avoiding bumps altogether; it's about learning to glide over them without losing direction.

Setbacks happen. They happen all the time when you're trying to make a difference. But what matters most is how you respond and whether you treat each one as a test that weakens your roots, or a moment that strengthens them. Rainmakers always choose the latter.

Psychological Flexibility: Adapting Under Pressure

Rainmakers don't freeze when things shift; they adapt.

The client changes direction. Priorities rearrange. A new stakeholder walks in and rewrites the rules. That's part of the job. Rainmakers don't dig in. They don't resist. They move, but with intent.

They bring an internal steadiness that allows them to bend without breaking. They read the moment, sense what's shifted, and adjust not with drama but with precision. While others get stuck in what *was*, they quietly recalibrate and keep going.

It's not rigid control. It's responsiveness. Like roots stretching sideways to find moisture underground, they stay connected to what really matters, even when the terrain changes.

Key Insight: Rainmakers don't cling to what should have happened. They stay open. They listen. They shift gears because they're grounded enough to know when and how.

Although some consultants get overwhelmed by noise, rainmakers tune into what counts. Where others hesitate, unsure of the next move, rainmakers step forward, clear-eyed and composed.

It's not about flair. It's not about making noise. It's about clarity.

They prepare for the hard conversations. They play out scenarios before the meeting ever starts. Increasingly, they use AI, not as a crutch but as a tool: testing assumptions, modeling client reactions, pressure-checking decisions. The tech helps.

But the mindset still leads.

Real agility doesn't start with tools. It begins with preparation. And when agility meets grounding, rainmakers bring something rare into the room: calm under fire.

Emotional Control: Choosing Calm over Chaos

One trait sets rainmakers apart, and it's not always visible. It's how they hold themselves when the pressure peaks.

Nobody gets it perfect every time. Let's be real. But the best consultants? They don't spiral. They don't lash out. They pause and find their footing. Then they act, not from instinct but from intention.

It begins from within. They know their own patterns. They feel the tension rising and manage it before it spills out. One rainmaker told us his technique is to count quietly to 10 when he feels the tension building. Doing so helps him stay in the moment, or read the room, and adjust where needed.

Key Insight: Rainmakers understand something most people overlook, and it is simple: Trust isn't built on facts. And influence? It's not just about what you say; it's about how you make people feel. When a room gets tense, rainmakers are the steady presence others gravitate toward.

In high-stakes meetings, on crisis calls, in make-or-break negotiations, rainmakers don't dominate. They anchor. They're not pretending to be calm; they *are* calm. And it shows.

For them, emotional control doesn't mean suppressing feelings. It means knowing which ones to follow and which ones to let go. It means staying focused when others lose their edge. It's not about being stoic; it's about being smart.

And that choice—to hold steady, to act with clarity—changes everything.

Conclusion: The Rainmaker's Engine

Rainmakers are driven by more than ambition.

Yes, they aim high, but what pushes them is a deeper drive: a commitment to excellence and a clear sense of purpose. And, importantly, the determination to shape outcomes that matter.

They're not in it for the spotlight. Their motivation runs quiet and deep.

Like top athletes, their edge isn't built on adrenaline or quick wins. It's forged in discipline, early mornings, long stretches of hard work, and decisions made when no one's watching.

Think of Simone Biles choosing to step back, not out of weakness but out of strength and self-awareness. Or Sara Hector, who spent years putting in the work before her Olympic moment. That kind of success doesn't come from talent alone. It comes from steady, often invisible choices made over time.

Rainmakers are no different. Their greatness is shaped in the moments most people overlook.

What keeps them going isn't hustle or hype; it's a system, a steady engine built below the surface.

Small, consistent habits: reviewing what went wrong after a tough meeting. Walking through a pitch the night before and getting up early to think before the day takes over.

They bounce back. They recalibrate. And through it all, they stay anchored to their purpose.

Over time, those unseen routines become their edge.

Not noisy. Just steady. Relentless. Sustainable.

That's the engine. Not burnout dressed up as drive, but brilliant performance built to last.

The kind that holds up when things get heavy.

The kind that endures.

Next: Looking Ahead

Resilience alone isn't enough.

With depth comes responsibility. With reach comes restraint.

Because rainmakers don't just influence outcomes, they shape systems, cultures, and decisions that carry real consequences. And the same root system that gives them strength must also keep them in check.

In the next chapter, we turn to the *root cap*, the protective layer at the edge of growth. It's what guides the roots forward through rugged terrain, sensing, filtering, and protecting.

So too must rainmakers lead with discernment, not just brilliance. We explore the ethical choices, responsibilities, and judgment that must accompany power.

Because in the end, what defines a rainmaker isn't only what they *can* do, it's knowing what they *should* do.

Let's begin.

CHAPTER

10

Root Cap: Ethics and Responsibilities

Careers Are Built on Ethics. They Are Destroyed When Ethics Are Abandoned

Strong roots anchor remarkable growth. But every root system, no matter how deep or expansive, depends on something easily overlooked: the root cap.

The root cap is the protective tip at the very front of growth. It shields the root as it pushes into new terrain. It senses direction. It filters what enters. And it guides where the root should and shouldn't go.

In the world of rainmakers, the root cap is judgment. Integrity. Responsibility. It's the ethical filter that determines not just how far you grow but *how* you grow, and whether your influence sustains or erodes.

When the root cap is healthy, rainmakers navigate complexity with discernment. They stretch into new ground without damaging themselves or others. They grow with purpose, not just pressure.

But when it's compromised, when ambition overtakes principle or shortcuts dull the edge of integrity, everything above becomes vulnerable. Sometimes the decline is slow: a slight erosion of standards, a silence when someone needed to challenge. Other times it's sudden: a decision that shatters trust, a misstep that can't be undone.

Either way, the damage runs deep.

Because in consulting, reputations are fragile ecosystems. The roots that sustain rainmakers—client trust, principled influence, and long-term credibility—depend on a firm, intact ethical core.

This chapter looks at how rainmakers protect what matters most, how they handle the tough decisions when the easy option would be to look the other way.

Their strength doesn't come from sharp thinking alone but from a strong sense of what's right. Because real growth isn't just about chasing more. It's about knowing where to draw the line.

The Ethical Terrain of the Rainmaker

Rainmakers put serious energy into building client relationships, sometimes through their own work, sometimes by backing up their colleagues in other parts of their firm. When those relationships are real, grounded, and well managed, everyone benefits. Conversations go deeper. Collaboration gets easier. The work starts to land in more meaningful ways.

But the stronger the relationship is, the greater the responsibility is to protect its integrity.

Trust, the very thing that makes a rainmaker valuable, can also be a risk. It's what opens doors, expands influence, and helps win new work. But it can also blur the lines. And the closer you get, the more carefully you need to navigate.

Because with trust comes access. And with access comes responsibility.

Academic research reinforces this tension. The concept of "moral licensing," explored by psychologists Dale T. Miller and Daniel A. Effron, shows that individuals who see themselves as ethical can unconsciously allow themselves to make unethical decisions if they feel their reputation has already been established.[1] In consulting, where personal reputation often precedes process, this form of moral licensing can be a real danger.

When Standards Are Tested

Rainmakers often work near power, senior leaders, high-stakes decisions, complex dynamics. And that closeness comes with risk.

The boundaries aren't always clear. One moment you're advising; the next, you're caught in something more blurry. The space between influence and overreach, partnership and complicity, isn't always easy to see in real time.

That's why judgment matters. So does a steady internal compass. Consider the following situations:

- A client asks you to lead a high-profile transformation while simultaneously slashing internal change management and people engagement budgets. You suspect the real impact will fall on employees, but it won't be your name on the consequences.
- You're invited to support a political or public sector client with a visible reform agenda. The work aligns with your skillset but not your values, and the client wants to use your credibility to neutralize criticism.
- A client asks you to validate a strategy and guarantee its financial justification before any work is done. The outcome is predetermined; the client wants your brand to legitimize it.
- You uncover improper conduct in a project. The client requests that the finding be removed before the report is finalized.

- A direct competitor of your client asks you to do similar work, a commercial opportunity that conflicts with loyalty and obligation.
- Your terms of reference don't include a serious issue you uncover midproject. Do you raise it? Or stay in scope?
- The chairman of your client's board requests private commentary on the CEO's performance. You work for the CEO.
- Your client offers a lucrative contract to take on decision-making functions within the company. Accepting the contract would blur your independence.
- A colleague asks for insights from a previous project to win a new bid. You know it contains confidential themes.
- A longtime, high-value client asks you to have one of your team members review a strategy paper and government grant application for one of his personal charities. He frames it as an "investment in the relationship," a no-charge favor, outside the formal engagement.
- You are a defense expert with security clearance in one country at the highest level, and you receive a request to share your industry insights with a colleague pitching on a defense project with another country that is currently in political conflict with the government where you work most of the time.
- You are the leading strategic advisor to governments in the Middle East on clean energy developments (wind, solar, hydrogen), and one day you get to share your CV with a colleague in another part of the world working on a massive coal mine expansion project.

None of these scenarios is hypothetical. They happen. And when mishandled, they lead to loss of trust, regulatory fallout, reputational damage, or worse.

The Firm Isn't Enough

Most modern firms have strong ethical codes. Contracts spell out expectations around conduct, confidentiality, privacy, and independence. Ethics training is standard. Conflict checks are embedded in systems.

In addition, client and engagement acceptance processes have become more rigorous, and for good reason. Over time, firms have strengthened their front-end filters to ensure they're not taking on work that is just profitable but appropriate. These processes assess more than legal risk; they evaluate reputational exposure, ethical complexity, strategic alignment, and potential conflicts of interest.

The processes and systems are not just about compliance; they are there to support judgment from the client-serving leaders. Because in a world where perception and trust are everything, the projects rainmakers choose to accept and those they have the discipline to decline say as much about their values as their results.

Key Insight: Rainmakers operate in gray zones. The most difficult decisions often come down to personal judgment, not policy. That's why the best rainmakers develop a personal code, one that goes beyond what's written.

International bodies like the International Council of Management Consulting Institutes (ICMCI), the Institute of Management Consultants USA (IMC USA), and even standards from professions such as accounting (IFAC Code of Ethics for Professional Accountants) or law offer robust frameworks for ethical conduct, objectivity, and independence. These frameworks are valuable. But they are not always known, taught, or enforced with the consistency required at the sharpest end of consulting: the boardroom, the war room, or the minister's table.

At the highest levels, with national governments, global corporations, and mission-critical transformations, these ethical standards don't fit in the room. They arrive with the individual.

Rainmakers must be that standard.

Because the higher the stakes, the murkier the questions. Should we advise a client to delay a critical disclosure? Should we continue supporting a program we no longer believe in? Should we flag a conflict that no one else sees or seems to want to see? These aren't scenarios a corporate policy can fully anticipate. They require personal discernment, grounded values, and moral clarity.

This personal code often includes:

- A clear boundary between consulting advice and client accountability
- A refusal to allow objectivity to be influenced or conclusions to be directed
- The right to reject work that conflicts with personal or the firm's ethical standards
- Refusal to participate in management or operational decision making for the client
- Confidentiality about findings, insights, or project details unless disclosure is explicitly approved
- A commitment to work with any client staff member professionally, without personal bias or judgment
- A promise to use lessons from projects to improve methods without ever disclosing client-specific insights

These boundaries are essential, not because they are legally required but because they protect trust. And trust, once lost, isn't easily recovered. The most effective consultants maintain both closeness and distance; they are embedded in the organization but not absorbed by it.[2]

At the top of the consulting profession, credibility travels ahead of you, and so do your values.

The Power of Personal Principle

Each rainmaker must define what they will and won't do, not just in theory but in the face of real trade-offs. Personal codes often go further than compliance. They protect integrity under pressure. Consider these:

- I will never behave unethically, illegally, or dishonestly on any client matter. Ever.
- I will not allow anyone on my team to be harassed, bullied, overworked, or victimized.
- I will not accept work that my team cannot execute to a high standard.
- I will walk away from a client if integrity is compromised.
- I will protect my firm's reputation and my team's well-being over personal gain.
- I will always be professional and expect my client to be the same.
- I will be prepared to sacrifice my client relationship should my ethical concerns not be addressed.

Transparency: The Hidden Pillar

One of the simplest and most underestimated ways rainmakers maintain ethical strength is through transparency.

It sounds obvious. But in practice, transparency can be uncomfortable. Many consultants avoid tough conversations for fear of jeopardizing the relationship or appearing uncertain.

Rainmakers see transparency differently. They understand that absolute trust is resilient. That transparency, even when awkward, deepens credibility. And that silence or omission, even with good intent, erodes the partnership over time.

They disclose early and often when:

- A team member is being replaced.
- A deliverable has slipped.
- A mistake has been made.
- A potential conflict exists.
- They've used AI and how it was used.
- They've referenced the client in another pitch.

These moments may seem operational. But in high-trust relationships, they're reputational. Each disclosure is a signal: *We're in this with integrity*.

But transparency doesn't mean going it alone. Rainmakers know that ethical judgment isn't a solo sport. Especially in gray zones where lines blur and stakes are high, they consult widely.

They seek input from peers, risk teams, mentors, and sometimes even clients themselves. They test assumptions, challenge blind spots, and ensure they're not rationalizing what feels expedient.

Key Insight: Transparency without consultation is risky, and consultation without transparency is hollow. Together, they form a powerful safeguard, not just for doing the right thing but for *knowing* what the right thing is.

Conclusion: The Long View

Ethics, at its core, aren't boxes rainmakers tick; they are something rainmakers carry.

The best consultants don't just focus on results. They look after the conditions that make results possible in the first place.

They know they're holding more than just a commercial relationship. They're holding trust. Reputation. The quiet confidence others place in them when the stakes are high.

That means protecting the roots, the unseen structures that support everything else: judgment, credibility, integrity. Not the things that show up in a proposal but the things that keep people coming back.

Rainmakers who take the long view don't just win work. They earn something harder to replace.

Because when the roots are damaged, when values erode or ethics are ignored, no one thrives. Not the client. Not the firm. Not the rainmaker.

But when the roots are strong and well tended? They nourish far more than a single success. They sustain a legacy of impact that endures across seasons, clients, and careers.

But before we turn to the core attributes of rainmakers, let's revisit the elements of a rainmaker's inner self: their roots.

PART

II

SUMMARY

The Roots: Inner Life of a Rainmaker

This part of the book has explored the invisible foundation, the root system beneath the surface, that enables rainmakers to grow, perform, and endure at the highest levels. While rainmakers' results are visible, their strength lies in what most people never see. These four foundational forces—self-awareness, purpose, resilience, and responsibility—shape everything that follows.

Self-Awareness: The Taproot of Growth

Rainmakers grow from the inside out. They start by understanding themselves honestly and without illusion.

They care less about being liked and more about getting better. They think for themselves, take time to reflect, and seek feedback not to defend their image, but to sharpen their impact.

Their identity isn't tied to winning the pitch or nailing the numbers. It's revealed in how they handle pressure with clarity, focus, and humility.

Purpose: The Lateral Roots That Anchor

What drives rainmakers runs deeper than the usual incentives. They're not chasing key performance indicators or external praise; they're led by purpose.

They care about the long view. About what their work changes, not just what it earns.

For some rainmakers, that conviction shows up in the causes they fight for alongside clients. For others, it's in the ideas they champion or the industries they shape. Whatever the focus, it's personal.

Recognition might follow. But it's never the goal.

Resilience: The Root Hairs That Sustain

No rainmaker builds resilience sitting comfortably. It's earned over time, under pressure.

They've had things fall apart. Deals go sideways. Situations turn personal when they shouldn't. But instead of snapping back to where they were, they move forward with more insight, more grit.

They learn fast. They carry the scar tissue. And when the ground shifts, they don't. They hold.

Others might lose their footing or grip too tightly to the original plan. Rainmakers adjust. Quietly. Decisively.

Not because they enjoy the pressure, but because they've trained for it. That steadiness doesn't come from some inner fire that never flickers. It comes from repetition. From choosing not to quit on tough days. From being anchored in something that doesn't shake when everything else does.

Real resilience doesn't shout. It listens, adapts, and keeps going.

Ethics and Responsibility: The Root Cap That Guides

Rainmakers grow with intention. They know trust takes time to build and seconds to lose.

They don't cut corners. They don't blur lines. When faced with a gray area, they ask the hard questions and choose the harder right over the easier wrong.

Their integrity shows when no one's watching.

They don't just benefit from a healthy system; they protect it. They treat their work, their clients, and their influence with care, knowing others are coming up behind them.

They don't just grow the tree; they look after the soil.

Review Questions for Potential Rainmakers

1. What am I not seeing about how I show up with clients, teams, or peers, and whom have I asked for feedback?
2. Where have my strengths become a blind spot, creating friction or resistance?

3. Am I building time for honest reflection, or just moving from moment to moment?
4. Is the work I'm chasing still aligned with what I care about most, or am I following momentum?
5. Do my clients and colleagues know my passion? Do I make it visible?
6. Do I feel pride in the impact I'm creating or pressure to perform?
7. Am I playing to my edge, the place where my passion and skill converge, or coasting inside comfort?
8. What habits, rituals, or relationships consistently restore my energy and focus, and am I honoring them?
9. How do I respond when things don't go my way? Do I blame, bounce, or build?
10. Where have I learned the most recently, and how have I applied that learning under pressure?
11. Have I stayed true to what's right, even when it was inconvenient, unprofitable, or unpopular?
12. Where have I let standards slide, in myself, my team, or the client, and what needs correcting?
13. Am I leading in a way that protects the soil, or am I just harvesting the fruit?

Looking Ahead: The Trunk: Core Attributes of a Rainmaker

With strong roots in place, the rainmaker begins to rise.

In the next part of the book, we explore the *trunk*, the core attributes that form the visible structure of rainmaker performance. These aren't personality traits. They're skills, habits, and postures that can be learned, practiced, and strengthened.

This is where *intention becomes action.*

Where *inner purpose* becomes *outward excellence.*

Let's begin.

PART

III

The Trunk

Core Attributes of a Rainmaker

CHAPTER

11

Overview of the Core Attributes

Attributes Are Not Taught – They Are Revealed Under Pressure, When the Stakes Are High

If the roots of a rainmaker represent identity, purpose, resilience, and responsibility, then the trunk is where those internal forces become visible, shaped, tested, and trusted in the real world.

The trunk is strong. Its structure. It gives rainmakers form, enabling them to stand tall under pressure, carry the weight of client expectations, lead teams forward, and support the complex strategies that grow above the ground.

These attributes aren't personality quirks or soft labels. They are observable, developable behaviors, the outward expressions of a deeply rooted foundation. When self-awareness is strong, purpose is clear, resilience is active, and ethics are intact, these attributes flourish.

Clients feel them in the room.

Teams draw confidence from them.

Leaders earn trust through them.

This chapter takes a close look at the 12 core attributes that shape how rainmakers operate, not just what they stand for but how they show up and deliver.

These qualities turn raw talent into momentum. They turn insight into influence. They give presence a direction.

Together, they form the trunk of the tree, the part that holds everything up.

It's what carries the weight.

It flexes when it needs to.

And it stands tall enough for others to follow.

Let's dig further.

What Do We Mean by "Attribute"?

In high-performance psychology, the terms "traits," "behaviors," and "attributes" are often used interchangeably. There's an overlap. But in this book, we define an attribute as an observable strength that meaningfully supports rainmaker performance and contributes to sustained success in high-stakes, client-facing environments.

At its core, an attribute is something that sets you apart. It's what you draw on when the pressure's real. It's what people notice when you're leading, especially when the situation gets tough.

It's what separates those who perform once from those who deliver again and again.

Attributes aren't handed to you. You build them, through experience, through hard feedback, through showing up when it would be easier not to.

Some develop gradually. Others take shape in sharp moments, a setback, a turning point, a conversation you can't forget.

Key Insight: Skills can be trained. Knowledge can be taught. But attributes? They show up in how you carry yourself, when things are unclear, when the stakes are high, and when others are watching to see how you'll respond.

Attributes become the traits people come to rely on. The things they count on you for. The part that sticks.

What the Research Tells Us

While no single study isolates the exact attributes of rainmakers in consulting, there's a rich body of research into the behaviors of top performers in business development, professional services, and high-trust advisory roles.

Emotional Intelligence

Take Daniel Goleman's well-known research from 1998.[1] He pointed to empathy, emotional self-control, and the ability to manage relationships as central to success, especially in roles where human dynamics are complex and fast-moving.

These aren't soft skills or optional extras. They're core to earning trust, handling uncertainty, and influencing without force.

Today, AI tools enhance this capability by surfacing emotional cues, analyzing language patterns, and suggesting adaptive responses. For rainmakers, these tools can augment, but never replace, their human empathy and emotional insight.

Top Sales and Advisor Research

Studies on high-performing sales professionals point to resilience, curiosity, adaptability, and emotional intelligence as core to sustained excellence. Trusted advisor frameworks reinforce similar themes:

credibility, *intimacy*, *reliability*, and *low self-orientation*. In other words, clients trust those who deliver value without ego and who show up for the long term.

Leadership Science

Research into effective leadership shows that the best leaders bring together clear thinking, integrity, self-awareness, and authenticity.[2] When they are grounded in their values and open about their intentions, they earn deeper trust and stronger followership.

Michael R. Kernis emphasizes that authenticity—the alignment of values, behavior, and self-awareness—is a cornerstone of trusted leadership.[3] Rainmakers integrate these elements not as individual traits but as a cohesive blend. Their edge comes not from having a single strength, but from integrating multiple strengths in high-pressure, client-facing environments.

A Practitioner's View: What Experience Reveals

Across our careers, we've assessed the performance of thousands of partners and directors, sat shoulder to shoulder in high-stakes pitch rooms and tense boardroom negotiations, walked the quiet corridors of client organizations at pivotal moments, and debriefed late into the night with teams under pressure, chasing clarity, alignment, or a breakthrough. We've worked on both sides of the table as global consulting leaders and as a senior executive commissioning over $700 million in major transformation work.

Regardless of city, we've seen how great consulting gets done and where it falls short. We've watched patterns emerge: a consistent set of strengths that separate the merely capable from the truly impactful.

Through these experiences and conversations with rainmakers, practice leaders, and aspiring partners across every major firm, we've identified what matters most, not in theory but in practice.

The next four chapters distill those insights, not into a list of traits but into a blueprint for becoming the kind of partner clients trust with their most significant, most consequential work.

We've identified 12 core attributes that appear time and again in rainmakers. (See Figure 11.1.) These aren't abstract ideals; they are observable, learnable behaviors that drive real impact. And to make them practical, we've grouped them into four categories, each aligned with a distinct part of the rainmaker's trunk, the central structure that supports and sustains everything above.

Category 1: Character and Connection—Heartwood

At the very core of the trunk lies the heartwood—strong, stable, and essential. Just like heartwood, these attributes represent who rainmakers are at their center. They embody integrity, trust, and authentic connection. This is where respect is earned, relationships take root, and deep client understanding begins. Without a solid core, nothing stands tall.

Category 2: Clarity and Presence—Bark

The outer bark protects the tree and shapes how it's seen. These attributes define how rainmakers show up—the clarity of their communication, the confidence of their presence, and the credibility they carry. Bark is what meets the world, and these traits help rainmakers read complexity, influence outcomes, and make others feel seen and heard.

Category 3: Action and Impact—Sapwood

Just beneath the bark lies the sapwood—alive, active, and always moving. These attributes are the lifeblood of rainmaker performance. They drive execution, results, and momentum. Like sapwood delivering nutrients, these traits power rainmakers to translate intent into real, measurable client and firm impact.

Category 4: Growth and Vision—Cambium

Cambium is the living layer that produces new growth—agile, adaptive, and always building. These attributes reflect how rainmakers lead into the future. They are about looking forward, creating new value, and expanding commercial opportunities. The cambium never rests, and neither do those with vision and drive to grow.

Each of these layers is vital. Together they form the living trunk for a rainmaker: resilient, visible, and foundational to everything that grows above.

The 12 Core Attributes of a Rainmaker

Now let's explore each attribute in turn. (See Figure 11.1.)

Build Lasting Relationships

Rainmakers don't "network." They *connect*. They build deep, trust-based relationships within their firms and across client organizations from the C-suite to the frontline, and they connect even when there is no work to be offered. Ten years ago, relationships were built over coffees and meetings; today they're built through presence, showing up with insight, relevance, and genuine care across every channel that matters.

Immerse in the Client's World

Rainmakers don't consult from a distance. They embed themselves. They know the client's people, pressures, and priorities deeply. What once meant understanding the industry now means truly understanding the ecosystem, data flows, digital signals, and unspoken culture shaping how the client really operates.

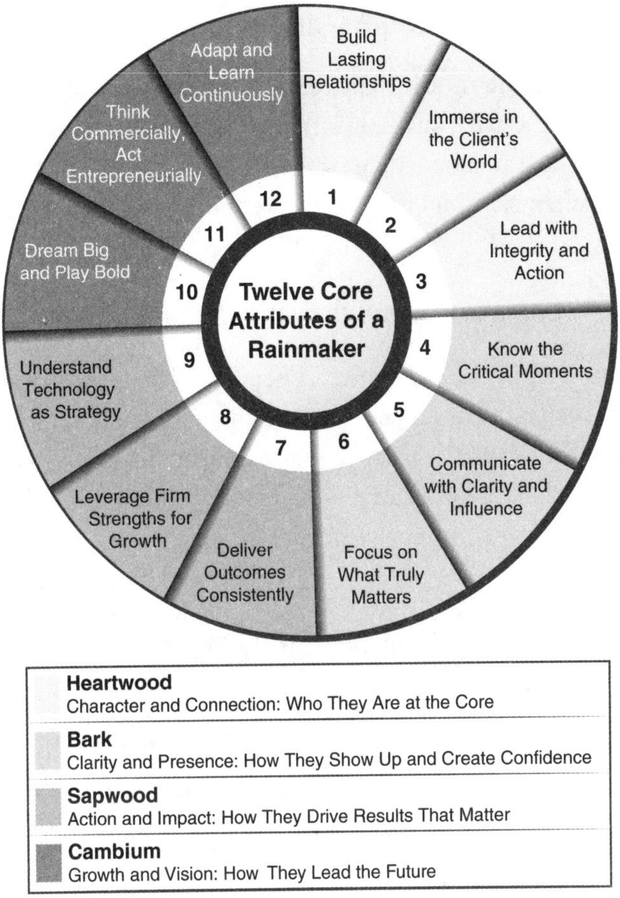

FIGURE 11.1 The 12 core attributes of a rainmaker.

Lead with Integrity and Action

Rainmakers do the right thing, especially when it's hard. They earn respect not through promises but through consistent values-driven behavior. A decade ago, integrity was about personal reputation; today it's also about transparency, accountability, and how you lead in full view of a digital world that never forgets.

Know the Critical Moments

Rainmakers read the room. They sense when things shift. And they lean in with empathy, clarity, and conviction. What was once about instinct in a boardroom is now about pattern recognition across multiple arenas, such as digital, hybrid, and human, where timing and tone define trust.

Communicate with Clarity and Influence

Rainmakers simplify the complex. They distill insight, shape compelling narratives, and influence decisions through clear, confident communication. Yesterday's great communicator inspired with words; today's rainmaker blends story with evidence, insight with emotion, turning clarity into competitive advantage.

Focus on What Truly Matters

Rainmakers cut through the noise. They help clients prioritize, focus, and act on the things that move the needle. Historically, focus was about efficiency; today it's about discernment, knowing what not to chase in a world overflowing with information and distraction.

Deliver Outcomes Consistently

Every interaction counts: a call, a meeting, an email, a text exchange. Even when there's no formal opportunity, rainmakers offer insight, ideas, value, and support that move the client forward. In the past, delivery was measured in reports and project milestones; now it's measured in value and moments: those small, consistent acts that build momentum and compound into trust.

Leverage Firm Strengths for Growth

Rainmakers don't work in silos. They mobilize the full capability of the firm—people, tools, and insights—to serve today's needs and anticipate tomorrow's opportunities. What used to mean "cross-selling" now means orchestration, connecting networks, data, and expertise to create value no single partner could deliver alone.

Understand Technology as Strategy

Rainmakers grasp how technologies like AI, cloud, and digital platforms shape business models, unlock value, and create new risks. A decade ago, technology was an enabler; today it's the core of strategy, the invisible architecture that determines who leads and who's left behind.

Dream Big and Play Bold

Rainmakers reframe the problem. They challenge small thinking. They imagine what's truly needed and pursue it with courage. Once "bold" meant confident; now it means creative, fusing imagination with data, daring to propose what technology makes newly possible.

Think Commercially, Act Entrepreneurially

Rainmakers see opportunity where others see obstacles. They shape new plays, balance risk and reward, and pursue growth with a focused ambition. Before, commercial thinking meant financial acumen; today it demands agility: the ability to read shifting markets and move before the crowd does.

Adapt and Learn Continuously

Rainmakers stay curious. They seek feedback. They evolve. The best rainmakers never believe they've "arrived." In the past, learning was formal and episodic; now it's continuous, self-directed, and fueled by feedback loops that keep rainmakers always just slightly uncomfortable and growing.

Conclusion

The attributes of a rainmaker are not abstract ideals; they are the visible strength of the trunk, revealed in decisions, conversations, and moments of consequence. When deeply rooted purpose meets disciplined behavior, something powerful emerges: credibility, momentum, and connection that compounds over time. These 12 attributes form that living structure. In the chapters ahead, we move from overview to practice, exploring how rainmakers bring these attributes to life when the stakes are highest.

Next: Attributes in Action

In the next four chapters, we explore these attributes in action—not as theory but as lived experience.

From our own experiences and those of others, you'll see how rainmakers earn respect, navigate complexity, influence outcomes, and transform relationships. You'll see these behaviors in high-stakes rooms, real-world conversations, and behind-the-scenes decision moments.

Most important, you'll learn how to start building these attributes yourself.

Not all at once. But over time, through reflection, practice, feedback, and commitment.

Because if the roots give rainmakers purpose and direction, the trunk provides them strength and shape.

Without that structure, even the deepest roots can't support growth.

Let's take a closer look.

CHAPTER

12

Heartwood: Character and Connection

Character Is Not About Being Liked. It's About Being Relied on When It Matters

Before rainmakers earn a seat at a senior client's table, they have to earn something deeper: trust. And trust doesn't come from titles or credentials. It comes from character and connection.

This is what forms the heartwood, the dense, steady core of who rainmakers are. Not the part on display but the part that holds everything together when the pressure builds. It's how they show up when no one's watching.

Rainmakers with real depth don't need to posture. They lead with integrity, and their empathy isn't performative; it's woven into how they work. They're curious in a genuine way, not just scanning for openings to speak but actually listening.

The connections they build don't fade when the project ends. Those relationships carry on through job changes, firm moves, entire career shifts.

That kind of trust isn't built from slide decks or quick impressions. It comes from time invested, from getting inside the client's world and staying long enough to understand what really matters.

It's not about being liked. It's about being trusted and being the person others rely on when the pressure's real.

In high-stakes environments, character isn't optional. It's part of the structure. The heartwood. The steady core everything else leans on.

These rainmakers don't chase the spotlight. They show up with a calm confidence that doesn't need to announce itself and clients notice.

In this chapter, we dive into the first three core attributes that set rainmakers apart. Rainmakers:

1. Build lasting relationships.
2. Immerse in the client's world.
3. Lead with integrity and action.

You'll hear stories from the field, real moments, not theory, alongside research that adds perspective. These aren't abstract ideas. They're lessons forged in the work itself. These are lessons you learn.

We start the chapter with a story from Neil; it's a story he's told often to partners wanting to make a bigger impact from their existing work.

Attribute #1: Build Lasting Relationships

It was early, far earlier than I would have liked. Around 6:30 a.m., I found myself in the corporate offices of a multinational mining company, bleary-eyed but alert. The fluorescent lights buzzed faintly. The air smelled of fresh paper and stale coffee.

Across from me sat a partner from a global strategy firm, one of the big three, a strong competitor in every sense. We were coleading a modest productivity strategy engagement. It was my first project for the client. Nothing glamorous, but solid, well scoped, efficiently delivered. The client seemed satisfied. Nothing flashy. Nothing remarkable. Just good, steady consulting.

And then everything changed.

The senior executive we reported to leaned forward. His voice dropped. He shared the high-level details of a confidential development that had just been sent to the stock exchange for immediate public release: a multi-billion-dollar acquisition had been proposed. A game-changing deal that would send shockwaves through the global resources sector.

What surprised me wasn't just the scale of the deal.

It was that the strategy consulting partner across from me had been anticipating this for months.

The client, unbeknownst to me at the time, had been a client of his for five years.

More than that, he had been preparing for this opportunity, if it was to eventuate, quietly, thoroughly, strategically. While I'd been focused on delivering the current project, he'd been shaping what came next. Not just a continuation but a transformation.

Within hours, another team from his firm arrived, flights booked. Briefings prepared. Integration planning is underway.

This wasn't improvisation.

It was the execution of a plan already in motion.

That morning changed everything about how I thought about client relationships, opportunity, and the role of the consultant.

Because my competitor wasn't just fulfilling a brief.

He was building off a long-term relationship, one built on trust, foresight, and shared ambition.

He was leading from the front.

Where I had a relationship with one sponsor, the strategy partner had cultivated an ecosystem.

He was in active conversation with the CEO, CFO, COO, and Head of Strategy, understanding how influence flowed across the organization. He'd mapped the decision makers, earned their trust, and positioned himself as a quiet, credible guide. Carefully, he helped each stakeholder see how their priorities intersected with broader organizational goals, all while maintaining discretion and fostering collaboration.

Rainmakers don't just manage stakeholders. They build trust architecture, formal and informal, vertical and horizontal.

They know that in complex organizations, authority is distributed. And they don't wait to be summoned.

They embed.

These days, AI tools can help map relationships in ways that weren't possible before, revealing hidden links, tracking shifts in sentiment, spotting patterns of influence.

But let's be clear: The technology and tools can take you only so far. They're a support, not a substitute. What still matters most is human: being present, listening well, and showing genuine empathy.

Andris A. Zoltners, Prabhakant Sinha, and Sally E. Lorimer found that enduring, cross-level relationships are among the strongest predictors of long-term client retention and high-value engagements.[1]

Rainmakers identify, nurture, and harvest the benefits of long-term relationships better than average consultants.

This wasn't a partner who just stayed close.

He stayed *valuable*.

Key Insight: Rainmakers don't just deliver well; they build enduring, multilevel client relationships rooted in trust, foresight, and presence. They embed deeply, anticipate change, and position themselves as indispensable before opportunity strikes.

Attribute #2: Immerse in the Client's World

To share the next core rainmaker attribute, let's hear a story from Robert. It's a hugely successful one, not because of a clever pitch or a breakthrough idea but because of something more enduring: a deep connection. It's a story about what happens when a consultant doesn't just advise from the outside but fully immerses in the client's world. Because rainmakers don't earn trust from a distance, they earn it by walking the same floors, facing the same pressures, and caring as much as their clients do.

Mia was a good consultant with a sharp mind, but what set her apart wasn't just intelligence; it was the intensity of her intent, the quiet determination to do whatever it took to make a real positive difference with her clients.

As a rising star in a global consulting house, Mia had worked on a couple of major corporate transformation programs under my leadership. She learned the frameworks well and applied discipline to program delivery. More important, she came to understand that achieving the optimal impact from transformational change requires not only the right strategy but also effective human connections. Mia saw that rainmakers and their teams can't deliver value on their own; the best results come when consultants embed themselves in the client's world until trust flows in both directions.

A few years later, newly promoted to partner and based in North America, Mia made a bold move. She didn't wait for the phone to ring. She wanted to take what she'd learned—the model, the mechanics, and the mindset—and lead a transformation of her own. Not just for a client, but to establish her business platform.

Mia's research led her to a $40 billion company headquartered on the West Coast in the United States, with 50,000 employees, global ambitions, and complex legacy systems. It was a candidate ripe to reap the rewards of transformation. But there was a catch. The company rarely used consultants. Internally, the organization was strong and proud. Externally, it was guarded.

Most consultants would have kept looking. Mia moved there.

She rented a small place just outside the city and quietly began showing up at the company. Mia organized meetings to introduce herself to key executives, found ways to learn the company's structure, its culture, and its internal language. She asked thoughtful questions and listened more than she spoke. Over time she picked up some pieces of work, small enough not to threaten the company's culture but significant enough to matter. These projects landed well. Gradually Mia's credibility as a trusted external consultant grew.

These efforts came at a personal cost. Mia still had to meet her firm's numbers. She was selling and delivering other projects across the country at the same time, often flying out at 5 a.m. on Mondays and back on the night's red-eye flight, to be in town for Tuesday meetings with her new West Coast client. It was exhausting. But Mia never stopped showing up.

Then came the opening. Mia determined that the time was right to pitch for something big. The client company needed to consolidate the rewards from customer growth it had achieved, and the market expected the company to improve its margins. Mia called the key members of the transformation team from whom she'd once learned, the same people who'd taught her the rhythm and nuance of complex corporate change.

We responded. We came from all corners of the globe. Not because we had to but because Mia had earned our respect. She orchestrated a presentation to the client's executive team that didn't just showcase capability, it showcased commitment. Mia's message to the client was clear. *This is what we can bring. We believe in your mission.*

Mia organized a dinner for us and the client. The moment that mattered came at that dinner. After exchanging pleasantries, we began a discussion. Mia kicked it off with the perfect introduction and then handed it to me. I told a story in the way Mia had choreographed:

- Leading with the results we achieved from previous transformations
- Speaking directly but with humility, admitting mistakes and learnings
- Explaining market reactions to the work

I paused after 10 or 15 minutes, and there was a moment of silence. Then the client's chief financial officer asked a question, not to me, but to Mia. Mia gave an answer that showed her insight and understanding, and they all leaned in to listen. The presentation became a free-wheeling discussion that went late into the night, with us sharing stories and the client opening up about their issues.

Mia didn't win with flash or forceful selling. She won by immersing herself in the client's systems and people, by understanding the company's pressure points and the aspirations of a client who wasn't asking for help. She embedded herself before she was invited. She brought the best of her firm's colleagues, but only after earning the right to do so.

Big projects followed. That night led to greater engagement with our firm and many more trips to the West Coast. The client became the firm's biggest client in the United States, and the company became one of the strongest growth performers in their market.

Mia's story is a story of how a rainmaker was created. Not overnight. Not by accident or by "being a natural." By showing up early, staying late, and getting to know both the organization and its people from the inside out, you can gain a deeper understanding.

Key Insight: Rainmakers don't wait to be invited in; they embed themselves early, learn the client's world intimately, and earn trust through presence, persistence, and purpose. They use this knowledge to create moments that matter. Real influence grows from immersion, not distance. Mia proved that.

Attribute #3: Lead with Integrity and Action

Neil has a story to bring this attribute to life. It was a pivotal moment, a fantastic client, a high-stakes opportunity, and the potential for a massive project. But then it wasn't.

It started with a text message at 7:12 a.m.

"Are you in town? Need 20 mins, just you."

It was from Scott, the group chief technology officer of a global logistics company. We'd worked together years ago on a digital twin pilot that became core to their network operations. Smart guy. Grounded. Constantly juggling too much.

By 9:00 a.m., I was in his office. Lights low, laptop open, black coffee in hand, no small talk.

"This thing is a mess," he said.

He pulled up a slide, a tangled architecture map, clearly patched together by multiple teams over a decade. Legacy systems, custom code, half-migrated platforms, brittle application programming interfaces. A fragile digital spine.

"We've got a board review in 17 days. They want a real plan, costs, risks, progress. And more than anything, signs that we're moving."

He looked up. "Can you help?"

What I didn't say, but knew instantly, was that our firm couldn't do this. Not properly. We had smart people. Good transformation credentials. But not the kind of deep infrastructure firepower this would take, not at the speed or scale required.

But I also knew this: Scott trusted me. Not to say yes. To tell the truth.

So, I took a breath and said:

"Scott, the truth? You're asking the right question. And I can help, just not the way you think."

He raised an eyebrow.

"I can help frame the problem, shape the story for the board, and get the right people in the room fast. But to fix this? You need specialists, people who've rebuilt systems like this under pressure. I know someone. I'll make the call."

There was a pause. Then he nodded. "That's why I called you."

By noon I was on the phone with a senior leader at one of our trusted technology alliance partners. We'd worked with them before but never handed them something this big. I kept it simple:

"This is a trust-based intro. Show up like a vendor, and you'll blow it."

By 3:00 p.m. the next day, we had Scott and his CTO of infrastructure in a virtual room with their top architecture lead, no sales pitch. No theatrics. Just solving problems.

For the next 12 days, I stayed involved. Quietly shaping the board narrative, guiding internal stakeholder prep, and clearing obstacles. My firm didn't earn a dollar.

Could I have tried to hold on? Absolutely. Assembled a few passable resources, built a shiny presentation, pretended we had the depth. We might have cobbled something together and stayed one step ahead.

But that would've been the wrong play. For Scott. For the board. For the relationship.

So, I let go of a $10 million opportunity and did what was right. I brought in the right team. I stayed close, but not in the way that demanded credit.

And when the board approved the roadmap, and again, six months later, when real progress showed up, Scott pulled me aside.

"You didn't just help me find the answer," he said. "You protected me from choosing the wrong one."

I smiled. That's rainmaking.

Not clinging. Not overpromising. Not pretending to be the answer to everything.

But showing up with clarity, leading with values, and standing in your client's corner, even when it costs you.

Because rainmakers don't earn respect and trust by talking about integrity.

They earn it when they have every reason not to act with it and do anyway.

Key Insight: Rainmakers do what's right, not what's easy, especially when there's money on the table. Integrity in action builds credibility, deepens respect, and ensures you're the first call next time.

Conclusion

Rainmakers don't lead with flash; they lead with character. Across these first three attributes, one truth stands out: Deep connection is earned, not assumed. It's earned through trust, consistency, and the way you show up when the pressure is on. These aren't surface-level traits; they're part of the structure. Like the trunk of a tree, they hold everything up, rooted in something solid at the core.

Because when all is said and done, clients remember who stood steady when it counted.

Next: How Rainmakers Show Up

Like the bark of a tree, the way rainmakers show up is what the world encounters first. It protects what lies within while shaping how they are perceived. Their clarity of communication, confidence of presence, and credibility form this outer layer. These visible qualities help rainmakers navigate complexity, influence outcomes, and ensure others feel truly seen and heard.

Let's check this out.

CHAPTER

13

Clarity and Presence

The Most Pivotal Consulting Moments Are Quiet and Unscheduled; Rainmakers Recognize Them and Then Ask What Others Won't

Let's now turn to how rainmakers show up and create confidence. When the pressure is high and the room is tense, rainmakers don't just speak; they shift the atmosphere. They bring clarity when others bring noise. They slow the moment down when everything is speeding up.

In the moments that carry weight—the tough client call, the tense boardroom exchange, the decision that just won't move—rainmakers don't try to control the room. They lift it.

They pick up on what isn't being said. They know when to press, when to pause, and when to stay quiet. Their presence is steady and intentional; not flashy, just firm.

Think of the bark on a tree. It doesn't draw attention to itself, but it protects, it holds, and it signals strength. You don't need to touch it to know it's solid.

In a world full of noise, complexity, and constant motion, these rainmakers stand out by cutting through.

They don't just explain complexity; they make it usable. They make it make sense.

Because when the pressure's on and decisions need to be made, no one remembers who talked the most. They remember who brought clarity. And that quiet, sharp clarity is one of the most powerful forms of influence there is.

In this chapter, we explore the next three core attributes of rainmakers, those that define how they show up and create confidence in the moments that matter:

4. Know the critical moments.
5. Communicate with clarity and influence.
6. Focus on what truly matters.

As always, we share stories, each one grounded in experience, each offering a valuable insight.

We begin with one of Neil's. It's a story he's shared many times over the years because it captures a moment that happens often in our industry but is rarely named, taught, or discussed. And yet it's in moments like these that rainmakers set themselves apart and where many consultants, often without realizing it, come up short.

Attribute #4: Know the Critical Moments

Some of the most critical moments in consulting don't happen in the pitch room or the boardroom. They don't arrive with a calendar invite or a formal agenda. They happen unexpectantly: in elevators, cafés, car parks, and corridors, even airport lounges. They're easy to miss. And most consultants do.

Rainmakers, though, learn to spot them. From experience. From feel. It's a skill that's hard to teach but unmistakable when seen.

Let me tell you a story Mary once shared with me. She's a senior partner at a major law firm, someone who moves fluidly between legal advice, risk, and strategy.

I've shared this story many times over the years, because it captures something we don't often talk about: presence.

Mary had arranged a meeting with one of her long-term clients at the client's office. No burning issue, just a regular check-in and a chance to walk through some new research her firm had put together. The conversation flowed easily. It was relaxed, familiar. They covered the material, traded a few updates. About halfway in, it seemed like the meeting had run its course. Another ticked box. Another meeting done.

And then something shifted. A moment.

The client's executive assistant walked in and handed the client a document. She glanced at it, paused, and softly muttered something like "Oh, no." Just enough for Mary to register it. Not enough for most people to act.

They continued chatting lightly, walking back through the office toward the elevators. And that's when Mary asked gently and sincerely: "Is everything okay? Are *you* okay?"

That moment, the tone, the timing, the choice to ask, was the moment.

The client hesitated. Then opened up. Something serious was unfolding. An issue had surfaced, quietly but critically. It was still in the early stages, and few people knew about it yet. But it had the potential to escalate: reputationally, operationally, and legally.

That conversation in the elevator turned into a longer coffee. The longer coffee turned into a working session. That session led to a two-year major remediation program involving legal, risk, technology, and governance transformation, one of the most impactful projects that the client had undertaken in years.

And it almost never happened.

It wasn't in the brief. It wasn't in the diary. It was a moment that could've slipped by. And for most consultants, it would have.

Here's the truth: The easy moments are when clients ask for help, such as when an RFP drops or a colleague refers you to one of their clients. Those moments are easy to spot.

The moments that matter most? They're subtle. They live in a change of voice on the phone. A frown midmeeting. A glance from an executive assistant. A hesitation in the hallway.

You don't find those moments from your desk. You see them by showing up, in person, with curiosity, with empathy, and with just enough courage to ask the question most people won't.

And when you do, everything can change.

Key Insight: The most pivotal consulting moments are often quiet, unscheduled, and easy to miss. Rainmakers spot them through presence, empathy, and timing and act with just enough courage to ask what others won't.

Attribute #5: Communicate with Clarity and Influence

Robert and I have seen this pattern many times, not through our delivery but in coaching the next generation of great consultants.

It's something we hear all the time from partners and directors:

"The client just didn't get it. We had the data. We laid out the story. The return on investment was clear. But they didn't bite. We lost the work."

Here's what they often miss. Being right isn't the same as being heard.

Rainmakers understand this. That's where they stand apart. They don't just present ideas; they make them land. They don't just share information; they connect in a way that moves people.

Real communication isn't just about transferring facts. It's about translation. It's helping someone not only understand what you're saying but feel it, enough to take action.

Rainmakers know how to do that. They simplify without dumbing down. They take complex ideas, strip away the noise, and deliver the part that matters, clearly, directly, and in a way that sticks.

They know when a story will cut through. When to build tension. When to pause. When to let a single line do the heavy lifting.

And they don't drown the room in detail. They layer it. If someone wants to go deeper into the model, the assumptions, the analysis, they're ready. But they always start with a clear signal. A sharp structure. A moment of clarity that tells the client: This matters. And here's why.

And rainmakers don't wait until the final presentation to do it. Influence starts early in hallway conversations, background documents shared in advance, and quiet chats before the big meeting. They seed ideas. They test resonance. They build alignment behind the scenes so that when the moment comes, the message lands.

This is especially true when the stakes are high. In crisis reviews, boardroom pitches, or major transformation updates, rainmakers don't wing it. They rehearse. They tighten the phrasing. They anticipate the tough questions. Not because they want to perform but because they respect the moment, the audience, and the potential impact.

They also understand the psychology of communication. That attention is fragile. That people are more likely to act on what they connect with emotionally. That a well-timed story can make the numbers matter. That influence often happens one person at a time, long before consensus is declared.

Great rainmakers make communication feel effortless. But behind that ease is craft. Precision. And a deep belief that every message is an opportunity to move someone forward.

That's what sets these rainmakers apart. Not the slides. Not the volume of information. But the way they bring insight to life—clearly, confidently, and in a way that changes the room.

Key Insight: Rainmakers know that being right isn't enough. Actual influence comes from clarity, connection, and craft. They translate complexity into meaning, shape messages that move people, and communicate with purpose long before the big moment arrives.

Attribute #6: Focus on What Truly Matters

In my practice leadership roles, one of the privileges I had was sitting down with senior clients to ask, candidly, why we won or lost a deal, how delivery was progressing, and what more we could do to support them. These were rarely easy conversations, but they were gold. I learned more in those quiet, behind-the-scenes meetings than in any formal review.

One in particular has stayed with me. I've shared it often in my reflections, but also in mentoring the next generation of consulting leaders.

It was one of those anonymous corporate offices. No logos on the glass doors. Identical floors, elevator doors and waiting areas that made you feel like you could be in any building in any city. I arrived early, sat in the neutral-toned waiting area, and was eventually shown to a high-floor meeting room. No fanfare. Just water in a jug and a view of the skyline.

The client was a seasoned executive: calm, sharp, and generous enough to give me 30 minutes to understand why we'd lost a recent pitch.

We exchanged the usual courtesies. He acknowledged the quality of our work, said we were known and trusted, *to a degree*. Then he paused. His voice softened, but his words cut through.

"In our company, we're surrounded by noise. Shifting priorities, endless pressure. The consultants who cut through that, who bring us the one thing that matters, those are the ones we remember. On this last piece, you told us everything that was wrong with our business and offered a generic way forward. It wasn't helpful."

He didn't want simplification for its own sake. He wanted clarity in the face of chaos.

In that moment, something clicked for me. He wasn't asking for more data or more slides. He was seeking clarity and the essential insight that mattered most. The one thing that could move a decision forward.

Rainmakers understand this instinctively. They don't try to prove how much they know. They curate. They edit. They say less, but with more weight. They separate the essential from the irrelevant and deliver it with calm conviction.

Cognitive load theory—the idea that our brains can process only a limited amount of information at once, so too much complexity quickly overwhelms understanding—reminds us that human attention is finite.[1]

When we flood clients with complexity, we don't create value; we dilute it.

Rainmakers resist that temptation. They don't hedge with 10 options. They show up with one powerful perspective, grounded in insight and tailored to the moment.

That, I've learned, is the rainmaker's edge: not in covering every angle, but in knowing exactly which ground to stand on and standing there with clarity, confidence, and care.

Key Insight: Rainmakers cut through complexity by focusing on what matters most. They don't overwhelm with detail: They curate with care, delivering clear, relevant insight that moves decisions forward and earns trust in high-pressure moments.

Conclusion

Rainmakers don't just show up; they shape the moment. These three attributes—knowing the critical moments, communicating with clarity, and focusing on what truly matters—are the heart of presence. They turn noise into signal, hesitation into movement, and complexity into confident action.

In a distracted world, clarity is rare. And rainmakers who master it don't just get heard; they get remembered, trusted, and called back. Like the trunk of a tree, these attributes provide strength and structure.

And like the bark that surrounds and protects that trunk, they shape how rainmakers are seen, felt, and experienced in the room. They shield against chaos, signal composure, and hold steady under pressure, supporting the entire ecosystem of influence, action, and growth that follows.

Next: What Drives Outcomes

Beneath the bark sits the sapwood, the part of the tree that keeps everything flowing. This is where movement happens and where potential turns into action. For rainmakers, these attributes, described in the next chapter, create momentum, fuel execution, and ultimately determine whether intentions become meaningful results for clients and their firms.

Let's examine this in detail.

CHAPTER

14

Action and Impact

Clients Remember Who Broke the Gridlock—Not the Models, Reports, or Decks

Rainmakers don't sit around waiting for the perfect brief or ideal timing. They make things happen. While others pause, weigh options, or play it safe, they step in and move.

In a profession where ideas often are left on a whiteboard or in meeting notes, rainmakers stand out by taking action: They make the call, send the email, organize a client catch-up.

For them, action isn't the last step; it's the point.

Clients rarely remember the smartest model or the slickest deck. What sticks is who helped them push past the gridlock. Who got them moving when it mattered.

These rainmakers pair relentless follow-through with an unwavering sense of purpose. They are builders, not just thinkers; catalysts, not just commentators.

Their impact isn't measured in volume but in velocity, in how fast they turn insight into change. Like the sapwood just beneath the bark, the attributes discussed in this chapter carry the lifeblood of momentum through the system. Constantly moving and always feeding and always translating potential into performance.

When the pressure's on, rainmakers bring what's needed most: focus, clarity, and follow-through.

In consulting, knowing what to do isn't enough. You have to be the one who makes sure it actually happens and that it sticks.

Faster. Smarter. Built to last.

That's what real impact looks like. That's where rainmakers earn their place.

In this chapter, we explore three more core attributes of rainmakers, those that define how they drive results that matter:

7. Deliver outcomes consistently.
8. Leverage firm strengths for growth.
9. Understand technology as strategy.

We keep sharing stories, real ones, drawn from experience, each with something worth taking away.

Let's start with one from Robert. It's a story he's told many times to newly promoted partners, the kind of people hungry to understand what really drives long-term success in selling more work than the rest.

Attribute #7: Deliver Outcomes Consistently

People often think rainmakers are relentless hunters, always chasing new leads, always searching for the next big client. But the opposite is usually true.

Across my consulting career, I worked at three different consulting firms. Through these moves, across firms and roles, one client stayed with me. Not a particular executive but an entire organization. My relationship lasted through client leadership changes, ownership shifts, and full-scale transformation. It began years earlier with a project that, at the time, felt small.

The project was a strategy piece for a small unit of a large, government-owned utility that would later be privatized. We delivered well: sharp analysis, clear options, and genuine engagement. But what mattered most was what happened afterward. The client invited us back to go deeper, to help implement the strategy, extract the value, and make real change stick.

That project became a door. From there, I was referred again and again, not through marketing or firm outreach but by client recommendation. The work grew. The conversations deepened. I was asked into rooms I hadn't originally expected to enter because I wasn't trying to sell. I was trying to help.

That's the shift. I never saw myself as a functional expert. I was never there to "own" a category or turn a particular solution into a product. I was there to be useful, to listen, bring clarity, and connect the right people and capabilities from across my firm to help solve the client's issues. I genuinely wanted to see the client organization do better. But I found that delivering outcomes consistently and without ego had a momentum of its own.

I learned a valuable lesson here that has stayed with me throughout my whole career. Projects that deliver excellent outcomes create advocates for your work. Rainmakers earn the right to use this advocacy to do more and have a greater impact. Over time I grew from a relatively timid consultant to someone who was always prepared to ask a happy client to be a referrer, make an introduction to a colleague, or support a bid for a new project.

Rainmakers don't always need to go searching. Sometimes they need to show up with insight, integrity, and a genuine intent to serve the client. Let's continue with another story from Robert.

Key Insight: Rainmakers don't win by chasing every opportunity. They get invited into the right rooms because they've delivered where it counts. When the outcomes are real, trust follows. And with trust come advocates: people who remember, who refer, who bring you into bigger, more meaningful conversations.

Attribute #8: Leverage Firm Strengths for Growth

The following story is a personal one, from my time as a senior partner at a global strategy firm. It came with real disruption for me and my family but ultimately delivered outstanding results for both our clients and the firm.

It started with a conversation about growth. Our firm was searching for bold ideas, something beyond incremental wins. I put one on the table, backing myself to take my local experience onto a global stage, but not expecting much. The next thing I knew, I was boarding a flight with my family and relocating to London for six months.

In my industry sector, we had some strong client relationships in Europe and the Americas, but they were narrow. In some cases, we had excellent access but not the right capabilities. In others, we had relevant capability but had never earned the client's trust. Meanwhile, I had deep experience leading complex enterprise transformations—driving productivity improvements, structural cost improvements, and reinvestment for growth—but I was based half a world away. I also had a good story to tell about a successful enterprise-wide transformation that exceeded market expectations and drew attention throughout the global industry. The idea was simple: Match capability to need. Not hypothetically. Physically.

Together with relevant local partners, I began a program visiting selected target clients; 20 in total, across Europe, the United States, and South America. In each boardroom or strategy workshop, I shared my story explicitly tailored to the audience: the work we'd done, the lessons we learned, the tangible outcomes we'd helped to deliver, and highlighting the relevance of the work to the target company. The story wasn't about me; it was about the ability of our firm to embed itself in understanding the client's challenges from a different perspective. It was a signal that we weren't global just in name but in action.

The response was immediate. Nine new deals resulted, across Canada, the United States, Germany, the Netherlands, Hungary, and Brazil. Three of these engagements became multiyear partnerships generating not just measurable value for clients but also new relationships, new opportunities, and deeper credibility with C-suites. None of the programs was identical to the original transformation I'd led. Some clients took parts of the model program, some added or adjusted elements, some sought to reshape the approach, but all embraced a transformation mindset and took learnings from our experience.

I learned that it was best not to cling too closely to the path taken in a case study. It was better to break down the key elements, identify the options considered, and discuss the reasons why the previous client chose the path they did. Doing this opens the discussion with the prospective client and allows local partners to engage with them in identifying what path best suits the client's specific needs.

Rainmakers don't just focus on what they can sell personally. They find ways to leverage their firm's full strength—its people, stories, track record, relationships—and connect these assets to where the client's needs are most urgent.

Key Insight: Rainmakers grow by mobilizing the full strength of their firm's capabilities, track record, and people and connecting them to real client needs, even if it means stepping outside their comfort zone.

Attribute #9: Understand Technology as Strategy

The next attribute isn't about knowing how to code. It's not about mastering platforms or getting certified in the latest enterprise software. It's about grasping—deeply, intuitively, and confidently—that in today's world, *technology is strategy*.

For both of us, this topic hits close to home. Not as technologists. But as veterans of the early waves of convergence, those murky years when consulting and technology firms were still learning how to dance together without stepping on each other's toes.

We remember one particular program well. A national telecommunications client. A fiercely intelligent CEO standing at the edge of a cliff. She didn't want another presentation or polished report. She wanted survival and then transformation. Regulatory change had swung the doors open to new competition. Mobile and data services were exploding. The company's once-golden fixed-line business was collapsing. Customers were furious. The future was unwritten.

We were brought in to chart a new course.

And what unfolded was messy, brilliant, bruising, and, ultimately, transformative.

We built a team made up of strategists, technologists, human-centered designers, process engineers, and customer experience leaders, some who had never worked together before, some who barely spoke the same professional language. The early months were painful. Half the team didn't know what the other half was doing. Misalignment was everywhere. Ideas collided. Jargon clashed. There was friction, fumbles, and more than a few difficult conversations.

But underneath the chaos, something new was taking root.

We were solving real problems. Together. We weren't writing reports for reports' sake; we were redesigning the business with technology embedded in every thread. New billing systems. Customer self-service platforms. Cross-channel experience design. Organizational redesign. New digital products and services. And, most important, a mindset shift from reactive infrastructure manager to proactive customer-first digital enterprise.

The client didn't want tech for tech's sake. They wanted business outcomes. But they understood, earlier than most, that the outcomes would come only if technology were core to the solution.

The engagement lasted years. And though we got there just barely and gratefully, it remains one of the most formative experiences of our careers. But here's the truth: If we tried to run that same program today the same way we did then, we'd be out of our depth. Executives today don't need to be convinced that technology matters. They expect you to know already *that it does*. They want you to speak fluently, not just in business, but in platforms, data, security, AI, cloud, and ecosystems.

Today, strategy *is* technology.

It's not a siloed workstream. It's not the "IT part" that comes later. It is front and center of every big bet, how the organization competes, how it serves customers, how it scales, how it survives. If you're not part of that conversation, you're not in the room where the real work is happening.

Rainmakers must learn to bridge that world. You don't need to be an expert. But you *do* need to bring the curiosity, humility, and fluency to engage to ask the right questions, to challenge shallow thinking, to connect the dots between technical possibility and business priority.

You need to partner deeply with your firm's technology leaders, not as a hand-off but as a true collaboration. Because when it works, when it clicks, it's magic. It unlocks growth, resilience, and relevance for your clients.

And for you? It's the difference between being a rainmaker or an afterthought.

This is the new rainmaker reality. Understand technology or get left behind.

Key Insight: Rainmakers must understand that technology is strategy, not an add-on. To stay relevant, they must engage deeply, speak fluently, and collaborate across disciplines to drive meaningful, tech-enabled business transformation.

Conclusion

Rainmakers known for action and impact are the ones clients remember and call back. They turn insight into movement, complexity into clarity, and ambition into measurable change. The attributes in this chapter aren't flashy, but they're foundational.

Like the trunk of a tree, they provide strength, structure, and support, and like the sapwood within, they carry the energy that fuels progress. This is the layer where real momentum flows. These rainmakers build respect with their clients through follow-through, shape momentum through discipline, and earn influence by delivering results that last.

In a world full of noise, these rainmakers stand apart, not by talking but by making things happen.

Next: Continuing to Grow

Just beneath the surface of the tree lies the cambium, the living layer responsible for new growth. It is where renewal begins and where the future quietly takes shape. Like the cambium, rainmakers sustain growth by continually looking ahead, creating new value, and opening fresh opportunities. In the next chapter, we explore the attributes that keep growth alive.

Let's move on.

CHAPTER

15

Growth and Vision

Rainmakers Don't Wait for Growth to Occur. They Build It

Rainmakers don't wait for growth to show up; they build it.

They keep one foot in the present and one eye on what's coming. Not chasing trends but spotting possibility early.

For them, growth isn't luck. It's not about being in the right place at the right time. It's what happens when vision meets discipline and when someone has the courage to lead commercially, not just follow.

Rainmakers are the ones who sense possibility early: in a shifting market, a new capability, an underserved segment, or a rising senior executive ready for more. They don't wait for clarity; they shape it. With a rare blend of imagination and commercial instinct, they stretch their firm's thinking while staying grounded in the client's world.

It's not about reckless bets or chasing buzzwords. It's about planting seeds before others see the soil as fertile and nurturing growth, where others see only risk. Like the cambium layer of a tree, which generates new rings each year, these attributes are where transformation begins, constantly renewing, continually expanding, always building toward what's next.

This chapter explores the attributes that drive that kind of growth: the vision, courage, and strategic investment rainmakers make to shape a future worth leading.

We're now down to the final three attributes that form the trunk of the rainmaker's tree; they are:

10. Dream big and play bold.

11. Think commercially, act entrepreneurially.

12. Adapt and learn continuously.

Attribute #10: Dream Big and Play Bold

In consulting, there are moments when you must take a bold, calculated risk, even when the voices inside your team say *Don't*. These are the moments that test more than just judgment; they test conviction. Because sometimes, to do what's right for the client or to open a door that may never appear again, you must be prepared to go all in.

And yes, sometimes, you must be prepared to lose.

The most powerful inflection points don't always come with perfect data or consensus support. They appear in the ambiguity, in a client's hesitation, in a half-stated concern, in a flash of possibility you either act on or let pass you by.

Rainmakers learn to spot those moments.

And act.

This is one of those stories.

It's the story of Laura, a highly successful global strategy partner working inside a Big Four consulting division. The environment was innovative, driven, and well resourced, but also fragmented. No one owned client relationships. Teams dipped in and out depending on the day of the week.

Laura was different. Known for her calm insight and quiet boldness, she didn't dominate rooms, but when she spoke, people listened. And when she listened, clients felt heard.

The consulting team was pursuing a program management office (PMO) engagement with a billion-dollar organization deep in internal change. It was a good opportunity. Manageable. Predictable. The team saw it as a straightforward win.

Laura didn't.

Where others saw a safe brief, she saw a bigger opening.

Before the request for proposal (RFP) landed, she arranged a conversation with the senior client, Julie. Newly appointed. Under pressure. Holding more questions than answers. Laura didn't bring a pitch. She brought stories. Cautionary tales. Lessons from other transformations. And she asked the kinds of questions that make people pause: *What story do you want to tell the organization? Where's the board really at? What would make this a turning point, not just another program?*

Julie opened up. The organization was stuck; structurally, culturally, and emotionally. Resistance to change was baked in. Energy was low. Systems were failing. People were tired.

Where others saw a PMO, Laura saw a possibility.

When the RFP arrived, it asked for PMO support. The internal team debated. Most leaned toward submitting what the client asked for. Laura pushed back.

She proposed two options. One addressed the brief. The other challenged it, a bolder, more strategic proposal built from everything she'd seen and heard. It wasn't just a bid for more scope. It was a reframe, an invitation to use the moment for transformational change.

It was a risk.

And it changed everything.

Julie didn't just read the proposal; she studied it. It gave her language for what she hadn't been able to articulate. It offered a path she couldn't see. It showed her that someone *saw* her and what she was trying to do.

When the decision came, she chose the bigger play.

What followed became one of the most significant client engagements Laura's firm had ever delivered, not just in size but in depth and impact.

Laura didn't win the work by sticking to the brief.

She won it because she looked past it and saw what was really needed.

Rainmakers aren't chasing certainty. They're aiming for impact.

They read the moment and trust their instincts, even when no one's asked them to.

They think bigger. They take the swing others hold back from.

Because those are the moments that change everything.

Key Insight: Rainmakers understand that some of the most important opportunities often live in the gray space, not in a client's brief. They notice what others overlook. It might be a hesitation, a passing comment, or a shift in tone. They notice it. And when the moment comes, they don't hang back; they trust their read, take the risk, and move.

Attribute #11: Think Commercially, Act Entrepreneurially

Of all the rainmaker attributes, this is the one that's hardest to grow, hardest to learn, and the most defining. It's the line in the sand, the quiet separator. The rainmakers who think commercially and act entrepreneurially are the ones shaping the real plays. They don't just respond to opportunity; they create it. And those who lack this instinct? They're not bad consultants. They're just not in the room when the deal is formed, not on the call when a client whispers their genuine concern, not even considered when a major strategic shift is being plotted. Because clients, senior, time-poor, pressure-filled, sense the difference. They know who's in it for execution and who's in it to help them win.

This attribute is the soul of the builder. It's the mindset of those who don't just solve problems; they scan the horizon, see the white space, and shape plays that others never imagined. When others stall in complexity, they move in. When a client hesitates, they lean forward, not recklessly but with calculated conviction.

We introduced you earlier to a few of the great entrepreneurial architects of the 19th and early 20th centuries: Morgan restructuring industries, Carnegie reimagining scale, Rothschild mapping capital like no one before, Shibusawa blending business and nation building, Tata laying the foundation for the modern Indian sector, and Sousa modernizing Brazil. These were visionaries, yes, but more than that, they were commercial engineers. They understood capital, supply chains, global dynamics, and risk. And they dared to act.

So too did the founders of our consulting tradition. Arthur D. Little didn't wait to be asked; he commercialized chemical engineering into advisory services. James O. McKinsey didn't wait for management science to become a thing; he made it one. They weren't merely analysts. They were market makers. They saw an emerging need, created language around it, and built capabilities ahead of demand.

Modern rainmakers share that same wiring. They think like owners. They tune into the economics of client businesses and of their firm. They know that commercial success in consulting isn't about more reports, more hours, more deliverables. It's about creating value that matters and claiming it.

They ask different questions:

- Where's the tension in this market, and who will pay to resolve it?
- What underutilized asset does this client have that we can help activate?
- If we win this piece of work, what are the next three plays?
- How do we turn this short-term project into a long-term partnership, one that reshapes our position in the account?

They also balance risk differently. Rainmakers don't chase every shiny object. But they know how to bet thoughtfully, boldly. They back their insights. They're comfortable being early, but not foolishly so. They test, adapt, and act fast enough to stay ahead.

And perhaps most important, they keep their ambition focused. This isn't about being a generalist opportunist. It's about knowing the client, the firm, the ecosystem, and moving precisely when others hesitate.

So, how do you grow this rarest of strengths?

Start here: Read the playbooks of commercial change agents. Not just in consulting. In healthcare, energy, fintech, logistics, space, and sport. Learn how innovators spot inflection points, reposition assets, form partnerships, and unlock trapped value. Study how they think, not just what they did. Then bring that mindset into your world.

Rainmakers don't wait for permission. They don't just hope to be included in the conversation; they earn it by seeing further, thinking sharper, and moving earlier than anyone else around them.

That's the difference.

And it's why this attribute doesn't just define the rainmaker.

It defines the future.

Key Insight: Rainmakers who think commercially and act entrepreneurially don't wait for opportunity; they create it. By blending bold insight with calculated risk, they shape the deal, influence direction, and consistently position themselves where value is made.

Attribute #12: Adapt and Learn Continuously

For this last attribute, we'll share a few crisp observations, drawn from years of working alongside the best-performing partners and consultants in the business, on how rainmakers adapt and learn continuously.

Adapting to Their Environment

The top rainmakers don't wait for the market to send them an email. They read the signals early and move. Here's what they do:

- They track the client's internal calendar as closely as their own. Budget cycles, board meetings, strategic offsites: They time conversations and proposals to land when decisions are being made.
- They flex their style, not their standards. With one client, they go deep on analytics. With another, they lead with story and impact. They know when to push, when to pause, and when to switch gears entirely without losing their edge.
- They embed in the client's language. They drop their own firm's jargon and adopt the client's terms. Not just to blend in but to connect because nothing builds trust like being truly understood.
- They learn the real decision-making structure. Not the organizational chart; the actual web of influence. Rainmakers map who matters, who blocks, who whispers in whose ear, and tailor their engagement accordingly.
- They respond to risk signals fast. If momentum dips or silence sets in, they act early, picking up the phone, getting in the room, and resetting expectations before problems grow roots.
- The reflect. They review their position and self-appraise their performance regularly and repeatedly.

Learning Continuously

Building on Carol Dweck's work,[1] we've seen the best rainmakers treat learning not as a phase but as a practice. Here's how:

- They conduct postmortems religiously, win or lose. After every deal or project, they ask: What worked? What didn't? What would we do differently? And they don't make excuses, they make adjustments.

- They reverse-mentor. They seek out younger colleagues or domain experts to keep them current, not just in technology but in culture, tools, language, and new ways of thinking.
- They read outside their lane. Public policy, behavioral science, geopolitics, industry trends. They draw insight from the edges to stay sharp at the center.
- They use AI, they don't just talk about it. Whether it's drafting thought leadership, modeling a client scenario, or summarizing board documents, they actively use AI tools to extend their thinking and execution. They don't wait for a playbook: They experiment, assess, and apply. And in this ever-expanding space, they read, explore, and enroll in self-development programs from a variety of sources.
- They seek feedback that stings. Not just "how did I go?" but "Where did I fall short? What could I have done better?" They want the unfiltered version because growth doesn't come from comfort.

This is how rainmakers grow: not just taller, but stronger. Season after season. Ring after ring.

Key Insight: Rainmakers grow stronger by staying alert and adaptable and by always learning. They tune into signals early, flex their approach without compromising standards, and treat feedback, reflection, and experimentation as essential disciplines, not optional extras.

Conclusion

Growth and vision aren't abstract ideals; they are the lived behaviors of rainmakers who sense what's possible before others do and move with purpose. They don't just follow strategy; they shape it.

They dream ambitiously, act commercially, and invest in futures not yet obvious.

Like the cambium layer in a tree, the living source of renewal and expansion, these rainmakers generate growth from within, season after season. By staying close to the client's world while looking beyond it, they help lead the firm and the market into what's next.

PART

III

SUMMARY

The Trunk: Core Attributes of a Rainmaker

As we close this part of the book, take a moment to pause. At the beginning of Chapter 11, we defined an attribute as *an observable strength that meaningfully supports rainmaker performance and contributes to sustained success in high-stakes, client-facing environments.*

These traits are not theoretical. They are lived, visible behaviors that shape careers and deepen impact. Many consultants will recognize our attribute categories and believe they are executing most of them. Rainmakers aim to execute all the attributes at an elite level, well beyond going through motions. This elite level sets them apart from the average consultant, as does their ongoing pursuit of excellence in all that they do.

Let's recap the 12 attributes and the elite standards targeted by rainmakers:

Character and Connection—Who They Are at the Core (Heartwood)

1. **Build lasting relationships:** Cultivate deep, trust-based relationships across all levels of the client organization.
2. **Immerse in the client's world:** Don't consult from a distance. Embed yourself. Know the client's people, pressures, and priorities deeply.
3. **Lead with integrity and action:** Prioritize long-term client value. Take the right path, even when it's harder. Follow through on what you say you will do.

Clarity and Presence—How They Show Up and Create Confidence (Bark)

4. **Know the critical moments:** Sense the subtle shifts, the openings where insight, empathy, and courage can unlock transformation.

5. **Communicate with clarity and influence:** Simplify the complex. Shape compelling narratives and guide decisions with calm, confident communication.
6. **Focus on what truly matters:** Cut through the noise. Help clients prioritize, focus, and act on the things that move the needle.

Action and Impact—How They Drive Results That Matter (Sapwood)

7. **Deliver outcomes consistently:** Add meaningful, forward-looking value, even before the client realizes what's coming.
8. **Leverage firm strengths for growth:** Mobilize the full capability of your firm to meet both current and emerging needs.
9. **Understand technology as strategy:** Grasp how technology is and can reshape business models, unlock value, and reduce risk.

Growth and Vision—How They Lead the Future (Cambium)

10. **Dream big and play bold:** Envision what's truly needed, not just what's requested. Play for impact, not just revenue.
11. **Think commercially, act entrepreneurially:** See opportunity where others see obstacles. Shape new plays, balance risk and reward, and pursue growth with focused ambition.
12. **Adapt and learn continuously:** Stay curious. Seek honest feedback. Evolve. Never believe you've arrived.

Each attribute is like a ring in the trunk, built over time. One adds strength. Another adds reach. Together, they support everything above. So now the question shifts to you.

At which of these attributes are you performing at an elite level? Which of these comes easily? Which one stretches you? And which are you ready to grow into?

Growth isn't about getting it all right. It's about choosing to grow with purpose. Rainmakers aren't born with these traits. They earn them, over time, with practice, with patience. Not all at once, but season by season. Through effort. Through reflection. With heart.

Review Questions for Potential Rainmakers

1. Have I maintained relationships with people that really matter? Have I lost contact with anyone that I value?
2. Am I sufficiently connected in the world of my clients? Have I met all key executives and been invited to the right events?
3. Am I doing the right things with all my current projects, leads, and proposals? How consistent am I in my actions?
4. Are there upcoming events that could provide moments that matter? Can I create circumstances for such moments to occur?
5. How do I communicate—fact versus impact, now versus future, detail versus succinct?
6. Are my relationship interactions on the right topics? Do I cut through the noise? Do I provide value in every interaction? Am I both interesting and interested?
7. Am I delivering outcomes consistently in all my interactions and projects, and am I leveraging these moments appropriately?
8. Have I identified a colleague with special knowledge or capability that I could introduce to my client?
9. What is my proficiency in emerging technologies, particularly AI, and connecting those technologies to business value?

10. Do I have a bigger proposition for any of my clients? Can I help one of my colleagues pitch to their clients? Can I export one of my good projects to another market?
11. How commercial am I compared to my peers? Do I have the right balance in my week between pursuing big opportunities, deepening existing or high-prospect relationships, and everything else?

Let's Keep Climbing

With a deep understanding of the soil, healthy roots, and a strong trunk in place, the rainmaker begins to reach upward.

In the next part of the book, we move into the branches, the four *strategies* the rainmakers use to win. These strategies don't replace the attributes. They express them. They are the outward systems that rainmakers build: hunting with precision, creating unmatched value, forging unshakeable trust, and mastering the routine of success.

Let's begin.

PART

IV

The Branches

Strategies Rainmakers Use to Win

CHAPTER

16

Four Strategies and Critical Links

Rainmakers Don't Work Harder; They Are Strategic, Deliberate, Focused, and Grounded in Routine

Rainmakers don't simply work harder; they operate with deliberate intention. Their efforts are strategic, focused, and grounded in disciplined routines.

You know the kind.

The colleague who somehow always has something significant underway. The one who rarely seems to chase clients because clients seek that person out. The consultant everyone seems to know and whose credibility is rarely questioned.

These are the individuals at the top: consistently winning work, consistently delivering impact for their clients, and consistently generating five to ten times the fees of the average performer. They are often the decisive force behind their firm's most important opportunities. They are the rainmakers.

But what truly sets them apart?

By this stage in the journey of the rainmaker's tree, we have already explored the deeper foundations of that success. We began with the soil, the environment in which consulting takes place and where opportunities first emerge. We examined the roots—identity, purpose, resilience, and ethics—that anchor the rainmaker beneath the surface. We reinforced the trunk with core attributes that give rainmakers presence, credibility, and strength under pressure.

But a tree does not fulfill its purpose by standing strong alone. For growth to occur, it must reach outward. That is the role of the branches.

The branches represent the strategies through which rainmakers extend into the market, finding and qualifying opportunity, shaping conversations, winning trust, and ultimately securing the work that allows the tree to flourish. It is through these outward-reaching strategies that the foundations built below the surface are translated into visible results.

Rainmakers follow four core strategies to win and grow work. These are not personality traits or lucky breaks. They are repeatable disciplines, developed through experience and strengthened through practice.

And here is the crucial insight: Rainmakers do not rely on one or two of these strategies.

They cultivate all four.

Like branches growing from the same trunk, each strategy strengthens the others. Together they create reach, balance, and resilience. Individually they matter; collectively they form the system that sustains consistent success. (See Figure 16.1.)

In this part of the book—"The Branches"—we explore these four strategies in depth.

FIGURE 16.1 The rainmaker's winning strategies.

Each extends the rainmaker's reach into the market.

Together they enable the tree to grow, flourish, and ultimately bear fruit.

Let's begin.

Strategy #1: Hunting with Precision

The first strategy is about *focus*.

Rainmakers don't chase every lead or fill their calendars with endless coffee meetings. They don't spread themselves thin across every opportunity. They aim.

They *hunt with precision*.

Rather than casting a wide net, they identify their *ideal clients*, the ones who need their expertise and are ready to act. They understand their market, know their buyers, and tailor their approach accordingly.

Precision is knowing where to look, when to step in, and how to make your approach stick. It's not about doing more. It's about doing what matters.

The moment you get clear, you stop wasting energy and start gaining ground.

Strategy #2: Creating Unmatched Value

Rainmakers don't just deliver services. They deliver *outcomes*. They don't sell time or tasks. They achieve results. They become essential. How?

By creating *unmatched value*. This value isn't generic. It's sharp. Relevant. Timely. Rainmakers solve problems others can't. They bring insights others miss. They anticipate needs that clients haven't even named yet.

When you shift your mindset from "delivering work" to "creating impact," everything changes. Clients stop seeing you as an option. They start seeing you as indispensable. That's the shift from transactional to transformational.

Strategy #3: Building Real Trust

Trust is what holds everything together. It's what turns a project into a partnership and a meeting into a seat at the table. Rainmakers earn it not just by delivering but by how they show up. They follow through. They take responsibility when things go wrong. They don't flinch when the pressure is on.

That kind of steadiness doesn't go unnoticed by clients. Clients remember. They mention your name. Eventually doors open, sometimes without you even knocking.

Strategy #4: Mastering the Routine of Success

Rainmakers don't leave growth to chance. They operate with rhythm and discipline. They have systems: simple, repeatable ones that drive consistent results. Whether it's a weekly prospecting routine, a follow-up process, or a thought leadership rhythm, rainmakers don't rely on bursts of inspiration. They build *momentum*.

This isn't about being robotic. It's about being *intentional*.

When you master the routine of success, you create a sustainable system that balances sales and delivery and keeps running, even when you're tired or distracted.

Critical Links

Rainmakers don't grow by relying on one strategy alone. Just as a tree cannot thrive with a single branch reaching skyward, no rainmaker succeeds by mastering only one move. The true power of these four strategies lies in how they *interconnect*, with each branch supporting, feeding, and strengthening the others.

When the strategies work in isolation, the system wobbles. However, when they're tightly linked, they form a resilient, self-reinforcing cycle, a dynamic ecosystem where momentum builds, trust deepens, value multiplies, and opportunities emerge.

Let's take a look at six key connections, the points where these strategies intersect and, together, lift rainmakers from good to truly outstanding.

From Hunting to Value: Making It Relevant

Finding the right client is only the beginning. What matters is what you do with that knowledge. Rainmakers take what they learn and use it to shape offers that land grounded in the client's world. It's not just about showing up with ideas. It's about making those ideas matter.

From Value to Trust: Proving It Counts

Delivering value isn't the end of the story; it's how trust starts. When outcomes are real, clients notice. And if you keep showing you can deliver where it counts, they begin to rely on you. That's when trust moves from a polite assumption to a genuine belief, built one result at a time.

From Trust to Routine: Becoming Essential

Trust opens the door, but consistency is what keeps you in the room. When rainmakers follow up, stay close, and bring fresh thinking without being asked, clients don't just appreciate it; they come to expect it. Over time, that rhythm creates something bigger: a relationship that's not just strong but built to last.

From Routine to Hunting: Momentum That Moves You Forward

A strong routine doesn't just keep things ticking; it creates movement. The cadence of delivery, outreach, and thinking out loud starts to surface new opportunities. You notice patterns. You spot openings. You become more visible in the market. That rhythm doesn't slow you down; it fuels your next move.

From Hunting to Trust: Starting on Solid Ground

Trust doesn't have to wait until after the first engagement. Rainmakers earn it early by showing they've done their homework, by offering real insights without a catch, and by respecting the client's time and context. Even in the early stages, their presence feels credible. That matters more than most realize.

From Value to Routine: Making Excellence Repeatable

Great work loses its edge if it can't be repeated. Rainmakers don't just rely on talent or luck; they build systems around what works. They turn strong delivery into habits, so value isn't a one-off; it's how they operate. That's how excellence becomes part of the rhythm, baked into the way they show up every time.

Together, these six links form a closed loop, a living cycle. Each strategy feeds the next. Each branch, strong in its own right, grows stronger still because of the others. And the whole system like the tree itself becomes more resilient, more productive, and more capable of withstanding storms.

Rainmakers don't just grow branches. They grow an ecosystem. And the branches that bear fruit are never alone.

Conclusion

The branches of the rainmaker's tree are where potential becomes performance. With strong roots beneath and a solid trunk to support them, these strategies extend outward into the market, reaching for opportunity, trust, and impact. Mastering all four is what allows rainmakers not only to win work but to sustain growth and consistently deliver results that matter.

Next: The Road Ahead

Over the next four chapters, we delve into the details of each of the four strategies that rainmakers use to win:

1. Hunting with precision
2. Creating unmatched value
3. Forging unshakeable trust
4. Mastering the routine of success

Apply these strategies, and you'll stop relying on luck or timing. You'll have a system. A rhythm. A way of winning that lasts. It's time to shift from a *reactive* to a *deliberate* approach. From good to great. From consultant to rainmaker.

Let's begin.

CHAPTER

17

Hunting with Precision

Knowing Where to Look, When to Step In, and How to Make Your Pitch Stick

It was a crisp morning in London when Neil met his colleague Sara at her favorite café. As they caught up on client strategies and growth plans, a newspaper on nearby table caught his eye. On the front page: a royal dressed head to toe in hunting gear, ready for game season.

Neil made a halfhearted joke about whether hunting was still legal in the United Kingdom. Sara didn't laugh. She said, "It's not about walking into a field and hoping for the best. Serious hunters plan everything. The timing, the terrain, the behavior of the game. Every move is calculated."

As they walked back to the office, Neil reflected on the parallels between game hunting and the way the best consultants pursue business development: not in the sense of conquest but in the discipline, patience, and preparation required to recognize opportunity and act decisively. Rainmakers don't wait for opportunity. They move toward it. With intent. With clarity. With precision.

This chapter marks the beginning of our in-depth exploration into the four core strategies rainmakers employ to win—the branches of the rainmaker's tree. If the trunk is built on attributes, then these branches are how those strengths are extended outward into the market. They are how impact is created, relationships are grown, and commercial value is realized.

This first strategy, *hunting with precision*, is foundational. It's how rainmakers identify where to play, when to act, and how to focus their energy. It's long because it's deep. We recommend reading it in one sitting or reading sections #1 and #2 together, then section #3, and then section #4.

Let's begin.

Section #1: What It Means to Hunt with Precision

Rainmakers don't chase every opportunity. They don't cast wide nets or default to busyness. They aim. They hunt with precision.

At the heart of this approach is one essential question: Where can I create the most value?

Rainmakers constantly scan the landscape for intersections where their expertise, their firm's strengths, and the client's most urgent needs converge. They ask:

- Where is value waiting to be unlocked for shareholders, citizens, regulators, or communities?
- What kind of impact could we create commercially, socially, operationally?
- Is this aligned to an outcome worth pursuing?

Importantly, value isn't always measured in fees. Sometimes it's about helping a government agency establish an emergency response capability. Sometimes it's equipping a chief executive officer (CEO) to lead through a reputational crisis. Sometimes it involves advising a national regulator on options to safeguard critical infrastructure better.

Rainmakers know that value is contextual. But they always seek it. And they guard their time accordingly.

Like all of us, rainmakers have only so many hours in the week. But unlike most, they are rigorous in how they invest those hours. Before committing to a pursuit, they ask:

- Is this strategically aligned?
- Is this a client worth building with?
- Is the challenge one we are uniquely positioned to solve?
- Is the potential value for the client and the system around them significant enough to merit our full attention?

They apply a mental valuation model. If the opportunity represents a meaningful transformation for the client, the sector, or society, they act. This echoes the principles of strategic opportunity evaluation found in the work of Igor H. Ansoff, who argued that alignment between internal capabilities and external opportunities is the cornerstone of strategic success.[1] If not, they respectfully decline and redirect their focus.

As we addressed in Part I, "The Soil," they gather intelligence. What's happening in the client's world? What shifts are underway: in leadership, regulation, strategy, performance? What's creating urgency?

Today, rainmakers are also using AI-powered tools to supercharge their market intelligence. Platforms and models that scrape public filings, track executive movements, and surface trend signals across industries enable consultants to identify inflection points quickly.

For example, many global consulting firms are now developing their own AI-powered tools to scan vast volumes of market data, industry reports, and client-relevant content, detecting weak signals, emerging issues, or shifts in strategic priorities across sectors. These proprietary assets are often supplemented by licensed technologies from external providers, combining in-house control with broader reach.

These tools don't replace human insight; they amplify it. The rainmakers still makes the judgment call, but with sharper, more timely data at their fingertips. What once took weeks of research can now be surfaced in hours, giving consultants an edge not just in analysis but in foresight.

They time their approach. Rainmakers don't try to sell just because they're ready. They wait until the client is. When a window opens—a new executive, a policy shift, a moment of change—they're already positioned.

They stay focused. While most consultants spread their energy too thin, rainmakers narrow it. They focus on high-value targets aligned with their strengths, and when a new opportunity emerges, they assess it quickly and act with purpose.

They understand the ecosystem. Who influences the client? Who are their trusted advisors? Where does power sit? Rainmakers map relationships with care and then move with intent.

This approach contrasts to the way many capable consultants work. These consultants focus their efforts internally, developing generic sales campaigns, capability statements, fine-tuning methodology documents, and crafting presentation templates. They spend hours refining messaging that rarely reaches a client, perfecting materials that are useful but seldom decisive. Their instinct is to start from their capability and ask "What can we sell?" rather than beginning with the client and asking "Where can we help most?"

Rainmakers reverse that logic. They start outside the office building, in the client's world. They invest more time in conversations than in reports or presentations, more effort in listening than in scripting. Their collateral is shaped by actual client engagement, not imagined scenarios. When they do create material, it's because a real conversation requires it, not because the firm needs something polished to file away.

They think like farmers of value, not just engineers of process.

A practical example: One colleague identified a critical client need not in a meeting but through an obscure regulatory shift in a niche financial sector that was published in a government gazette that didn't attract much media attention. When the legislation passed, its implications would be vast. She crafted a point of view, engaged the client early, and within three months had secured a multiyear engagement, positioning her firm as the lead advisor for a sector-wide compliance transformation.

Another example: In the wake of severe flooding, a senior consultant observed that a government emergency response agency was operating at its limit. Without waiting for a formal brief, he offered pro bono mobilization support. That early move turned into a multiagency strategic planning and services support contract.

In both cases, the rainmaker didn't wait. They anticipated. They acted with precision. This is what it means to hunt with purpose. Not chasing every deal. Not following every signal. But asking, again and again: *Where can I make the most significant impact, not just for my firm but also for this client and the system they operate within?*

Rainmaking begins here: with discernment, discipline, and a deep belief that value grows when you focus not on everything but on what truly matters.

In the rainmaker's world, this is the first branch to grow: focused opportunity. It reaches out from the solid trunk of core attributes, finding the right clients, at the right time, with problems that truly matter.

This is where real growth takes root.

But opportunity isn't just strategy and timing. There's a human side to the chase: emotional, messy, and real. Let's dig into that now: the lived experience of prospecting, and everything that comes with it.

Section #2: The Emotional and Practical Realities of Prospecting

Let's be honest: Prospecting in consulting is hard.

You can follow every rule in the book, be strategic, methodical, precise, and still walk away empty-handed. And when that happens, it doesn't just sting. It bruises your confidence.

So, let's name the truth: This part of the rainmaker's work can feel like wandering in a wilderness. You show up with insight, offer ideas, invest time, and listen closely, only to realize the client isn't ready. Not now. Maybe not ever.

That's the reality of consulting.

There's a myth that if you're good enough, persistent enough, clever enough, you'll win every time. But here's the truth that every rainmaker eventually learns: Sometimes, despite your best effort, the alignment isn't there.

And that's not a reflection of your value. It's a reflection of timing, appetite, and fit.

The statistics speak clearly. Economy-wide, only about 5% of business-to-business (B2B) are in the market at any given time,[2] and conversion rates vary by sector, with professional services and healthcare typically in the mid-single digits. In our experience, high-end consulting is no different, with only about 10 to 15% of sales leads eventually leading to engagements. This sobering reality underscores the critical importance of lead quality, nurturing, and precise sales strategies. Consider this reflection from Neil.

I remember pursuing a senior executive for over a year. She was sharp, respected, and led a public agency facing complex environmental and regulatory challenges. On paper, everything points to opportunity. Our conversations were promising. She engaged with my ideas. She encouraged me to "stay close."

So, I did. I followed up after the events. I sent articles. I offered informal strategy input as the agency approached major reform. But she never moved—no meetings beyond the informal. No scope. No proposal.

Eventually I had to face what I didn't want to admit: She wasn't going to buy. Not from me. Not from anyone. She wasn't a buyer of consulting services in any absolute sense. It simply wasn't how she chose to solve problems.

That experience changed me. Because it taught me one of the hardest and most liberating truths of precision hunting: Sometimes it's not about your performance, it's about the fit.

Some executives aren't buyers or aren't buyers of significant consulting services. Not because they lack ambition, or pressure, or insight, but because consulting isn't the way they solve their challenges. And even in the case where they ask for a proposal, often they have done a lot of the prework themselves. The *Harvard Business Review* reports that B2B buyers often complete much of their project discovery journey before asking for help, making budget and timing major obstacles in many deals.[3] This is the cold, hard truth: You might have the right solution, but timing or organizational readiness can often derail even the most promising prospect.

This is where empathy matters. Executives are often navigating legacy cultures, constrained budgets, and political scrutiny. Research by Neil Rackham and John DeVincentis highlights that high-level buyers are typically skeptical and emotionally guarded, especially when confronted with unfamiliar solutions or internal conflicts.[4]

Past consultants have also burned many executives. Some are guarded. Some are indifferent. A few are quietly hostile. Even when your insight is sound and your timing feels right, the answer might still be no.

Especially in large, complex organizations, access is not the same as appetite. You might have C-suite conversations but no internal sponsor. No true urgency. No alignment. You may be respected but not truly needed. Yet.

Rainmakers get it. They've been through it. What sets them apart is how they handle it. They don't take it as failure; they take it as a signal.

They ask the hard questions: *Is this real? Or am I chasing something that just isn't ready?*

And if it's not the right time, they step back. Not with frustration but with clarity. They walk away without burning energy or the relationship.

Here's the difference: They don't vanish. They keep the connection warm, a light, thoughtful presence that adds value without pressure. Because things shift. Priorities move. People move.

And when the timing's finally right, they're still there, not as the one who kept chasing but as the one who always understood.

Let us share another story.

A colleague had been cultivating a relationship with a senior executive in the transportation industry for nearly 18 months. The signals looked good. The organization needed transformation. He shared insights, offered pro bono support, and connected the client to experts. Still, nothing landed.

Six months later, that executive moved on. Her replacement? Someone my colleague had worked with five years earlier. Two weeks into the new appointment, he got a call: "Let's pick up where we left off." One month later, he was leading the market strategy for a significant transformation.

That's the game. You can misread timing. You can be ahead of the curve. You might not win the work, but you can still sow the seed that grows into your next breakthrough.

And, yes, this part is tricky. Emotionally hard. It tests your patience, your resilience, and your sense of worth. You're investing in conversations with no immediate return and planting without knowing when, or even if, the rain will come.

By using tools like ChatGPT and other AI writing assistants to craft tailored, timely follow-ups, articles, notes, or perspectives aligned with the client's industry or evolving context, AI can help rainmakers maintain a light-touch presence during quiet periods.

Some rainmakers even use AI to help track and score their prospecting cadence, identifying when a nudge might be most welcome or when a lead has resurfaced due to a market change. AI doesn't replace human persistence; it helps you persist with precision.

But this is also where the magic lives.

Because every time you show up with clarity and care, you're tending a branch. If you nurture enough nodes with discernment, with generosity, with precision, some will strengthen. Some will flourish. And some will reshape the whole tree.

So, yes, be commercial. Protect your energy. Choose your efforts wisely. But don't measure your worth by whether a deal lands today.

Because when that long-awaited "yes" finally comes, the client won't remember how many times you followed up. They'll remember how it felt to be heard and understood.

And in that moment, you won't be an option. You'll be the obvious choice.

Section #3: The 12 Key Sources of Opportunity

Rainmakers don't bet on one lead. They build a whole portfolio, a mix of prospects that keep their practice alive and growing.

Like branches reaching toward the sun, they stretch in different directions depending on the season, the soil, the conditions.

They read the environment. They stay flexible. And they keep testing new paths to see what takes. Their approach isn't scattershot; it's intentional, adaptive growth.

Key Insight: Not all opportunities and not all sources of opportunity are weighted equally. Rainmakers are purpose-driven and precise in their hunting. They're not chasing activity; they're aiming for *impact*. Their focus is on big-ticket consulting sales, the kinds of engagements that lead to meaningful client change, long-term relationships, and commercial traction.

That doesn't mean they won't take a smaller job. However, they do so deliberately when it comes from a senior executive with whom they have a Level 4 or 5 trust relationship, or when there's a high probability that it will lead to a significant engagement. And, of course, there are exceptions: The rare requests from the CEO of a Fortune 500 company, a board member, or an official in government are often prioritized or thoughtfully handed to a trusted colleague with the right expertise and positioning.

This part of the chapter explores 12 such sources of opportunity. Not all are created equal. We include them all here to show the breadth of the field but also to offer a warning: If you're not careful, you can waste enormous time and energy chasing prospects that are unlikely to convert. Worse, you can distract your firm from more promising ground.

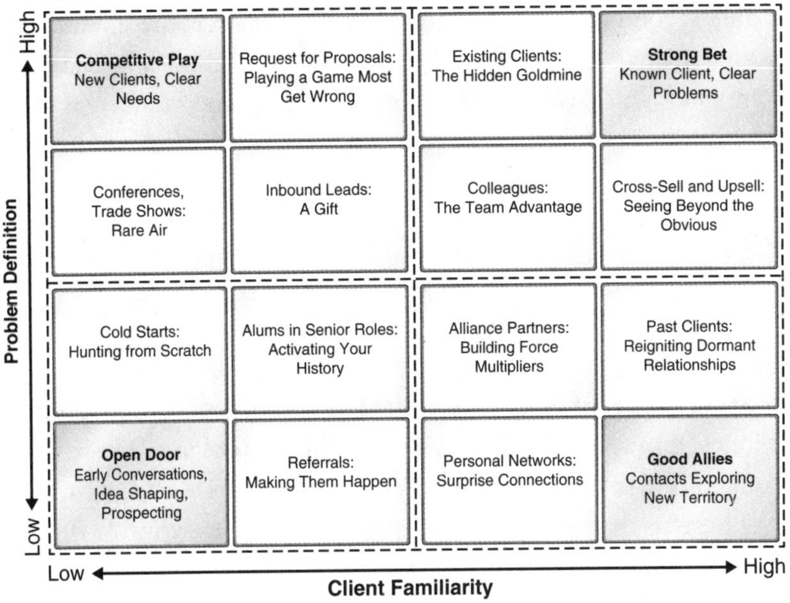

FIGURE 17.1 The Consulting Opportunity Source Matrix.

Before diving in, take a moment to reflect on the earlier chapters on soil, the bedrock, the subsoil, the topsoil, and the surface layer. These layers form the context in which opportunities either take root or wither. The issues that drive opportunity are rarely visible on the surface alone. To hunt effectively, you need to understand the terrain beneath your feet.

Remember, rainmakers are focused. And like Sara said in the café, "*Serious hunters plan everything: the timing, the terrain, the behavior of the game. Every move is calculated. It's all about precision.*"

To help make sense of the terrain, we offer a simple but powerful lens: the Consulting Opportunity Source Matrix. (See Figure 17.1.)

Making Sense of Opportunity: The Consulting Opportunity Source Matrix

The first dimension is *client familiarity*. Do you know the client, their world, their pressures, their soil? Have you earned credibility with them, or are you still a stranger? What's the competitive position?

The second dimension is *problem definition*. Has the client clearly articulated what they need or shared their most important challenge? Or are they still circling the issue, exploring, uncertain, making no traction, or innovating? Or have you done your research, and can you see a significant problem that no one at the client is fully and successfully addressing?

When you place these two dimensions on a 2 × 2 matrix, four categories of opportunity source emerge, each with different implications for how you may invest your time.

- **Strong Bet** sits in the top right. These sources are high-potential ones, known clients facing well-defined problems. There's trust, deep understanding, there's clarity, and, often, there's urgency. These sources tend to convert quickly and are your most direct path to big-ticket opportunities. Rainmakers fast-track these.
- **Good Allies** occupy the bottom right. These are past clients, alliance partners, or individuals you know well in broader networks, but the problem persists. There's ambiguity, but also openness. This is where co-creation, early-stage design, and thought leadership thrive. These sources can grow your future pipeline, but some can also be ghost prospects—they might look like valuable sources but aren't really. Be careful.
- **Competitive Play** is in the top left. The problem is clear, but the client is new to you. These opportunities often show up as requests for proposals, tenders, or formal proposal processes. They can be won, but rainmakers qualify the sales opportunity deeply before jumping in, knowing the odds are lower if they have limited access or influence with the client.
- **Open Door** lives in the bottom left. You're still building the relationship, and the client's needs are still forming. These are exploratory: the early coffee meetings, roundtables, and thought pieces. Rainmakers use these sources highly selectively and strategically for longer-term bets.

The matrix helps you balance short-term pipeline growth with long-term positioning. It enables you to match your energy to where it can have the most return.

Here is a list of the 12 sources of opportunity:

1. Cross-Sell and Upsell: Seeing Beyond the Obvious
2. Existing Clients: The Hidden Goldmine
3. Colleagues: The Team Advantage
4. Past Clients: Reigniting Dormant Relationships
5. Alliance Partners: Building Force Multipliers
6. Personal Networks: Surprise Connections
7. Alums in Senior Roles: Activating Your History
8. Referrals: Making Them Happen
9. Cold Starts: Hunting from Scratch
10. Requests for Proposals: Playing a Game Most Get Wrong
11. Conferences, Trade Shows: Rare Air
12. Inbound Leads: A Gift

In this, the longest part of the chapter, we aim to explain what rainmakers do differently in each of the opportunity source areas and summarize a real-life example to highlight how a significant deal came about.

Let's begin with the closest and often most overlooked source of opportunity: the work already underway.

Cross-Sell and Upsell: Seeing Beyond the Obvious Rainmakers don't view current engagements as single projects. They see them as broader deals and opportunities to learn more about the client. They treat every project as a chance to listen more deeply, look wider, and connect dots across the client organization that others overlook. While others stick to the brief, rainmakers are already exploring what's next, uncovering the hidden needs, untapped potential, and the value behind the request.

To a rainmaker, cross-selling and upselling aren't about pushing services; they're about enhancing customer value. They're about expanding impact. It's not "What else can we sell?" but rather "Where else can we help, where else can we add value?"

Take a senior colleague at Big Four firm who was engaged to run a modest governance review for a midsize financial institution. On paper, it was a low-complexity and fixed-fee job. But she didn't just go through the motions, hand it off to a more junior team member, and move onto something else. She invested her time to deeply understand the client's real pressure points and asked thoughtful questions to each client executive she met. In these interactions, she noticed hesitations, inconsistencies in how decisions were made. As she listened more closely, she began to uncover deeper issues, tensions between leadership layers, unclear accountability, and cultural fragmentation.

Rather than overstepping, she invited conversation. She framed what she was seeing, shared insights from similar organizations, and gently posed the question: "Is this governance issue a symptom of something broader?"

That one moment shifted the trajectory. The client asked her to stay on and explore the broader context. She brought in colleagues from organizational design, leadership, and change. What began as a governance review evolved into a comprehensive transformation of an entire division. For the client, it delivered far greater value than anticipated. For the firm, it resulted in over 10 times the original fees and an enduring relationship anchored in trust.

Rainmakers are constantly asking themselves:

- What's the bigger challenge behind the brief?
- Who else is in the client organization is feeling the impact of this issue, even if they're not in the room?
- What inflection points are coming up that could reshape the client's priorities?
- What insights or experiences can I share that open new possibilities?

That's how rainmakers create exponential value: not by selling more but by seeing more.

Existing Clients: The Hidden Goldmine Rainmakers know that the richest soil is often right beneath their feet. Existing clients, where trust is already established and doors are already open, offer some of the most significant opportunities to deepen impact and expand value.

But rainmakers don't treat delivery as the end of the sale. They treat it as the beginning of discovery. Every meeting, every milestone, and every challenge at a client is a listening post, a chance to tune in to what is said and what is left unsaid.

Rainmakers stay curious. They look beyond the task at hand and ask:

- What's not being said in meetings?
- Who's feeling the impact beyond our immediate stakeholders?
- What new priorities are quietly gaining traction internally?

During a cyber risk assurance project, one consultant overheard the CIO mention concerns about third-party vendors in passing. That single offhand remark led to a deeper conversation and, within weeks, a proposal to address supply chain vulnerabilities. Approved quickly. Delivered effectively and trusted deeply.

Rainmakers often build quiet, informal pictures of their clients' worlds, the personalities, pressure points, and patterns of influence. They watch for inflection points. They stay close to budget owners. They align their firm's strengths with emerging needs.

Key Insight: Rainmakers don't upsell. They help. And because they've already built a connection and they're already trusted, their advice lands with less friction and more speed.

Take Jerry. His journey with a key public institution began six years ago with a simple functional review: a small project with a low profile. But Jerry delivered with care. He built rapport with the assistant chief financial officer (CFO), followed through on promises, and took time to understand the organization beyond the numbers.

As that assistant CFO rose to become chief operating officer (COO), Jerry stayed connected and offered genuine support, fresh perspectives, and ideas that added value.

Then came the pivotal moment. Late one night, Jerry received a call from a client. A wage theft crisis had just been uncovered by someone in the client's team, affecting thousands of employees and exposing them to decades of risk. The COO needed help, fast. "I'll be there by 6:30 a.m. with a team," Jerry said. And he was.

By sunrise, they had a plan in place. Though the immediate fees were modest, the trust Jerry had built paid off. That response led to the opportunity to help shape, advise on, and deliver a significant digital transformation engagement, a multiyear, multi-million-dollar deal that reshaped the institution.

Rainmakers ask themselves four questions in every client engagement:

1. Where is this organization quietly hurting?
2. What signals suggest something bigger is coming?
3. Who do I know well and who else do I need to understand?
4. How can I help before I'm asked?

That's how rainmakers unlock the goldmine: not by digging harder but by seeing deeper.

Colleagues: The Team Advantage Rainmakers know that one of the most overlooked sources of opportunity is the people sitting right beside them. In a world where clients demand integrated solutions and rapid value, rainmakers don't just sell what they know; they unlock what their firm knows. Doing that starts with collaboration.

The myth of the lone rainmaker is precisely that, a myth. Rainmakers are connectors. They constantly scan and connect with teams and individuals across service lines and surface hidden insights. They utilize AI-enabled platforms to understand who else in their firm has similar client relationships, detect overlaps, and identify patterns of unmet needs. But more often they pick up the phone, grab a coffee, or listen carefully during internal presentations.

Take the strategy partner who overheard a colleague from his firm's international trade team mention a client's global supply chain issue that had been discussed unfavorably in the media that morning. Rather than nod politely and move on, the partner and the colleague teamed up. Together, they proposed a multifaceted solution that addressed the client's challenges and opportunities holistically rather than tackling a single issue. The result was a multiyear global engagement that neither could have secured alone.

Or Shu Ning, a partner at a large global consulting firm, who took a 9:00 a.m. call that changed everything. A US colleague reached out: A Nasdaq-listed client's headquarters had launched a restructuring initiative that required setting up a 600-person Global Business Services center in the Philippines, quickly. But the real story began years earlier. Shu Ning had invested time in building strong connections with US stakeholders in her firm, consistently providing valuable insights long before any significant opportunity arose. When the moment came, she was the obvious choice. Over six months, she led a global team that not only delivered the center on time but also established a multiyear relationship grounded in trust and shared success.

Then there's Judy, a technical expert in complex merger and acquisition work. She was giving an internal talk when Rob, a senior client relationship partner, happened to drop in. A month later, one of Rob's clients announced a significant acquisition. Rob sent the public documentation to Judy, who spotted a critical flaw. Within 48 hours, they were in front of the client's global CFO. That insight not only won a high-impact, high-value engagement but also significantly strengthened the client relationship and unlocked a blueprint used in a dozen other deals worldwide.

These stories remind us: High-performing consultants don't win alone. They ask themselves:

- Who in my firm could see what I can't?
- Where might our strengths combine to solve bigger problems?
- Am I known inside the firm as someone who creates opportunity or captures it?
- What relationships do I need to deepen before the next big moment comes?

Rainmakers know the advantage isn't just in the market. It's in the team around them, if they're willing to invest.

Past Clients: Reigniting Dormant Relationships Your next deal might come from your last client, or even a client from several years ago, or a client of a colleague from several years ago.

Rainmakers never underestimate the power of shared history. Even when the project ends, the relationship doesn't. They stay connected, not with generic check-ins or recycled pitch presentations but with timely and tailored insights that matter.

Reconnecting with dormant client relationships isn't about reliving the past. It's about reearning trust. Sometimes this takes time; other times it can happen quickly.

> **Key Insight:** Rainmakers do their homework. They stay attuned to client moves, industry shifts, and leadership transitions. And when the time is right, they don't hesitate. They reach out with confidence and purpose.

Take the senior managing director of a global technology organization who had led a successful transformation for a multinational retail client three years earlier. The work was complete. The team had moved on. So had the client, literally. The former client executive had moved to a new company and taken on a new role as the COO.

The rainmaker noticed the move in his feed and paused. He didn't send a congratulatory note. He dug in.

Within 48 hours, he had briefed himself on the company's recent market activity, financial analyst reports, new product directions, and board-level priorities. He then pulled together a short, two-page insight-rich paper outlining how leading companies in adjacent sectors were tackling exactly the kind of challenges this COO was about to face.

He sent the two-page image via text with a simple message: "Saw the news, congrats. I've been thinking about how others in your space are tackling similar strategy pivots. Thought this might help."

The COO responded within the hour.

They met the following week, not to reminisce but to explore. The conversation was sharp, current, and high value. Within a month, they were scoping a significant piece of work, something the client had intended to initiate but hadn't yet found the right partner to lead.

That one moment of relevance reignited a dormant relationship and sparked a new multi-million-dollar engagement. More important, it reestablished the rainmaker as a trusted guide in a new context.

Rainmakers routinely ask themselves:

- Who have I worked with that's facing new challenges today?
- What unique insight could I offer right now that earns their attention?
- Am I staying visible to my full network of contacts in a way that adds value, not noise?
- How do I reconnect with relevance, not nostalgia?

In the hands of a rainmaker, the past isn't a closed chapter. It's an open door if you know how to knock.

Alliance Partners: Building Force Multipliers We've said before, rainmakers don't hunt alone. They build ecosystems. They know that to solve complex client problems, you often need more than one set of tools.

That's why rainmakers forge strategic alliances with technology and software vendors, legal advisors, banks, specialist boutiques, and anyone who sees the client from a different angle and brings complementary strengths.

But these partnerships don't start with a pitch. They begin with trust. Rainmakers give before they ask. They help their partners win. They show up with generosity and insight, and when the time is right, they co-create something neither could deliver alone.

Consider the partner from a boutique strategy and risk firm who was supporting a multinational on environmental, social, and governance (ESG) compliance. The company's legal advisors, a top-tier global law firm, were already working with the same client on regulatory positioning. Rather than staying in their respective swim lanes, the partner reached out, not to compete but to collaborate.

They offered to share insights from recent ESG benchmarking projects and invited the law firm's partners into a working session with the client to align messaging and strategy. No fees were exchanged. No contract was signed. But the value was real.

That session turned out to be pivotal. The client saw, and appreciated, an integrated approach and a new way of tackling a challenge. Trust was earned through action, not intent.

Fast forward six months.

That same legal partner picked up the phone. One of their FTSE 100 clients was undertaking a review of its digital assets in response to new regulatory expectations, and it needed a consulting partner who could deliver quickly. Without hesitation, this partner referred the consultant in. Why? Because the partner didn't see the consultant as a vendor but as part of their ecosystem.

The engagement landed. But more important, it opened up a multiparty relationship that became a reliable source of future deals, shared insights, and joint value delivery across multiple clients.

Rainmakers know that great partnerships don't just extend reach; they deepen roots. They routinely ask:

- Who do I trust outside my firm that sees the same clients from a different angle?
- Who else can I combine our strengths with to tackle a larger challenge?
- What can I give before I ask?
- Am I showing up as a partner or a competitor in disguise?

Rainmakers view alliance partners not as optional extras but as force multipliers.

Personal Networks: Surprise Connections Rainmakers know that new deals don't always come from boardrooms. Occasionally they emerge from unexpected places: a conversation after a community fundraiser, a chat on the sidelines of a local soccer match, or a quiet moment at a charity event. These aren't channels you build a pipeline around. But rainmakers stay open because once in a while, a surprise connection turns into something substantial.

Take the example of a senior partner at a strategy advisory firm who volunteered on the board of a regional arts foundation. It was never about business; she believed in the cause and enjoyed the work. Over several years, she built relationships with other board members, most of whom were local leaders from diverse sectors, including finance, logistics, and health.

One evening, after a planning session for a major exhibition, a fellow board member, the CFO of a growing health services group, lingered. "You know," he said, "we've just acquired three new clinics and we're struggling to integrate the systems and teams. I hadn't connected the dots until now, but this kind of challenge is right in your wheelhouse, isn't it?"

It wasn't a pitch. It was presence, trust, and credibility built steadily over time and recognized at the right moment.

The partner followed up with a short diagnostic checklist, not to sell but to help him clarify the challenge. A few weeks later, she was brought in by the CFO to lead a postmerger integration review. That led to an 18-month engagement.

Rainmakers don't force these moments. They don't overplay the room. But they do stay engaged, generous, and curious, even outside "work." In rare moments, a long-standing connection allows them to be seen not just as a peer but as a trusted expert. And that can change everything.

Alums in Senior Roles: Activating Your History A shared past is a robust foundation, if you know how to use it.

Rainmakers don't let former colleagues drift into memory. They pay attention to where the alum is. They reconnect with purpose, not platitudes. And when the timing is right, they create something new, grounded in the credibility of history but driven by today's needs.

Why does the reconnection work? Because alums already know how you think. They remember the late nights, the high standards, the tough calls. The trust was built when there were no deals to close and no work to be done. That history becomes a shortcut to credibility if approached with relevance and context.

Take the story of a rainmaker who worked under a senior manager in a major consulting firm many years ago. They lost touch after the senior manager moved on to industry, eventually landing a senior strategy role at a global food and beverage company.

Two years passed. One day the rainmaker saw a press release stating that the company was entering new growth markets in Southeast Asia. He paused. Instead of sending a "congrats" text message or a generic note to catch up, he went back to an old email where the senior manager had shared their personal email account when he had left the firm. He took a few hours to build something useful.

He crafted a short document of insights from previous projects, regional consumer trends, and examples of agile supply chain models. He attached a brief note that said: "*Saw the expansion announcement. Thought this might spark some ideas, happy to talk it through if helpful."*

The reply came the same day: "*Thank you, this is gold. Can you meet next week?*"

They met, not to reminisce about the old days but to discuss the future. That initial conversation led to a $1 million market strategy engagement and, more important, reestablished a working rhythm based on mutual respect. Within six months the rainmaker's team was supporting the client's mergers and acquisitions team on acquisitions, divestments, and integration planning. The relationship spanned two years, not because of the past but because the rainmaker had reactivated the past with relevance.

Rainmakers regularly ask themselves:

- Which former colleagues are now in positions of influence?
- What's changed in their world, and what can my firm offer that's timely and valuable?
- How can I, or anyone else in my firm, reconnect with insight, not nostalgia?
- Am I staying in touch with the people who already trust how I work?

Key Insight: Old roots, when watered with care, often grow new branches. Rainmakers know precisely when and how to tend them.

Referrals: Making Them Happen Rainmakers don't wait for the phone to ring. They earn referrals by design.

They know an outstanding client experience isn't just a win. It's an opening. The right moment isn't weeks later during a generic follow-up. It's right after impact has landed when the client says, "*This was exceptional.*" That's when rainmakers act.

They time the ask. They make it easy. And they give the client something worth sharing, not a hard sell but a smart takeaway, a compelling insight or a simple tool that helps others see the value.

Take the managing director of a national consulting firm focused on healthcare infrastructure and strategy. She had just wrapped a multiyear capital transformation program with a major hospital group in the Northeast of the United States, one of the most complex facility upgrades in the region. The work spanned clinical redesign, technology integration, and funding strategy. It finished ahead of schedule, under budget, and with outstanding clinical feedback.

During the final executive session, the group CEO turned to her and said, "You've made a real difference here. This is one of the best-run programs we've had."

She didn't let the moment pass.

She replied, "That means a lot, thank you. I was wondering, is there anyone in your network who's facing a similar infrastructure challenge who you could introduce me to?"

The CEO paused. "Yes. There's a peer in the South managing a similar portfolio and they've been asking how we pulled this off."

She followed up the next day with a crisp one-page "results snapshot," a visual summary of the program's outcomes, lessons learned, and potential applicability. The CEO forwarded it with a personal note.

Two weeks later, she was on a call with the leadership of the southern group. That conversation turned into a substantial engagement to plan and deliver their next phase of hospital upgrades.

Referrals don't just happen. Rainmakers make them happen by delivering value, recognizing the right moment, and making the connection easy to share. Doing this aligns with the findings of Arndt (1967), whose foundational and influential work on word-of-mouth communications revealed that trust-based referrals significantly outperform other forms of marketing and promotion in influencing B2B decisions.[5]

Rainmakers ask themselves:

- Which client executive just had a great experience from working with us and might share it?
- What's the best format to help that client tell the story?
- How can I time the ask so it feels natural, not transactional?
- Am I closing the loop and thanking the referrer?

Rainmakers don't rely on hope. They turn trust into momentum, one well-timed referral at a time.

Cold Starts: Hunting from Scratch This is rainmaking in its purest form. Sure, at the start, it can be energizing, but the truth is, it is hard and low probability. No warm introductions. No legacy relationships. Just belief, insight, and discipline.

Rainmakers don't shy away from cold starts; they approach them with precision, doing the necessary homework and asking tough questions: Why does the client need help now, and why would they switch from an incumbent provider? Rainmakers know that building trust from zero is hard, but it's also one of the clearest tests of value. When you have nothing to lean on but your thinking, your questions, and your persistence, what you offer has to matter.

That's why rainmakers pick their ground carefully. They don't spray and hope. They:

- Target sectors in motion: new regulation, leadership changes, strategic pivots.
- Build credibility slowly: with insight, not self-promotion.
- Give value before asking for anything: benchmarks, provocations, sharp questions.

Take Thomas, a partner in a Big Four consulting firm who decided to reengage a large customer services organization that his firm hadn't worked with in over five years. No active contacts. No warm leads. Just a hunch and a belief that the firm could help.

It took four months to land a meeting. The business development manager worked tirelessly to secure a meeting with a newly appointed senior executive. The firm sent a team of five, including Thomas, to the session.

But it started poorly.

Everyone wanted to speak. Everyone wanted to sound impressive. The firm's representatives spoke too much about themselves, their credentials, past wins, and service lines and not enough about the client. The conversation lost rhythm. The client leaned back.

Then, with just minutes left, Thomas was invited to speak.

He skipped the preamble. In 30 seconds, he posed three bold, insight-driven questions, each rooted in research, each focused squarely on the client's customer experience model. Questions the executive hadn't heard phrased that way before. Questions that landed.

The meeting ended. It felt like a loss.

But three days later, Thomas got a call. The client wanted a whiteboard session. That led to a board paper. That paper led to a second engagement. Over the next four years, the relationship evolved into one of the firm's most strategic, unlocking multi-million-dollar projects and shaping critical transformation programs.

Cold starts aren't cold forever. They warm with time, relevance, and respect.

Rainmakers ask themselves:

- Is the opportunity worth earning from scratch?
- What insight would prompt someone to attend a cold meeting?
- Am I ready to lead with questions, not my credentials?
- If I only had 30 seconds, would it change the conversation or end it?

Every cold start holds heat if you know where to strike.

Requests for Proposals: Playing a Game Most Get Wrong Clients increasingly use RFPs to hire consultants. But rainmakers rarely win by responding. They win by shaping.

Most consultants treat RFPs like exams: Read the question, show your credentials, submit the correct answer. Rainmakers take a different view. They treat RFPs as a test of perspective, not a test of compliance. They qualify hard and fast and ask five fundamental questions before they decide to play:

1. **Do we already own the conversation behind this brief?** Have we shaped the client's thinking early, built trust, and framed the issues before the RFP landed, or are we being invited to validate someone else's narrative?
2. **Can we bring something no one else can, something that truly matters?** Do we have a point of difference that changes the game for this client (e.g., unique insight, experience, or method that solves their challenge in a higher-value way)?
3. **Do we have the right people, time, and energy to do it justice?** Can we craft a proposal that reflects our best thinking, or will this be a rush job that dilutes our standards and drains our team?
4. **Will winning this strengthen our position or stretch us off course?** Does this pursuit deepen our core story and market credibility, or would it pull us into work that looks good on paper but weakens our brand?
5. **If we win, will both sides feel like they've chosen well?** Will this be a partnership built on trust, respect, and shared success or a transactional race to the bottom?

If the answer to some of these questions is no, they walk. Proudly. Because chasing every RFP is a recipe for mediocrity. Saying no isn't a loss; it's a strategic focus.

But when they do lean in, they go all in.

They don't submit a brochure. They submit a point of view. They write as if they've already earned the work. They listen between the lines of the RFP, and if the brief feels off course, they reframe it, respectfully but clearly.

Take the partner of a large financial advisory firm who was responding to a significant RFP from a government investment authority. The ask was straightforward: Deliver valuation and advisory services on a series of distressed infrastructure assets. Most competitors responded with track records, pricing tables, and templated approaches.

But the rainmaker saw something different. He noticed the brief framed the challenge solely around financial optimization, assuming the assets needed to be either divested or restructured. Instead of accepting the premise, he added a two-page section titled "An Alternative Lens." In it, he laid out a second set of assumptions. This counterfactual scenario positioned the assets not as financial liabilities but as long-term strategic platforms, if viewed through the lens of intergovernmental collaboration and ESG-linked financing.

It was bold. But not reckless.

He wrote with care. He referenced global case studies. He made the client look forward, not just inward. And he did it all while showing deep respect for their original brief.

The result? His firm won, not because they ticked the boxes but because they saw the problem differently.

Rainmakers don't play the RFP game the way others do. They rewire it. And in doing so, they often walk away with the win.

For more on hunting with precision in a predominantly RFP market, see Appendix A.

Conferences, Trade Shows: Rare Air Conferences and trade shows are vital for firm visibility. They're where thought leadership is broadcast, booths are branded, and panels are populated. But let's be honest: They are rarely fertile ground for serious consulting opportunities, especially for rainmakers chasing senior-level work. The most senior clients don't usually attend. If they do, they're whisked in for a keynote, then gone by the next coffee break.

For rainmakers, these events are about presence, not pipeline. But, and it's rare, sometimes the timing hits just right.

Take a senior supply chain partner at a Big Four consultancy. He was invited to speak on a panel at a global logistics and trade conference in Singapore. It was a solid marketing play for the firm; global branding, fresh insights, nothing more. But that week, everything in global trade changed. The US president announced sweeping tariffs on all imports, a policy shift that sent shockwaves through global sourcing and supply chains.

After the panel, while chatting near the stage, a man approached. "I run global procurement for a major consumer brand," he said, offering his card. "We import 90% of our products from China. I'd love to talk."

The supply chain partner didn't rush in. He followed up with a thoughtful perspective on strategic responses to trade shocks. They exchanged notes, met again, and explored scenarios. Months later, that hallway conversation evolved into a board-level engagement to redesign the company's entire supply chain, from sourcing to distribution. It became the most critical transformation project that the business had undertaken in a decade.

These moments are lightning in a bottle. Rainmakers don't bet on them. But when lightning strikes, they're ready with insight, presence, and the ability to turn chance into change.

Inbound Leads: A Gift Rainmakers don't wait for the phone to ring because it rarely does. Not anymore.

A generation ago, clients might have reached out after reading a white paper or hearing your name at a board meeting. That world is gone. Today's clients have teams, gatekeepers, and procurement processes. If they're looking for help, they don't cold call consultants they don't know; they crowdsource opinions, search online, or quietly test options through their networks.

And yet very rarely—once in a career, if you're lucky—the phone rings anyway.

A former colleague was working for a successful national financial advisory firm. The firm did excellent work but wasn't on the radar of the country's largest corporations. One quiet afternoon he was waiting for a call from a friend. When his cell phone rang with an unfamiliar number, he almost ignored it. But something told him to answer.

On the line was the assistant to the general counsel of a major multinational, a name he recognized instantly. "You don't know me," the assistant said, "but I was told you might be someone my boss should speak with today, in confidence. Are you available?"

He said yes. And he showed up. That one call turned into a discreet meeting that afternoon, then into a six-week diagnostic and ultimately into a two-year engagement to unwind a failed $10 billion merger. It was a high-stakes separation, a restructuring of two intertwined businesses that had never integrated appropriately. The project became a turning point for both companies, restoring strategic focus and investor confidence.

Later my colleague asked: "How did you get my name?"

The assistant replied, "That doesn't matter. But let me tell you, you weren't the first person I called. I called two others. They didn't answer. You did."

Rainmakers don't count on inbound leads. But when one arrives, they treat it like what it is: a gift. And they're ready.

The Nodes of the First Branch

Each of these 12 sources of opportunity is a node on the first branch of your rainmaker tree—the points where the leaves, fruit, or flowers will emerge. You won't use them all equally. Some will bear more fruit, some less. But the strength of your canopy depends on how you cultivate it.

The most successful rainmakers don't rely on one node to carry their weight. They build an ecosystem that can weather any storm and thrive in any season.

So, look at the nodes on your prospecting branch. Which ones are strong? Which ones are underdeveloped? Which ones could you develop further?

Because the more qualified and diverse your sources, the more resilient your growth.

That's how rainmakers hunt.

And that's how their trees grow tall.

Section #4: Identifying and Qualifying Opportunities with Precision

You've done the hard work, scanned the horizon, worked out which opportunity sources work for you, cultivated relationships, listened for signals, and spotted a spark of potential. Now comes the moment that separates capable consultants from rainmakers: Do you go all in or walk away?

Rainmakers don't chase every breeze that rustles the branches. They don't mistake motion for momentum. They qualify—ruthlessly, intelligently, and with an unwavering focus on where real value can be created and captured.

Why Most Consultants Get Stuck in the Undergrowth

Too often, consultants fall into the trap of feeling flattered by interest. A client shows some interest in you, and suddenly there's a slide deck in production, a team assembled, a proposal half built, all without asking the crucial questions:

- Is there a real and urgent client need?
- Is the budget available or even being discussed?

- Are we talking to the actual decision makers?
- Is this aligned with what we do best?

Rainmakers never skip this step.

They know their time is their most valuable resource. Every hour spent on a low-quality opportunity is an hour stolen from a higher branch.

The Rainmaker's Filter: Qualification as Strategy

Rainmakers use structured thinking to sort signal from noise. They don't guess. They assess.

Increasingly, top-performing firms are integrating AI into their qualification processes. Some use predictive analytics trained on past pursuits to score new opportunities based on win likelihood, relationship depth, and market timing. These systems flag misaligned or low-probability pursuits early, saving hundreds of hours a year. But rainmakers know: The tool is only as good as the judgment behind it. They use AI to inform the gut, not replace it.

This section explains five powerful qualification models, each one used by rainmakers to decide whether to climb or cut loose. Rainmakers don't apply them blindly; they assess their market, context, and personal strengths first and then select the model that best fits their style and circumstances.

BANT: Budget, Authority, Need, Timing Simple, sharp, and timeless. BANT is the fast filter rainmakers often run in their head midconversation[6]:

- **Budget:** Is money allocated, or can it be?
- **Authority:** Are we speaking to someone who can say yes?
- **Need:** Is there a pain point or strategic goal worth solving?
- **Timing:** Is now the moment or is this just idle curiosity?

Example: A rainmaker was approached by a midsize bank with a vague request for "support on culture change." Using BANT, she quickly uncovered that while the head of human resources was enthusiastic, no budget had been assigned, the CEO was unaware of the request, and the timing was vague. She parked the idea but stayed in contact. Six months later, the CEO initiated a formal program, with funding and urgency. Because she hadn't wasted capital too early, she was ready and won it.

MEDDIC: Metrics, Economic Buyer, Decision Criteria, Decision Process, Identify Pain, Champion In complex environments, MEDDIC is the gold standard[7]:

- **Metrics:** What key performance indicators (KPIs) matter most?
- **Economic Buyer:** Who holds the purse strings?
- **Decision Criteria and Process:** How will the choice be made?
- **Identify Pain:** What's truly keeping them up at night?
- **Champion:** Is someone advocating for us from within?

Example: A consultant pursuing a global logistics company's digital transformation dug into MEDDIC and realized the team engaging her had no internal champion yet. She spent time building trust with the COO, surfaced critical operational KPIs (delivery accuracy and cost to serve), and codeveloped a shared vision. That same COO became her champion, introduced her to the CFO, and unlocked a multiyear engagement.

SPIN: Situation, Problem, Implication, Need-Payoff Rainmakers don't pitch. They guide by asking SPIN-style questions.[8]

- **Situation:** What's happening now?
- **Problem:** Where's the friction?
- **Implication:** What happens if nothing changes?
- **Need-Payoff:** How could things improve?

Example: A rainmaker noticed an insurance client exploring the use of automation. Instead of jumping to offer a solution, he asked SPIN-style questions. The client revealed inefficiencies in claims processing. The rainmaker helped them see that delays were costing millions in lost renewals and customer churn. By guiding them to articulate the implications and envision the payoff, he didn't sell automation, they asked for it.

CHAMP: Challenges, Authority, Money, Prioritization CHAMP adds nuance to BANT especially in crowded, chaotic environments.[9]

- **Challenges:** Is this a burning issue or background noise?
- **Authority and Money:** Who makes the decision, and is funding aligned?
- **Prioritization:** Where does this sit among the client's top initiatives?

Example: A consulting partner was referred to a health agency facing significant regulatory change. She sensed opportunity, but CHAMP revealed the challenge was real, the decision maker supported her, and money was earmarked. However, it wasn't prioritized; a public inquiry had shifted its focus. Rather than push, she built mindshare, offered insights, and waited. Months later the client circled back ready to act. Trust had been banked.

Account-Based Qualification In major accounts, rainmakers zoom out. It's not just about one opportunity, it's about long-term strategy:

- What's our positioning across the account?
- Where are the power bases and areas of tension?
- Who else is selling here, and what gaps do they fill?
- What could open new branches in the client tree?

Example: At a major telco, a rainmaker knew a proposal for a narrow procurement efficiency review wouldn't change the game. However, by examining the account details, he realized the CFO's team was struggling with fractured data and poor spend visibility. He set about earning trust with the finance function, reframed the value narrative, and landed a broader transformation. That work branched into analytics, governance, and, eventually, geographic and product expansion.

Reading the Signals: Subtle but Telling

Rainmakers are master readers of the unspoken. They look for green lights:

- Invitations to bring others into the room
- Forward-looking, tactical questions
- Writing notes of conversations
- Willingness to share risk, urgency, or vulnerability
- Signals that the organization is already moving and needs help

And they watch for red flags:

- "We're exploring options" with no urgency
- Stakeholders are missing from key meetings
- Endless interest but no next step
- No clarity on who decides or how

Rainmakers don't ignore these signals. They translate them into action.

Go/Wait/Walk: The Rainmaker's Decision Matrix

Every opportunity lands in one of three buckets:

1. **Go:** The fit is strong, value is high, and urgency is real. Go deep.
2. **Wait:** There's promise but not yet momentum. Stay close, nurture.
3. **Walk:** The energy isn't there. Walk away with grace.

Rainmakers don't see walking away as failure. They see it as a focus.

A Story from the Field: When Neil Chased the Wrong Client

Years ago Neil was invited to pitch for a flagship transformation. Big client. Big stakes. Real budget. The kind of opportunity that quickens the pulse. But in hindsight, it was the wrong chase. Let's hear his story and the lesson that stayed with him.

At first, the opportunity looked like momentum. Our firm had delivered a handful of smaller strategy pieces, tight turnarounds, solid work, and excellent feedback. But those were all with a senior general manager, three levels below the CEO. He had energy, vision, and a real appetite for change. But he didn't have the money; that was with his boss. And while he talked often of "my boss" and "leadership alignment," we'd never been in the room with anyone above him. Not even once.

Then came the signal: "Something big is brewing," he told us, "and we want you involved." We were flattered. Excited. We polished a capability statement. Spent days repackaging previous successes and sent them across. A brief "Thanks, this looks great, let's catch up soon" followed.

Then silence.

Weeks later we were informed that the client's internal business case was being developed and he wanted a set of global benchmarks. So we mobilized. We interviewed overseas experts. We gathered competitive intelligence. We even hired a contractor to analyze sentiment data across the client's customer base. The material was substantial: sharp, relevant, original.

We sent it. No reply.

Still hopeful, we pressed ahead. Built a team. Held daily war room conversations. Brought in alliance partners and started lining up the pitch, rehearsing the playbook. But the phone never rang. No RFP came.

The transformation was delayed and/or canceled. Or done by someone else. We never really knew.

What we *did* know was this: We'd invested hundreds of hours. We'd spread ourselves thin. And we'd ignored the signals: weak access to power, vague timelines, and an "opportunity" that seemed to ask for everything without committing to anything.

I've never forgotten that lesson.

In today's world, there are more clients fishing for ideas than ever before. Some are genuinely exploring; others are just testing the water. And a few—not many but enough—were never looking for serious help to begin with. It's easy to mistake early interest for intent. But it's not the same thing.

That's why today is about focus. About spending time where it matters. It's about pursuing the winnable opportunities and resisting the pull of low-probability pitches, those flattering invitations that sound promising but rarely lead to real work. Too many consultants confuse curiosity for commitment, adding names to a long pursuit list that looks healthy on paper but, if qualified properly, would be half as long and twice as strong.

Now I qualify harder. Earlier. Smarter. Rainmakers know the difference between a mirage and a market. They ask the tough questions. They look for proof points, not polite enthusiasm. They listen for buying signals beneath the surface and aren't afraid to walk away when they don't hear them.

Because when you're chasing the wrong thing, no matter how exciting it looks, the cost isn't just time.

It's traction. And traction is what rainmakers protect above all.

Your Superpower: Precision Qualification

Here's the truth: Every "yes" you say should be backed by a dozen or two dozen "nos." Precision isn't about volume. It's about judgment.

The real test for a rainmaker isn't finding opportunity; it's knowing which one is worth the climb. Because when you direct your focus to what truly matters, something shifts.

Growth isn't just steady. It's alive. It's deliberate. And the whole tree thrives.

Conclusion: Hunting with Precision

In this chapter, we explored the first of four core rainmaker strategies: the art of *hunting with precision*, the foundational branch of the rainmaker's tree.

Rainmakers don't chase every scent. They move with intent. They qualify with clarity. They ask not just "Where is the work?" but "Where can I grow the most value?"

They're clear-eyed and committed. Strategic, yes, but always grounded. They care about revenue but also about impact: commercial, social, structural.

In this chapter we explored:

- The mindset behind sharp targeting: focused, ambitious, and anchored in purpose.
- The emotional reality of prospecting: the uncertainty, the long game, the resilience it demands.
- Twelve distinct sources of opportunity: not a funnel but a living, evolving landscape.
- The discipline of qualification: the filter rainmakers use to protect their time, their energy, and their name.

Because here's the truth: Not all opportunities deserve your pursuit.

Rainmakers understand the cost of chasing the wrong ones. They grow with intention, reaching only for the strongest branches, and building something that lasts.

Next: The Power of Creating Unmatched Value

Hunting with precision is just the start.

In a crowded market, access isn't enough. What sets you apart is the value you bring: clear, meaningful, and impossible to ignore.

In the next chapter, we step into that shift: from chasing work to being sought out. From credible to essential. From presence to pull.

That's where rainmakers change the game.

Let's find out how.

CHAPTER

18

Creating Unmatched Value

Shifting Your Mindset from "Delivering Work" to "Creating Client Impact"

It's a story we've seen far too many times. A talented consultant lands a career-defining opportunity, the kind of engagement that comes around only once or twice in a decade. He's done the work. Built trust. Helped the client see what's possible. Now, after months of relationship building, problem solving, and shaping a shared vision, he stands on the brink of securing a major transformation program: a back-office overhaul that promises not just efficiency but real, enterprise-wide impact. Lower costs. Higher productivity. The freedom to invest in growth and customer experience.

This is the moment to seal the deal. And yet, with just hours to go before the proposal is due, he and his team turn their attention for the first time to the question of pricing. How much should we charge? What margin do we need? What do we think the client is prepared to spend?

It becomes a hurried scramble. A few last-minute tweaks to a spreadsheet. A quick phone call about precedent pricing. Some finger-in-the-air assumptions about value. No real link to impact. No clear articulation of how success will be measured or what outcomes will be achieved. No definition of value, let alone proof that the value on offer is worth the investment.

It's an all-too-common pattern: Pricing is often an afterthought, and value is assumed to be inherent. No matter how good the solution, the final proposal falls short because it fails to give the client the confidence to say yes. The consultant walks away confused. Frustrated. Wondering how such a strong opportunity slipped away.

In this chapter, we explore what rainmakers do differently.

They know the opportunity isn't won just by identifying the problem or proposing an innovative solution. It's more complex than that; it involves framing value early, clearly, and consistently. Rainmakers understand that the most challenging part isn't designing the work; it's getting it done. It's creating a case so compelling and outcome aligned that the client can't imagine saying no.

This is the branch of the rainmaker's tree where all that inner strength—purpose, insight, empathy, discipline—finally reaches outward, where it becomes real. Visible. Measurable.

Rainmakers do six things better than the average consultant when it comes to creating unmatched value. In the pages that follow, we explore each of them with stories, research, and practical examples so you can do the same.

Defining Unmatched Value

First, let's start with a definition: "Unmatched value" is defined by *impact that endures beyond the engagement*—impact that reshapes decisions, strengthens internal credibility, and advances the client's goals in ways they could not have achieved alone.

It is, fundamentally, a relational and contextual concept, not a transactional one.

Where traditional consultants focus on *output*—reports, frameworks, and deliverables—rainmakers focus on *outcome* and *trajectory*. They don't just hand over solutions; they accelerate progress. As Parasuraman, Zeithaml, and Berry established in their seminal work on service quality, value is perceived not in what is delivered but in how reliably, empathetically, and insightfully it meets the client's actual needs, often before those needs are fully articulated.[1]

Unmatched value also demands psychological closeness. Allan R. Cohen and David L. Bradford's model of informal influence in organizations highlights that genuine impact stems not from positional authority. But from embeddedness, the ability to operate within the client's strategic agenda as a trusted voice, not an external vendor.[2] Rainmakers do this instinctively. They shift the conversation from "What do you want us to do?" to "What are you trying to achieve and why now?"

That proximity enables another essential dynamic: trust. As Donald R. Lichtenstein, Nancy M. Ridgway, and Richard G. Netemeyer showed, trust is not a by-product of value; it is its precursor.[3] In high-stakes advisory work, clients are most likely to experience value when they feel the consultant truly *gets* them, their pressures, aspirations, blind spots, and politics. This is why rainmakers work hard to establish consistency in insight, responsiveness, and results. These aren't soft skills; they are strategic prerequisites for impact.

Moreover, research by Berend Wierenga and associates reveals that solutions that connect to the client's deeper motivations—the "why" beneath the "what"—are stickier and more likely to succeed.[4] Rainmakers probe until they uncover the deeper why. They know that unmatched value is not about dazzling with breadth but aligning with precision.

And perhaps most critically, unmatched value is not assumed. It is defined, tracked, and tested. As Kumar Rahman, and Kazmi argue, consultants who tie their work directly to measurable business impact and who are willing to be held accountable for it generate higher trust, stronger partnerships, and greater client satisfaction.[5] Rainmakers bring this discipline into every engagement. They formalize what value means, how it will be delivered, and how it will be proven.

In this way, unmatched value becomes more than a philosophy. It becomes a practice rooted in empathy, defined by relevance, enabled through accountability, and delivered through trusted relationships.

To sum it up: Unmatched value is the ability to shape decisions, deliver meaningful change, and earn the right to be in the room, again and again. Not because you completed the project, but because the client was changed by what you helped them do.

The Six Levers of Unmatched Value

Rainmakers don't stumble into value; they build it. Not through one-off ideas or flashy moments but through steady, deliberate effort.

They work with tested, practical, and powerful levers, applied in combination, not isolation. And always shaped to fit the client, the context, and the moment.

Here are six ways they create value that stands apart:

1. Shift from transactional delivery to transformational impact.
2. Practice deep empathy and contextual relevance.
3. Anchor all work in accountability and measured value.
4. Offer thoughtfully designed options that empower clients.
5. Extend targeted generosity, not overdelivery.
6. Use pricing as a strategic lever.

Individually, each of levers is powerful. Together, they form the architecture of trust, relevance, and impact that clients not only respect but also rely on. (See Figure 18.1.)

Let's take a closer look at how rainmakers use each lever to turn good work into indispensable value.

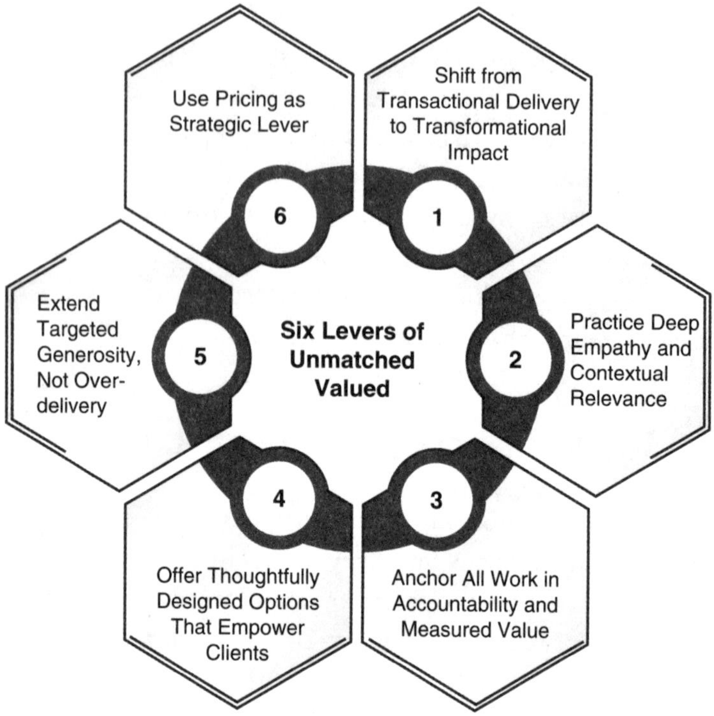

FIGURE 18.1 Six levers of unmatched value.

Lever 1: Shift from Transactional Delivery to Transformational Impact

Rainmakers don't win work by promising outputs. They win by delivering outcomes that matter. Most consultants see an engagement as a project, tasks to complete, deliverables to hand over, milestones to hit. Rainmakers see something else.

To them, the work is a turning point. A chance to shift the client's direction in ways that last well beyond the final slide. This approach is the first and most foundational lever of unmatched value: reframing the engagement from transactional delivery to transformational impact.

Rather than asking "*What will we deliver?*" rainmakers ask, "*What will be different because of this?*" They begin with the end in mind, not the contract close but the after-state the client is striving for. What change will this work enable? What clarity will it unlock? What business decision, cultural shift, or performance leap will it accelerate?

That shift in mindset changes everything.

It moves the consultant from vendor to partner, from executor to strategist. And it forces a new kind of discipline, one rooted not in activity but in impact.

As Jenny, a senior partner at a Big Four consulting firm, regularly reminded her teams: "*Our job isn't to do the work. Our job is to make a difference.*" Before any proposal was written, she challenged her team to answer three questions:

1. Why is the client asking for this now?
2. What differentiated value will we bring that no one else can?
3. How will the client feel and think differently if we're successful?

This framing demanded more than technical excellence. It required deep understanding, insight, and accountability. It forced consultants to think like owners, not just of their work but of the client's outcome.

Increasingly, rainmakers are pairing this mindset with AI-powered tools that help them visualize transformation in real time. Many firms are building proprietary platforms tailored to their consulting approach while also licensing the best of the latest tools being released across the market. These systems track forward-looking indicators, such as sentiment, momentum, or decision readiness that reveal whether a client is undergoing meaningful change. These signals don't replace judgment, but they help consultants stay on course, adjusting as they go to remain aligned with what truly matters.

That's the heart of the matter: Deliverables are not the destination. They're a vehicle. The real value lies in what the client becomes capable of doing because of your work.

In the rainmaker's tree, this is the branch that bears real fruit. It's not just decoration. It provides nourishment to the client, to the firm, and to the relationship.

So, when a rainmaker steps into a room, they're not thinking about what slides to present or what outputs to tick off. They're asking "*What future are we helping this client walk into, and how will they know they're getting there?*"

Ultimately, transformation is the only deliverable that genuinely matters.

Lever 2: Practice Deep Empathy and Contextual Relevance

Rainmakers don't just solve problems. They understand people.

Behind every brief, every request, every project, there's a person or a team carrying risk, pressure, and expectation. Rainmakers recognize this. They know that to deliver real value, they first must understand the client's lived reality, not just the organization, recognizing that they are dealing with individuals navigating uncertainty, internal politics, and personal stakes.

This is where the second lever of unmatched value comes in: deep empathy and contextual relevance.

In many firms, empathy still gets dismissed, seen as too soft, too personal, not part of the strategy. But for rainmakers, it's the core to how they work. It's what turns a standard engagement into a trusted partnership.

They don't just listen. They pay close attention. They ask the hard questions. They notice the pause in a client's voice. They pick up on the politics behind a decision, the quiet push for influence, the silence that signals resistance.

This isn't guesswork; it's a skill. Built over time. Sharpened through experience. And now, in some firms, it's being amplified.

Looking ahead, it's likely that AI tools, in the right context and with the right guardrails, will support consultants by analyzing tone, pace, and sentiment in client conversations. For rainmakers, these tools won't replace instinct; they'll sharpen it. They'll help surface tension points, missed cues, and patterns that deserve a second look. When used thoughtfully, these AI tools won't make interactions less human, they'll make empathy more precise.

Because genuine empathy isn't about agreeing; it's about *understanding*.

Understanding that a client's request for a "strategy refresh" might be a bid for organizational relevance under a new CEO. That a transformation roadmap might be driven less by market demand and more by pressure from an activist investor. That the "what" rarely tells the whole story; the "why" does.

Rainmakers move quickly from the surface-level ask to the more profound need.

They don't jump to solutions. They create space. They establish psychological safety. They allow the client to say "Here's what I'm worried about." And that's when the conversation gets real.

Research backs this up. The Wierenga et al. study in the *Journal of Marketing* found that consultants who uncover a client's deeper motivations are significantly more likely to deliver effective and lasting outcomes.[6] Similarly, Kent Grayson and Radan Martinec demonstrated how symbolic cues such as empathy, attentiveness, and cultural fluency shape perceptions of trust and strategic credibility.[7] When consultants demonstrate emotional and contextual understanding, they're seen not just as capable but as essential.

Jenny, a highly successful partner, understood this without needing a playbook. Her first question on any potential opportunity was never "What is the client asking us to do?" It was "Why is the client asking for this now?" That single question often cracked open the real issue and reshaped the entire approach.

Another powerful example came from Rose, a partner in a global firm based in the United States.

Over time, Rose had become a trusted advisor to a major North American company. Her impact went beyond results; it came from how she showed up. She built deep, lasting relationships across the business.

The company's CEO had fostered a culture of decentralized autonomy. Each business unit made its own strategic and operational calls. That structure could easily confuse an outsider. But Rose didn't try to force a top-down solution. She earned the trust of each unit leader individually, showing up, delivering, and staying consistent.

She wasn't seen as a vendor. She wasn't even an external partner. She was one of them. Then came the disruption.

A landmark merger reshaped the entire industry and the company. A new executive from the merged entity was appointed to lead post-merger integration. The mandate? Achieve the promised benefits quickly, visibly, and centrally.

The new executive issued a request for proposal to multiple consulting firms, including Rose's. However, the brief called for a top-down approach, stripping business units of decision-making power, which directly contradicted the culture Rose had come to know, respect, and serve.

The stakes were enormous. Rose's firm had built years of goodwill. However, the new executive had now invited in a rival firm, one with which the company had a long-standing relationship. Winning the work might mean bending to a model that risked alienating the business unit leaders who had been Rose's strongest allies. Losing it could unravel the firm's standing altogether.

At the internal strategy session, two options emerged:

1. Submit a compliant response, aligned with the new executive's vision and hope to stay in favor.
2. Take a stand and propose an alternative approach grounded in cultural continuity and the firm's proven track record with the client.

Rose consulted with several rainmakers in her firm. She made her case to the people in her company, firmly and clearly: "We should not tailor our response to win favor. We should tailor it to deliver impact. That means respecting what's worked here and showing how we can generate benefits without breaking the very culture that made this company successful."

She pushed for a "noncompliant" proposal, one that met the business objective but challenged the method. It detailed the levers to unlock merger value but insisted those levers be deployed in a way that preserved local accountability and respected the company's DNA.

Before finalizing the proposal, Rose did something bold: She consulted the business unit leaders themselves. She listened. Tested assumptions. Refined the approach. Her empathy wasn't passive; it was active. Strategic.

The result? The business unit leaders endorsed her proposal. So did the CEO. Rose's firm retained the relationship not by capitulating but by demonstrating deep contextual understanding and the courage to act on it.

Rose didn't win by playing politics. She won by practicing empathy at a strategic level, understanding not just what the client asked for but what the organization needed to succeed.

That's what rainmakers do.

Key Insight: Rainmakers are part analyst, part anthropologist. They read the room. Decode the brief. And see the whole board, not just the next move.

In consulting, value resides in relevance. And relevance requires empathy.

Rainmakers don't just deliver a solution; they provide a solution that drives results. They show they *get it*. And clients remember that long after the work is done.

Lever 3: Anchor All Work in Accountability and Measured Value

Rainmakers don't just promise value. They prove it.

This approach one of the most overlooked yet powerful disciplines in consulting. Where average consultants focus on the pitch, rainmakers concentrate on the proof. They know that unmatched value isn't just felt; it's measured, tracked, and communicated. That approach is what elevates them from trusted vendors to strategic partners.

From the moment the engagement begins, rainmakers take a different path. They don't wait for a contract to expire or a client to ask

"Did this work?" Instead, they embed accountability into the project's fabric with clarity, discipline, and intent.

Doing this starts with co-creating a value definition. Not a vague ambition or a boilerplate key performance indicator set but a specific, client-relevant agreement on what success will look like. A few examples:

- Reduce decision-making cycle time by 40% within six months.
- Shift stakeholder sentiment in the target region from neutral to net positive.
- Achieve 20% cost recovery through operational redesign by Q3.

This practice isn't about padding the proposal with performance metrics. It's about building shared ownership, creating a roadmap that both parties commit to and believe in.

Rainmakers don't stop there. They establish deliberate value checkpoints with the client sponsor: not just internal reviews but transparent moments of accountability. Often these checkpoints are led by an objective peer or senior advisor who is a step removed from the client engagement and who can ask the hard questions:

- Are we delivering what we promised?
- Has the context shifted?
- Are new risks emerging?
- Are we truly aligned with what matters most to the client?

This practice does more than course correct. It signals something deeper: *We are as invested in your success as you are*. It shifts the dynamic from service delivery to joint performance management.

And at the end of the engagement? Rainmakers return to the original definition of value. Not to check a box but to test the outcome. They ask:

- Did we deliver the promised results?
- Can we quantify the impact?

- What changed commercially, culturally, and operationally because of this work?
- Where did we exceed expectations, and where did we fall short?

Many firms avoid this conversation. Rainmakers lean into it.

Because they know that the measured value is the remembered value. Clients are busy. Focused on their internal priorities. If value isn't made value visible, it can be invisible, regardless of how hard you work.

That's why rainmakers build the value story as they go. They use dashboards, impact scorecards, and tailored executive updates. They translate results into the client's language: not just inputs and activities but outcomes and implications. They even equip the client with the narrative they'll need to tell their own board or executive team.

This is how rainmakers create loyalty. This is how reputations are built.

Ultimately, unmatched value is not just about what gets done; it's about what gets done *well*. It's about what changes as a result and how that change can be observed, shared, and celebrated.

Lever 4: Offer Thoughtfully Designed Options That Empower Clients

Rainmakers know that the path to value isn't always linear and that clients rarely arrive with total clarity on what they want.

That's why one of the most powerful levers rainmakers use is this: They offer thoughtfully designed, well-differentiated options that help clients move forward with confidence, clarity, and control.

Just as what Rose did with that North American corporation, rainmakers don't offer open-ended menus. They don't ask the client to choose between five vaguely defined service levels. Instead, they bring two to three *wise, structured choices*, each aligned to a different level of ambition, urgency, or risk tolerance. Or, as Rose did, they offer a different method. Each one is grounded in outcomes.

This approach does more than respond to a client brief. It reshapes the conversation, moving it from a sales-purchase discussion to codesign session. From *"What's your price?"* to *"What future are we building together?"*

Here's the key: Offering options isn't about upselling. It's about leadership.

It's about saying to the client *"We understand your position. We've thought ahead. Here are credible paths forward, each one viable, but tailored to different needs."* This strategy demonstrates foresight. Strategic empathy. And above all, relevance.

Contrast this with the all-too-common trap of overdelivering: Many consultants, trying to signal value, pile on more resources, deliverables, and content. However, as decades of research demonstrate, more doesn't necessarily equal better.

Parasuraman et al.'s SERVQUAL (Service Quality) model revealed that client satisfaction depends on *reliability, empathy, and tangibles* rather than on volume.[8] Katherine N. Lemon, Roland T. Rust, and Valarie A. Zeithaml demonstrated that in transactional contexts, clients often overlook when firms exceeding expectation that are not relevant to clients.[9] At worst, doing so creates confusion. At best, it goes unnoticed.

And yet consultants still fall into the trap of adding 60-slide "thought leadership" documents that no one asked for. Including appendixes to demonstrate effort, not insight. Stretching the scope to look generous and diluting the focus that creates impact.

Rainmakers do the opposite. They are disciplined. They ask one straightforward question before adding anything to their work: "Will this be meaningful to the client right now, in this context, with their priorities?"

If the answer is no, they prune the idea. Not out of laziness, but out of respect. Respect for the client's time, attention, and decision-making clarity.

Instead of pitching one big solution, they offer real choices each designed with purpose.

Take a client exploring a major transformation. A rainmaker might lay out three distinct paths:

1. A short diagnostic to uncover what's blocking progress and build alignment early. Quick, focused, and low risk.
2. A full transformation program, built to go the distance with capability building woven in from the start.
3. A tightly scoped pilot, with clear outcomes and a path to scale if it delivers.

Each path stands on its own. Each ties to real impact. And none is there just to fill out the slide.

This approach empowers the client to choose a path that fits their readiness, politics, and ambition while positioning the rainmaker as a copilot, not just a supplier.

Because in high-stakes consulting, clarity *is* a valuable asset.

And when clients are offered clear, well-considered choices, not more noise but more relevance, they respond with trust, conviction, and action.

Rainmakers know great consulting isn't about doing more. It's about helping the client make better choices.

Lever 5: Extend Targeted Generosity, Not Overdelivery

It was the final phase of a high-stakes strategy engagement. The client's executive team had been cooperative but cautious: aligned on paper but privately divided on what came next. The work was intense and essentially done. The roadmap was sound, and all the analysis and reports were packaged to be handed over. But something wasn't landing.

Rather than add another appendix or revise the final report for the fifth time, Maya, the lead consultant, did something else.

She called her client sponsor and asked a quiet question: "*What's holding us back from alignment?*"

The client hesitated, then admitted: Several midlevel leaders didn't feel heard. The big picture made sense, but the nuances of execution, the cultural tensions, and operational pain points hadn't been captured enough to build confidence across the business.

Maya didn't scramble to produce more slides. Instead, she pulled her team into a short-burst effort: four days of targeted, confidential interviews with key stakeholders. Then, over the following weekend, she distilled what she heard into a two-page synthesis, plain language, clear themes, and a list of unresolved concerns.

She didn't charge for it. She didn't frame it as extra. She sent it to the client with a note: "*We thought this might help unlock the next conversation.*"

And it did.

That short document reframed the final steering meeting. It gave voice to the room. It helped the client move toward alignment, not just logically but emotionally.

That's targeted generosity. Not more. Just *right*.

Lever 6: Use Pricing as a Strategic Lever

Rainmakers see pricing for what it really is: a signal.

It's not just about numbers. It shapes how the work is perceived by the client, by stakeholders, and often by the market. Pricing reflects how well you understand the stakes, the context, and the value you intend to create.

Many consultants treat it as a final step, something to plug in once the proposal is done. Rainmakers don't. For them, pricing is part of the story. It carries meaning. It sets the tone. Handled well, it's not just a number; it's a lever.

How you price is one of the clearest signals you send about the quality of your thinking, the strength of your offer, and the kind of relationship you want to build. Done well, pricing becomes a natural extension of the rainmaker's branch, shaped with intention, anchored by trust, and grown to support weight over time.

However, pricing is both an art and a science. It requires judgment, creativity, and courage.

Six Questions Rainmakers Ask Before They Price Rainmakers don't start with the model. They begin with questions, ones that shape the conversation and calibrate the offer:

1. What value will this engagement create, and for whom?
2. How can that value be measured, financially, operationally, or reputationally?
3. What pricing model best aligns our interests with those of the client?
4. What level of risk are we prepared to take and share?
5. How can we use pricing to reinforce our role as a high-impact advisor?
6. What are our strengths and weaknesses versus those of our competitors?

These questions don't guarantee the perfect answer. But they frame the conversation in a way that roots the branch in fertile soil, built for long-term trust, not short-term convenience.

Four Common Approaches to Pricing Rainmakers use four common approaches in pricing. Let's explore each one:

1. Value-based pricing
2. Fixed fees versus time-based billing
3. Tiered pricing
4. Risk-sharing models

Value-Based Pricing: Focus on the Outcome, Not the Effort Rainmakers don't charge for time; they price for impact. The fee reflects the result, not the hours. Because clients aren't buying effort. They're buying what changes.

A landmark *Harvard Business Review* article by James C. Anderson, James A. Narus, and Wouter van Rossum found that firms using value-based pricing captured more of the value they created *and* built stronger, more trusted client relationships.[10]

This model works best when:

- The client has a clearly defined strategic goal (e.g., growth, market entry, efficiency).
- The impact can be estimated or measured.
- There is mutual trust in your ability to deliver.

Common metrics include:

- Revenue uplift.
- Cost savings.
- Speed to market.
- Regulatory risk mitigation.
- Strategic enablement (e.g., launching a new product or capability).

Even when the numbers are hard to pin down, value-based pricing still reframes the conversation: from *what we do* to *what the client gets*.

Used well, it turns the consultant into a co-investor in the client's success, a branch not just offering shade but bearing fruit together.

Fixed Fees Versus Time-Based Billing: Trust Versus Flexibility The second key pricing choice is structure.

- Fixed fees offer predictability. They give the client budget clarity and reinforce trust.
- Time-based billing can provide adaptability. It suits projects where the scope is unclear or likely to evolve.

Joseph P. Cannon and Walter D. Perreault Jr. found that when buyers perceive contractual arrangements to be clear and aligned with their expectations, such as through predictable pricing, trust in the provider increases significantly.[11] Fixed pricing, when used well, can send a strong message: We know the work, and we stand behind it.

Rainmakers ask simple but important questions before deciding on which pricing method to choose:

- Does the client need certainty or room to adapt?
- Is the scope clear or still evolving?
- Has trust been built, or is it still early?

Often the answers aren't either/or. A blended approach works best: fixed fees for clearly defined work and time-based billing for what's still taking shape.

The goal is to support the work as it grows, steady where it needs to be, flexible where it matters.

Tiered Pricing: Creating Choice Without Confusion Tiered pricing gives clients choices.

It lets them pick a path that matches their needs, budget, and ambition.

Rainmakers don't use tiers to push for more. They use them to make decisions clearer:

- What's included and what's not
- What changes at each level of investment
- Where the real return lies

A typical structure might look like this:

- **Foundational:** Core analysis and key recommendations
- **Strategic:** Deeper insight with targeted support
- **Transformational:** End-to-end change, with capability built in

Each option stands on its own. No filler. No pressure. Just clarity.

Research from the field of psychology helps to explain that people feel more confident after decisions when using clear processes and well-defined options. The key? Each option must address a distinct problem angle; otherwise, it creates confusion rather than clarity.[12]

Risk-Sharing Models: Contingent and Success-Based Pricing

Linking your fee to the client's results through gainsharing, contingency, or outcome-based pricing can be effective, but the method isn't something to use lightly.

It only works when a few things are true:

- The value has to be clear. Not abstract or subjective.
- The timeline needs to be tight enough to track. You need real influence over what happens, not just advice from the sidelines. Everyone has to know who's doing what.
- And the numbers? They need to add up, with no guesswork.

When all those pieces are in place, the model can work. Without them, it can backfire.

We've found through experience that risk-based pricing for some clients can improve trust and collaboration, but only when expectations are clear and both parties are aligned on success metrics.

Rainmakers use these models strategically. They ask:

- What is the client trying to derisk?
- What part of that risk are we willing to share?
- Can we structure pricing in a way that preserves trust even if outcomes shift?

And they always document the rules: how success will be judged, by whom, and on what timeline.

Strategic Questions to Shape Pricing Before finalizing their approach, rainmakers use one last filter, a set of simple, strategic questions to test alignment:

- What does success look like and for whom does that success transfer to, and who defines it?
- How will we demonstrate progress and outcomes?
- What's the client's risk tolerance?
- What kind of relationship are we trying to build?
- Does our pricing reflect ambition, alignment, and confidence?

These aren't box-ticking exercises. They're pruning shears, helping shape the branch of value so it grows clean, strong, and client facing.

Final Thought: Pricing Is a Window into Your Mindset At its core, pricing reveals what you believe about your client, your offer, and yourself. Weak pricing signals one of two things: a lack of clarity about the value you bring or a lack of confidence in your ability to deliver it. Rainmakers avoid both.

They price with confidence and not afraid to request a large fee as they know there will be a large return. And they price *with* the client, not just *for* the client. Because in consulting, pricing isn't just about revenue. It's about positioning.

And done well, pricing becomes one more branch to extend your impact.

Reflection: Making Value Your Edge

Delivering real value isn't about doing more. It's about doing what matters with focus, care, and intent.

Rainmakers walk into each engagement with a clear purpose: not just to meet expectations but to shift something. To help clients get to a place they couldn't reach on their own. To spot the opportunity others miss. To step into the hard parts others avoid.

They're not chasing deliverables. They're aiming for change, connecting what they do to what the client truly needs.

And they don't let that value stay hidden. They track it, share it, and make it felt. Through data, through feedback, through the way the story carries.

Clients might forget the model or the milestones. But they'll remember what moved. What shifted. Where they gained clarity, confidence, and ground. That's what stays with them.

This is the growth principle behind every strong branch in the rainmaker's tree. Not haphazard, overgrown effort. But value, well shaped, well rooted, and reaching in the right direction.

Rainmakers don't get there by accident. They get there by asking:

- What will move the needle for this client?
- What's the impact behind the ask?
- What would make us indispensable, not just useful?

They build their work around the answers to these questions. And when they deliver, they don't hope the value is recognized. They ensure it is. They package it. They measure it. They equip the client to retell the story with clarity and pride.

They make value a habit, not a highlight. That's the difference. In the end, value isn't the slide deck or the deliverable. It's what clients can now do that they couldn't before. But that's only part of it.

Insight, on its own, doesn't always land. Even the best idea can stall if the client isn't ready to act or doesn't fully trust the source.

That's why rainmakers go further. They don't just bring value. They earn trust. Not surface-level rapport but trust built over time. Trust that opens doors, speeds up decisions, and turns clients into long-term allies.

Next: Forging Unshakeable Trust

In the next chapter, we look at the third rainmaker strategy: *forging unshakeable trust*. You'll see how trust becomes the branch that feeds everything, relationships, results, and long-term growth. And why, in the consulting forest, the trusted voice is the one that's called when the storm hits.

Let's turn there now.

CHAPTER

19

Forging Unshakeable Trust

In Complex Engagements, Clients Choose Trust over Innovation. They Bet on Character

If there's one branch of the rainmaker's tree that's been discussed more than any other, it's this one: *trust*.

Every consultant knows it matters. Every firm claims it as a differentiator. And every keynote, panel, and proposal seems to mention it.

However, despite the considerable airtime trust receives in our industry, it remains the least well understood, especially when it comes to the kind of trust that rainmakers forge with senior client executives. The type that earns them the right to step inside the most sensitive, complex, and high-stakes matters. The kind that gets them invited back, not just to deliver but to advise as well.

This chapter is about that kind of trust; the kind that is *experienced* in the field, in the room, and in the moments that matter.

Here's what we cover:

- First, we define what trust is in consulting and break it down into five distinct levels. Most consultants operate at Levels 1 to 3. Rainmakers live at Levels 4 and 5, and we explain why those levels are different, rare, and powerful.
- Then we dive deep into the actions and behaviors that distinguish rainmakers at the highest levels of trust. This is where the work happens and where the returns are most significant.
- We explore how trust varies across cultures, how it plays out across layers of a client organization, and why building internal trust with colleagues is just as critical to your success as any client relationship.
- Throughout, we share real stories, research-backed insights, and hard-won lessons, not just about how trust is built but about how easily it can be lost.

Before we delve into what makes trust strong, we begin by illustrating just how fragile it can be, with a couple of stories that every consultant should carry with them. This isn't about learning to be liked. It's about learning to be trusted with what matters most.

We start with a legacy story, one where trust wasn't just talked about: It was earned, tested, and held over time. This is the level rainmakers work at. High stakes. Limited access. Relationships that matter. But the lessons aren't just for senior partners.

They're for any consultant ready to step into more where trust isn't a buzzword but the thing that gets you in the room and keeps you there.

When Time Means Nothing

Real trust doesn't fade. It doesn't weaken with distance or dilute with time. When the stakes are highest, clients don't reach for the most polished bio or the biggest brand. They come for the person they trust to stand beside them, not just to advise but to carry the weight of their burdens.

It was 2:13 a.m. when the call came through. A senior partner at a global advisory firm, half a world away, picked up on the second ring.

"Sorry for the call at this hour. I need you and your team in London within 36 hours." The voice was steady but urgent. The CEO of one of the world's largest resource companies. A man the senior partner hadn't worked with in four years.

The crisis was unfolding fast: A catastrophic event—environmental, financial, and deeply human—had sent the company into freefall. Stock markets had panicked and the company's stock had been suspended trading. The CEO, based in North America, was under pressure. Public backlash was building. The board was unsettled.

The senior partner understood the weight of the crisis. But what stood out wasn't the headlines; it was the CEO's voice.

They'd weathered tough moments before. This one felt different. Closer.

And in that moment, the partner didn't need to ask why he'd been called. He already knew.

Years earlier, they had worked together on a complex transformation. It wasn't just another project. The senior partner took the time to understand not only the business but the pressures the CEO was under.

There were late-night calls, some about strategy, others about what wasn't working. And now and then, the conversation drifted to life outside the job. The CEO had shared how hard it was to stay present at home while carrying the weight of global leadership.

When a family member became seriously ill, the partner didn't stay silent. He checked in. Quietly. A short message on a Sunday afternoon. No agenda, just asking how things were going.

It wasn't about the work. It was about being there.

And it wasn't just during crises. Over the years, the senior partner had kept in touch regularly, not in a self-serving way but by sending occasional emails with industry updates, market research, or even articles about the CEO's biggest competitor. Simple gestures, like the occasional text message or a quick call to share some insight he thought might be helpful, not with an agenda, but because he genuinely wanted to help. Those quiet, thoughtful moments were how trust took root.

It wasn't just about business; it was about understanding the person behind the title. The senior partner took the time to connect the CEO with others in his network, building alignment across his organization before any tough decisions needed to be made. The partner wasn't just there to fix things. He made sure the solutions worked, not just for the CEO, but for the broader team. They were practical, lasting, and aligned with the direction the organization needed to go.

Over time, that showed up in the small things. In the way he listened. In the way he brought others in. Every exchange—every call, every note—added weight to the relationship. Not rushed. Not performative. Just steady, thoughtful, and shared.

So, when the crisis hit and the CEO needed immediate support, he didn't turn to his current consultants or scramble for someone new. He reached out to the person who had been a constant, even in the silence between major projects. The senior partner's ability to execute in high-pressure moments wasn't just about his expertise. It was about the trust he had cultivated over the years, the quiet commitment that no matter the distance or the time between calls, the partnership would endure.

Within days, that partner had mobilized 60 consultants across disciplines, working shoulder to shoulder with 450 client staff to bring order to the chaos. Not with theatrics. With calm, focused execution.

The team didn't show up with big claims or staged urgency. They concentrated on what mattered, getting organized, pulling the right people into the right conversations, and making sure everyone was clear on what had to be done.

They weren't just there to fix the immediate problem. They were thinking longer term, about stability, recovery, and what it would take to keep the business moving forward.

Rainmakers understand that trust doesn't appear in the moment. It's built quietly, often long before the pressure arrives through consistency, honesty, and showing up when it's inconvenient.

In a crisis, no one looks for the best pitch. They look for the person they believe in. Trust doesn't need a headline. But when everything else is unclear, it's what holds the room together. Because when people look back, they won't remember the deck or the detail. They'll remember who stood with them and didn't flinch.

Defining Trust in Consulting

In consulting, trust is what separates service providers from strategic partners. Without it, you're one of many. With it, you're in the room when it matters most.

The academic literature offers a strong starting point. Roger C. Mayer, James H. Davis, and F. David Schoorman define trust as *a willingness to be vulnerable based on a belief in someone's ability, benevolence, and integrity.*[1] In simple terms: Can you do the job? Do you care about me? And will you do what's right, especially when it's hard?

Most consultants focus on the first ability. They highlight credentials, case studies, and delivery track records. This approach builds credibility but not necessarily trust. Trust also requires belief in your intent and character that you're here to serve the client's interest, not your own.

David H. Maister, Charles H. Green, and Robert M. Galford sharpened the lens further, identifying four dimensions of trust in their book, *The Trusted Advisor*[2]:

1. **Credibility:** You know what you're talking about.
2. **Reliability:** You do what you say you will.
3. **Intimacy:** You create a safe space for the client to be honest with you.
4. **Self-orientation:** You prioritize the client's needs over your agenda.

Most consultants excel in terms of credibility and reliability. But the deeper dimensions, intimacy and self-orientation, are where rainmakers distinguish themselves. They show up with empathy, humility, and consistency. They make space for hard truths. They earn permission to walk with the client through uncertainty, not just deliver outputs.

This shift is especially critical in today's world. As we're finding, AI tools can make it easier to generate content, and clients are asking: *What can you give me that a machine can't?* The answer is trust. Not just information but judgment. Not just analysis but emotional intelligence. Not just frameworks but presence.

Successful professional relationships rely heavily on trust, which is a multidimensional construct involving cognitive, emotional, and behavioral components. Trust develops through demonstrable competence and integrity, clear communication and alignment of expectations, and the building of personal rapport and goodwill. Trust is experienced as a leap of faith based on sociocognitive and emotional exchanges, making it a dynamic process rather than a static attribute. This multidimensional and procedural understanding of trust has been specifically studied in client–consultant relationships, highlighting its essential role in sustaining successful and high-stakes partnerships.[3]

And that kind of trust doesn't grow from capability alone. It grows from conduct. It grows when consultants meet expectations and then exceed them in the moments that matter: when the pressure is on, when the politics are complex, or when the client needs someone to speak the truth, not just what's convenient.

While competence is the cost of entry, trust is the multiplier. It grants access. It accelerates momentum. And it transforms consultants from outsiders to insiders.

Key Insight: Here's the truth: Access is relative. Not all consultants are invited into the same rooms. Not all are trusted with the same opportunities. And that difference, often invisible from the outside, is what separates the good from the truly exceptional.

That's what we're about to explore in our *Five-Level Client Trust Model.*

Let's unpack what that means.

The Five-Level Client Trust Model

Not all trust is equal. In consulting, access is relative and shaped by the depth of trust you've earned. Some consultants are trusted to deliver the brief. Others are trusted to shape it. And a rare few are trusted with far more: the judgment calls, the gray zones, the personal stakes.

This understanding that there are different levels of client trust is the foundation of our Five-Level Client Trust Model, a practical framework that describes how trust evolves, what behaviors signal each level, and what kind of matters a client is likely to entrust you with. (See Figure 19.1.)

Rainmakers operate almost exclusively at Levels 4 and 5. Most consultants never rise beyond Level 3.

Let's explore each level in turn.

FIGURE 19.1 The Five-Level Client Trust Model.

Level 1: Functional Trust—You Deliver What You Promise

Functional trust is the foundation of any professional relationship. The client trusts that you're dependable, that you'll do what you say you will, when you say you'll do it. At this level, trust is based on execution, not insight. You deliver what was promised. The work gets done. You're seen as dependable but easy to swap out.

Key behaviors:

- Timely, error-free delivery
- Professional responsiveness
- Adherence to project scope and budget

Typical client matters and issues:

- Standard project execution
- Compliance reviews
- Implementation projects
- Project management

These are low-risk engagements from a client perspective and follow standard methodologies.

Level 2: Relational Trust—You Understand Me

At this stage, trust starts to grow. The client feels that you understand their world, the pressures, the pace, the way decisions really get made. You're not just delivering. You're paying attention to them. You're adjusting.

The dynamic shifts at this level. It's less transactional. More personal. The client starts to see you as an someone who understands them and their world, not just someone who gets the work done.

Key behaviors:

- Asking thoughtful, context-rich questions
- Remembering unspoken preferences or constraints
- Showing empathy for pressures beyond the brief

Typical client matters:

- Department-level transformations, restructures, and operating model design
- Operational strategy alignment
- Change management planning

These engagements are still scoped, but there's more room for nuance and more opportunity to differentiate through insight.

Level 3: Advisory Trust—You Guide Me

At this point, the client isn't just asking you to deliver; they're asking what you think. They want your perspective. They expect you to push back on them or their team, in the right way, when something doesn't feel right. When things are unclear, they look to you for direction.

You're not just solving problems. You're helping shape how those problems are understood. That's where real consulting starts.

Key behaviors:

- Offering forward-looking ideas
- Constructively challenging assumptions
- Framing risks and opportunities in strategic terms

Typical client matters:

- Executive-led strategic reviews
- Market entry or innovation planning
- Early-stage digital or merger and acquisition readiness assessments

These projects often involve competing interests, fuzzy briefs, or emerging priorities and require confident, nuanced guidance.

Level 4: Strategic Trust—You Help Me Win

At this level, you're not reacting to strategy, you're helping shape it. The client sees you as a long-term partner. You're invited into early-stage conversations, before the path is clear. There's trust in your ability to navigate ambiguity, to bring clarity, and to focus attention where it matters most.

You're not there to help them keep up. You're working with them to set the pace and stay ahead.

Having this level of trust enables you to:

- Shape long-term vision and positioning.
- Facilitate alignment across senior leadership or the board.
- Design solutions that look beyond the immediate brief.

Typical client issues include:

- Organization-wide transformation.
- Leadership change or restructuring.
- Growth planning and capital allocation.

This is where rainmaking moves from influence to impact, where you help set direction, not just support it.

Level 5: Personal Trust—I Count on You

This level of trust is uncommon, and it's built slowly. The client doesn't just involve you. They lean on you when the path is unclear, when the pressure is personal, or when the stakes stretch beyond the business itself.

It's not about your qualifications. It's about showing up and staying steady when it matters most. You're in the room when the real decisions are made.

Having this level of trust enables you to:

- Keep confidence without needing to be asked.
- Be present during difficult moments, not just to advise but to stand beside.
- Take the late call, not to deliver but to listen and offer perspective.

Client issues at this level often include:

- Sensitive leadership tensions or internal politics.
- Crisis management and reputational pressure.
- Early conversations about succession or major shifts still under wraps.

At this point, you're more than a consultant. You're trusted at a personal level, someone they turn to, not because they have to but because they want to.

Earning Strategic and Personal Trust: What Rainmakers Do at Levels 4 and 5

Most consultants aim to earn credibility. Rainmakers earn unshakeable trust. At Levels 4 and 5 of the Five-Level Client Trust Model, *strategic trust* and *personal trust*, consultants are no longer seen as external vendors or even reliable advisors. They are viewed as partners in progress, steadying hands in uncertainty, and critical voices in the decisions that matter most.

Key Insight: Where other consultants focus on delivery, rainmakers concentrate on depth of insight, relationship, and presence. They don't just meet expectations. They reset them. And they do it with one quiet, consistent message in their behavior: "*I'm in this with you.*"

Here's how they earn that rare trust and keep it.

They Build Relationships of Depth, Not Just Utility

Rainmakers don't just show up when there's work to be won. They're there when there's nothing on the table, asking better questions, listening without an agenda, paying attention to the client's world.

They invest in learning:

- What success means to the client personally, not just professionally
- How decisions get made, not just what's on the org chart
- Where the pressure is, and who's carrying the weight
- What myths, assumptions, or fears are shaping client thinking

This relational groundwork is invisible on a Gantt chart. But it becomes the root system that supports every future engagement.

They Earn the Right to Stretch the Conversation

Rainmakers don't barge into strategic space. They're invited in because they've first delivered something helpful, timely, and that shows they understand the client's world.

They challenge, but never to provoke. They stretch thinking with questions, not declarations:

- What would need to be true for this to scale?
- If this succeeds, what changes for your leadership team?
- Where do you feel uncertain, even if no one else is saying it?

Because they've earned credibility, their provocations land. They aren't threats; they're signals of commitment.

They Co-Create, Not Just Deliver

Rainmakers treat the client as a co-architect, not an audience. They replace polished presentations with working sessions. They use whiteboards, working drafts, and shared language. They pull insights from AI tools in real time to explore possibilities, not to overwhelm but to engage.

They know shared ownership builds belief. And belief is the fuel of trust.

They Stay Present After the Deliverable

When the project ends, most consultants move on. Rainmakers don't. They stay in touch. Not to pitch, just to stay connected. A short note. A useful article. A heads-up about something taking shape in the market. There's no agenda, just the sense that they still care.

Clients notice. Not because it's loud, but because it's rare. It feels real. And it tells them the relationship wasn't just about the work.

They Behave Like Trusted Insiders, Not External Experts

Rainmakers show up with a posture that says:

- I'm listening.
- I've thought this through.
- I'm here for your success, not my next contract.

They don't claim trust. They model it. And over time, that behavior earns them access that others never get.

Five Signals You've Reached Levels 4 or 5

A retired, highly successful consulting partner once said, "Trust doesn't show up in contracts. It shows up in quiet moments." Here's how you'll know when you're at Level 4 or 5.

- **They take your call after hours:** It's not about availability; it's about importance. Your voice carries weight, even outside of work hours.
- **They confide in you about what they don't know:** Uncertainty is rarely shared in formal settings. When clients admit their fears or doubts, you've created psychological safety.
- **They bring you into strategic decisions before the brief exists:** Being looped in early, even before there's scope, means you're part of the conversation, not just the execution.
- **They refer you without being asked:** An unprompted referral is a reputational risk. When clients stake their name on you, they're telling the world: "I trust this person."
- **They respect your time by trusting your judgment:** You're not micromanaged. You're given space because they know you'll speak up when needed and deliver without making a fuss.

The Waffle Referral

At this point, there's a story from Robert's time as a senior corporate executive that's worth sharing. It speaks directly to one of the points just mentioned, being referred without being asked. And it's a reminder that referrals can come from anywhere, often when you least expect them.

I was in Denver, Colorado, visiting a global contact center outsourcing company. It provided services from the Philippines, and I was there to learn more about their operations, to apply the insights gained to a corporate transformation program I was leading at the time.

The CEO of this business happened to be a close friend of one of the most successful and highest-paid media executives in the United States. This media executive had been aggressively acquiring companies across Europe and was now facing a massive challenge: how to consolidate operations, realize benefits, and build a new operating model at speed. The stakes were high. Failure wasn't an option.

The CEO asked if I'd be willing to meet with his friend while I was in town. I said yes. And early the next morning, in a local pancake parlor, I found myself sitting across from a stranger, eating waffles and drinking bottomless coffee.

I came prepared to share insights from both sides of the table, my corporate and consulting experiences. And I did get to share a few. But before long, he cut to the point.

"Who do you trust to get a job like this done?"

That was it. No slide decks. No methodology comparisons. No discussions about capability statements or daily rates. He didn't want options; he wanted a name. I gave him one.

We spent the rest of our breakfast talking about the meaning of trust, what shapes it, how it lasts, and how quickly it can be lost. I gave a few examples, not to persuade, just to be clear about my view. When we finished, we shook hands, and I flew home.

Months later, I heard he'd gone with the firm and the name that I'd suggested. Maybe their proposal was strong. Maybe the plan made sense.

But that's not what got the firm in the door; it was a warm referral from someone the client trusted. That alone was enough.

The Crucial Role of Trust in High-Stakes Moments

That breakfast in Denver was a rare encounter, a chance moment that opened an unexpected door. But many of the defining moments in a client–consultant relationship don't unfold over coffee or in calm conditions. They arrive during a crisis when reputations are on the line, when regulators are circling. When leadership is under siege and the path forward is unclear.

And in those moments, clients don't choose the flashiest deck or the loudest voice. They back the person they trust as someone operating at Level 4 or 5 in our trust model.

As we explored earlier, Mayer and coauthors found that when the stakes are high, trust hinges not just on competence but also on integrity and benevolence.[4] Clients need to believe two things: *You can do the job*, and *you're on their side*.

Kurt T. Dirks and Donald L. Ferrin demonstrated that trust accelerates decision making.[5] When the pressure mounts, it's trust that clears the fog and moves things forward. Elayne M. Whitener, Sue E. Brodt, Ann L. Korsgaard, and John M. Werner added a further layer: In sensitive environments, it's discretion and restraint, not dominance, that earns trust.[6]

Why does this understanding of trust matter? Because the biggest, boldest, most complex engagements don't go to the most innovative team. They go to the most trusted. When the heat is on. When the timeline is brutal. When the consequences are real.

Clients don't bet on charisma. They bet on character.

Rainmakers win these moments not with promises but by becoming the kind of branch clients can rely on—solid, seasoned, and steady under pressure. A visible extension of strength that can hold the weight when others falter.

That's what makes rainmakers indispensable.

Trust Travels—But It Doesn't Always Translate

The story you just read shows what strong trust can unlock. But there's a catch: Trust isn't one-size-fits-all. It depends on context. Culture, company, setting—Each shape how trust works.

For rainmakers, reading that context is part of the job.

In some places, trust comes through expertise and a strong track record. In others, it grows over time through shared meals, informal conversations, or simply being present.

What works in New York might feel out of place in Tokyo. What lands in São Paulo may miss entirely in Berlin.

The work is the same. The way you build trust isn't.

Trust is also layered within organizations. A midlevel sponsor might trust your judgment while a senior executive still sees you as a vendor. Or the CEO may value your advice but the project lead won't return your calls. Rainmakers know that access at one level does not guarantee access at all levels. You have to earn it, again and again, up and down the chain.

And then there's internal trust, the kind that lives inside your firm. Too often overlooked, it's one of the most critical enablers of rainmaker success. Why? Because your colleagues are your first clients. They're also your amplifiers, introducers, validators, and collaborators.

Key Insight: Many of the biggest, most transformative opportunities don't arrive in your inbox. They come through the trust you've earned with others, quietly, behind the scenes, when you're not in the room.

In the next section, we explore the cultural, structural, and interpersonal dimensions of trust. We look at how trust is built, broken, and rebuilt across geographies, hierarchies, and teams, and why the best rainmakers work just as hard to earn trust inside their firm as they do outside of it.

Cultural Differences in Trust in the Client–Consultant Relationship

In consulting, especially when selling to senior executives, understanding how trust is earned across cultures isn't a soft skill. It's a strategic imperative. Consultants often lean on the wrong things: polished slides, sharp frameworks, strong resumes. In many places, those are not what sets you apart. They are the starting point.

What makes the difference is trust. Not the kind built on contracts or credentials, the kind built in person, over time, with real attention. And that trust doesn't go to the smartest person in the room. It goes to the one who listens, who shows up, and who understands how things really work in that context.

Neil learned that firsthand in Brazil, so let's hear his story.

It was a warm, sticky evening in São Paulo. The churrascaria was buzzing, the scent of grilled picanha in the air. I was there to support a senior local partner on a significant opportunity, bringing global experience and capability to the table. At first glance, my role was to help lead the conversation.

But that changed quickly. "Selling consulting in Brazil," my colleague said over dinner, "isn't about credentials or clever ideas. It's about trust. And trust takes time."

The client, a sharp, reserved CEO of a leading financial institution, wasn't interested in slides or international case studies. He'd seen all of that. What he needed was someone who *got* him, his business, his people, and the unspoken pressures of his world. And that wasn't going to be me, not because I lacked expertise but because I hadn't earned that trust in his eyes.

My colleague had.

He didn't pitch. He didn't push. He listened. Asked the right questions. Took time to visit branches, speak with staff, and get close to how the business actually worked.

I stayed in the background, stepped in when needed, but never tried to lead. Because in that setting, I knew trust couldn't be handed over. It had to be earned, face to face.

Months later, in a quiet moment, the CEO looked at both of us and said: "Most consultants hand me a proposal. You gave me something better, you took the time to understand us."

That insight wasn't mine; it was my colleague's. And it was the product of patience, presence, and cultural fluency.

That experience changed the way I think about trust in consulting. In some markets, trust can't be flown in, no matter how strong your resume. It has to be earned, on the ground, over time.

Rainmakers know that the real differentiator isn't just what you know. It's what you understand and how deeply you've taken the time to do so. Because in high-stakes, cross-cultural consulting, trust doesn't follow the pitch. Trust *is* the pitch.

How Culture Shapes the Trust Equation

Across decades of research, Hofstede's Cultural Dimensions Theory remains a valuable entry point.[7] Two of Hofstede's dimensions are especially relevant:

1. **Individualism versus collectivism:** In individualistic cultures like the United States, the United Kingdom, Australia, or Germany, trust is professional, built on competence and delivery. Clients value directness, logic, and results. You earn trust through precision and performance. In collectivist cultures like Japan, Indonesia, or Saudi Arabia, trust is personal and slow growing. It hinges on relationships, loyalty, and social harmony. Rainmakers take the time to build rapport, show humility, and honor the group dynamic.
2. **High-context versus low-context communication:** In high-context environments, often found in East Asia or the Middle East, a lot of business is communicated implicitly. Meaning is embedded in tone, history, and relationship. Silence matters. Indirectness is respectful. In low-context cultures like the United States or Germany, trust is built through clarity. People expect structure, direct communication, and open debate.

Rainmakers learn to work across both settings. In high-context environments, they pay attention to what's not said, watch the dynamics, and avoid forcing the conversation. In low-context cultures, they're clear, organized, and quick to name issues before they grow.

Real-World Contrast: Same Client, Two Cultures

Neil once observed a global energy client with operations in Texas and Southeast Asia. In the United States, leadership expected direct advice, firm opinions, and fast decision making. They appreciated the challenge.

In Southeast Asia, that same company expected deference, careful relationship building, and reverence for hierarchy. Consultants who pushed too quickly lost credibility. Same client. Same strategy. Different trust currencies.

Rainmakers adapt. They:

- Lead with relationships in collectivist cultures.
- They are explicit and structured in low-context settings.
- Respect hierarchy and adjust when and how you challenge.
- Read nonverbal cues and subtext.
- Wait to offer solutions until trust is seeded.

They don't abandon who they are. But they flex how they build trust because they know that, in many cultures, how you show up is as important as what you bring.

Academic Backing: Why Cultural Sensitivity Builds Trust

Francis Fukuyama argued that in low-trust environments, personal relationships often outweigh contracts.[8] Fons Trompenaars and Charles Hampden-Turner demonstrated how ignoring norms erodes trust, even with good intentions.[9]

These insights are not theoretical. They're tools. Rainmakers use them with cultural humility and curiosity.

Bottom Line

Trust doesn't travel on autopilot. It must be grown in local soil.

Rainmakers understand that what builds trust in one setting may bruise it in another. So, they adapt, subtly, thoughtfully, and with deep respect for the cultural canopy they're operating under.

When you tune into your instincts, shift your stance, and honor the norms of the people around you, something powerful happens: You show respect. And respect, in every culture, is where trust begins.

Trust Building Across Different Client Levels

One of the most significant misunderstandings in consulting is the belief that trust is built the same way at every level of the client organization. It's not.

The board member. The CEO. The divisional or functional leader. The frontline project sponsor.

They all require trust, but the form, focus, and foundation of that trust vary wildly.

Rainmakers know this. They don't approach every client the same way. They read the room, listen between the lines, and adapt how they show up because what earns trust in one client may undermine it in another. (See Figure 19.2.)

However, there's a nuance: While there are apparent differences between the levels, there are also critical linkages. Trust building can't be reinvented for every layer. If it is, the consultant comes across as inconsistent, inauthentic, even false. And once trust erodes at one level, the erosion spreads. Rainmakers understand that trust must be tailored, not fractured.

Consistency of character is nonnegotiable. You can't be inspiring and strategic with the board, then detached and transactional with delivery leads. Nor can you show empathy and presence to functional

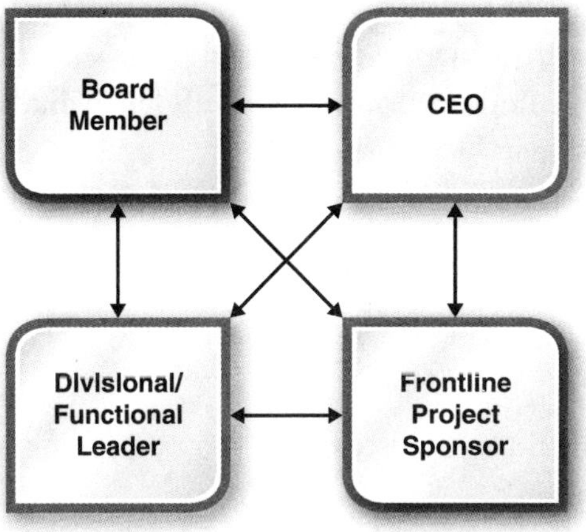

FIGURE 19.2 Trust building across different client levels.

heads while being overly theatrical or shallow with the C-suite. These fractures, often subtle, undermine credibility fast.

That's why rainmakers work deliberately across all levels to build trust in a way that is values-based, strategically attuned, and emotionally intelligent. They calibrate tone, depth, and emphasis, not values. They shift gears, not personas.

Rainmakers know trust doesn't flow in just one direction. It needs to hold across the organization, not just at the top but across teams and levels. The links between those people matter just as much as the titles.

Rainmakers adjust how they show up, not by changing who they are but by meeting each relationship on its own terms. Like shaping different branches to support the whole tree, they stay rooted while adapting their reach.

Let's look at how trust is built at each level and how rainmakers move with it.

Board-Level Trust: Strategic Insight, Gravitas, and Discretion Board members think in decades, not deliverables. They focus on governance, long-term performance, and existential risk. They don't want slides. They want a signal.

To earn trust here, rainmakers demonstrate strategic fluency, offer foresight beyond the obvious, and project judgment that can withstand scrutiny. Most of all, they exude calm confidence, like a sturdy limb of a tree that won't snap in a storm.

What builds trust at the board level?

- **Insight over information:** "Here's how your peers are preparing for AI and climate regulation—the issues boards are focused on."
- **Discretion:** Boards trust those who operate quietly and protect confidentiality.
- **Judgment** is demonstrated through thoughtful, balanced advice grounded in commercial and political awareness.

Rainmakers speak with brevity and weight. They educate, not pitch. They offer board education sessions with an expert on a relevant topic. They never outstay their welcome.

C-Suite Trust: Blending Strategic Alignment with Operational Relevance C-suite leaders live in tension between strategy and execution, vision and constraint. They want partners who can move seamlessly between the canopy and the roots.

Rainmakers build trust at this level by showing that they get the whole picture and the fine print.

What builds trust in the C-suite?

- **Contextual fluency:** Connecting business model, market forces, and internal dynamics
- **Presence in critical moments:** Showing up when the pressure peaks
- **Clarity in ambiguity:** Bringing simplicity to complex decisions without dumbing things down

Rainmakers bring frameworks, not just facts. They help leaders think, then act. They show, not tell, how others have worked through similar challenges and emerged stronger, providing real stories with tangible impact.

Functional Leader Trust: Practicality, Precision, and Empathy Functional heads shoulder the burden of execution. They are aware of the operational bottlenecks and political minefields. They don't want theory, they want traction.

What builds trust here?

- **Execution credibility:** "Have you done this in a business like ours?"
- **Co-creation:** Involving them in shaping the solution, not just receiving it
- **Respect for complexity:** Understanding that what looks simple on a whiteboard is rarely so in practice

Rainmakers empower, not override. They make the client the hero and themselves the trusted guide.

Project and Delivery Leads: Consistency, Responsiveness, and Psychological Safety Project managers often operate below the strategic spotlight, but their perceptions shape the client's overall experience. Win their trust, and you reinforce the whole ecosystem. Lose it, and the tree weakens at the base.

What builds trust with delivery teams?

- **Follow-through:** Keeping promises, big and small
- **Listening without defensiveness:** Valuing their voice in the feedback loop
- **Recognizing their success:** Building loyalty by acknowledging contributions

Rainmakers create safety and shared ownership. Delivery becomes not just execution but about education, transferring knowledge and skills, and coauthoring a story of success.

Most consultants miss this nuance because they default to a single style. They pitch the same way to a CEO and a project management office lead and wonder why trust doesn't take root.

Rainmakers are different. They calibrate.

They ask:

- What does this person care most about?
- What does trust *look like* in their world?
- How do I help them win, not just the project but in their role?

They treat trust building like arborists shaping a tree, knowing which branch to strengthen, which one to lighten, and how to help the whole system grow stronger.

Trust and Relationships with Colleagues: The Rainmaker's Secret Fertilizer Let's now turn our attention to the inside of the firm.

When people discuss trust in consulting, they typically focus on clients. But the truth is, no rainmaker thrives alone. The most influential consultants—those who lead complex transformations, shape industries, and unlock game-changing results—share a quiet but powerful truth: Brilliant collaboration with colleagues is often the secret fertilizer that nourishes the whole tree.

Internal trust isn't just a nice-to-have; it's what turns individual excellence into scalable impact. You can't win the firm's most significant opportunities on your own. You can't staff the best team, shape the sharpest pitch, or deliver at pace and scale without people who want to work with you, not because they have to but because they trust you. Because they know you'll show up, speak up, share credit, and do what it takes.

These internal relationships may take different forms. Sometimes the trust is built, as with a colleague you'd go to war with. At other times, the respect is earned: a mutual understanding of high standards, even if the personal connection is slight. Both matter. Both work.

Rainmakers recognize that not every relationship needs to be the same. Some are forged in fire. Others, in quiet consistency. Nuance is part of the terrain.

That nuance reflects the nature of consulting itself. Consulting is not a conventional workplace. It's fast, fluid, and fiercely individual. It's competitive and collaborative. Short-term sprints and long-term partnerships. Local hustle and global scale. You can work side by side for 18 hours straight one week, then not again for six months. You might pitch with someone in Singapore, coauthor a report with someone in Stockholm, and deliver with a team in Sydney, all in the same quarter.

And yet alignment is expected. That's the paradox. We operate in an environment that's structurally fragmented but culturally high performing. There are a few rules, but the standards are high; few formal hierarchies, but enormous pressure. Trust here's not institutional; it's personal. It must be earned, expressed, and constantly renewed.

Rainmakers don't leave internal relationship building to chance. They put in the time. They check in on their people, not just their output. They respond to requests promptly. They learn how others work and flex accordingly. They reach out, curious to learn from others, especially the ones they don't know well. They say thank you. They show up on camera. They follow up. These are small acts, but they compound into something powerful: belief. And when belief is mutual, when the chemistry is right, the values are shared, and the ambition is collective, the results are extraordinary.

Because when your internal ecosystem is rich with trust, generosity, and mutual belief, it's not just the rainmaker who grows. It's the whole tree.

Building New Executive Relationships Despite their strong focus on relationships and connection, even rainmakers face situations where they need to build rapport with a senior executive they do not yet know. This may involve a newly appointed CEO or CXO at an existing client, someone who has joined the firm another market or industry. It could be the CEO of a target account where the firm has had no prior presence or the leader of a company in another market where the rainmaker is supporting the local firm on a significant opportunity.

In each case, rainmakers need the same skill and judgment to develop a trusted relationship.

Questions to consider include:

- Who do I or my firm know who could make an introduction?
- Does an alliance partner have a strong relationship that I can leverage?
- What value can I provide that demonstrates immediate relevance or impact?
- Is there a meaningful way to get in front of this person, perhaps through research or another contribution I am involved in?
- Can I invite this person to a bespoke firm event with peers from other organizations to help build a connection?

There is no selling involved in these interactions. The purpose is to build connection and trust. Importantly, developing these relationships also requires a genuine level of personal investment.

Conclusion: Trust Sets You Apart

In consulting, plenty can be copied: the models, the language, even the way ideas are pitched. But trust can't be copied. That has to be earned. And it can't be faked.

Trust is the ultimate differentiator. It gives you access to the conversations that matter most. It opens doors to the most strategic projects. It allows you to say what needs to be said, not just what the client wants to hear. And most important, it binds your value not to what you do but to who you are in the eyes of your client: a partner, not a provider.

Rainmakers know this. They don't just build trust; they embody it. Every interaction, every promise kept, every difficult conversation navigated with care becomes part of a larger trust narrative. One that positions them not as interchangeable consultants but as indispensable allies.

For rainmakers, trust is not hidden underground or locked within; it is one of their visible, outward-facing branches or strategies. Alongside hunting with precision, creating unmatched value, and mastering the routine of success, it reaches out into the world. It's where others see the difference, where clients feel it. And where trustworthy reputations are formed.

If value gets you in the room, trust keeps you there. If insight earns the contract, trust earns the relationship. If capability wins the work, trust wins the future. And when your clients face moments of risk, crisis, transformation, or opportunity, they'll turn not to the best-decorated pitch or the cheapest bid but to the person they trust. The person who has walked beside them, not just ahead. That's what it means to be a trusted advisor. That's what it means to be a rainmaker.

But rainmakers don't rise to the top by chance.

While precision hunting, unmatched value, and forged trust are critical, it's the daily discipline, the habits, rhythms, and routines that turn talent into consistency and potential into performance.

Next: Systematizing Success

In the next chapter, which covers the final outward-facing branch that differentiates rainmakers, we explore how the most successful consultants systematize their success. You'll discover the behind-the-scenes practices rainmakers use to stay focused, build their pipeline, deepen relationships, and show up at their best, every single day. Because in the end, it's not just what you know or even who you know.

It's what you do repeatedly that defines your trajectory.

Let's get started.

CHAPTER

20

Mastering the Routine of Success

Discipline and Routine Separate Occasional Wins from Sustained Success Year After Year

In consulting, success doesn't rest on one brilliant idea or the occasional big win. It comes from what you do every single day. Routines and habits aren't optional extras; they're the basis of a rainmaker's career. Without them, you might manage to get by, but you won't stand out, and you certainly won't lead.

Top performers across every field understand this. The late Phil Walsh, the much-respected Australian Rules football coach, put it plainly: *Success doesn't come looking for you. You've got to chase it, and as a team the only way to do that is through hard work and elite habits.*

His message was as sharp as it was simple. Natural talent will take you only so far; the real difference lies in the discipline of daily actions. In sport, the champions aren't always the most gifted athletes but the ones who turn consistent habits into unstoppable progress.

The pattern repeats in other professions. Surgeons don't enter an operating room without carefully practiced rituals. Soldiers drill until their responses under pressure are instinctive. Leading trial lawyers refine their arguments again and again until delivery feels effortless. What looks like confidence on the surface is, in truth, the product of hard-wired routines.

What has changed is the speed and intensity of the environment in which those routines now operate. AI is accelerating every aspect of consulting: how clients gather information, how quickly they form views, and how rapidly they expect results. Decision cycles are shorter. Expectations for impact are higher. Personalization is no longer a differentiator but a baseline, delivered at scale through technology. In this environment, weak or inconsistent habits are exposed quickly. Strong habits, by contrast, become a multiplier, enabling rainmakers to keep pace, cut through noise, and consistently show up with relevance, precision, and trust.

In this faster, more demanding environment, rainmakers rely on these same disciplines, but with greater intent and consistency than ever. Their edge doesn't come from a single burst of effort but from steady disciplines: writing sharp notes each morning before client meetings, setting aside time each week to review their pipeline, rehearsing stories until they sound natural, and following through on every commitment without fail. Over time, these routines create momentum, reputation, and trust.

In Chapter 19, Robert showed how rainmakers earn trust that lasts when the pressure is on. Here we focus on where habits form. This is about the daily practices that shape consulting careers quietly but decisively. About the routines that separate those who level off from those who grow into rainmakers.

The Monday Morning Rainmaker

Let Neil begin with a story he has shared with his team many times, one that shows what happens when routine and discipline become the real engine of success.

It was 7:30 a.m. on a Monday morning, and I found myself at a small café tucked around the corner from one of our biggest clients. I wasn't there for a meeting—at least, not officially. I was there to observe someone who was.

His name was Alex, and he was a senior partner in a global consulting firm.

Every Monday, without fail, he'd be there. Same table. Same long black. Laptop open. Earbuds in. And for the next three hours, he wasn't just working, he was orchestrating. Tapping out emails. Following up with clients. Making a few well-placed phone calls. And just as important, greeting familiar client faces as they came through the door.

Alex wasn't the loudest or flashiest person in his firm. But year after year, quarter after quarter, he delivered five to 10 times more work than his peers. He knew where to focus his time and how to earn the confidence of senior-level executives in his sector. His results—client impact and profitable revenues—were outstanding. But the real secret wasn't just *what* he did; it was *how* he did it.

His edge wasn't built on charisma or hustle. It was built on structure. On rhythm. On a routine so precise, so intentional, that it became a flywheel for performance.

Alex made a habit of staying close to his clients. He didn't spend time caught up in internal calls or chasing distractions. He was out in the field, where the real work happened.

He didn't choose that café at random. It was where his clients worked, passed through, or stopped for coffee. It gave him a place to listen, to catch things early, to stay in step with what was going on.

There was no performance to it. Just consistency. Every Monday, no matter what other things were going on in his firm, he showed up to reset, to listen, and to stay focused on the work that made the difference: building connection, one conversation at a time.

Alex's routine was simple, but it ran deep. He understood something a lot of people miss: that consistent performance doesn't come from talent alone. It comes from structure. From habits repeated over time, until they become second nature. Every Monday he followed the same rhythm. Same place. Same time. It gave him space to think, reconnect, and get ahead of what mattered. It worked.

That routine built confidence. It kept him close to his clients. It gave him room to think clearly and act early. And, over time, it made his business stable, focused, and less reactive—and very successful.

Routine is often what separates high performers. Not big moments but quiet discipline. They don't rely on bursts of inspiration. They rely on rhythm.

In this chapter, we take a closer look at that kind of rhythm, not as a productivity tool but as a way to stay sharp, steady, and ready for the work that matters.

We explore the three essentials to mastering that routine: the what, the why, and the how. (See Figure 20.1.)

1. **The what:** Time. It's the most limited, valuable, and misused asset in consulting. We examine what top performers do with their time and how they structure their weeks to prioritize what matters most.
2. **The why:** The science. We unpack the behavioral and psychological foundations behind habits, why routines stick, how they shape identity, and what research tells us about building high-performance behaviors.
3. **The how:** The actual routines that rainmakers follow including how the smartest ones are now using AI to sharpen, accelerate, and extend their edge.

This strategy is one of the stronger branches of the rainmaker's tree, a branch that endures year after year and provides support and

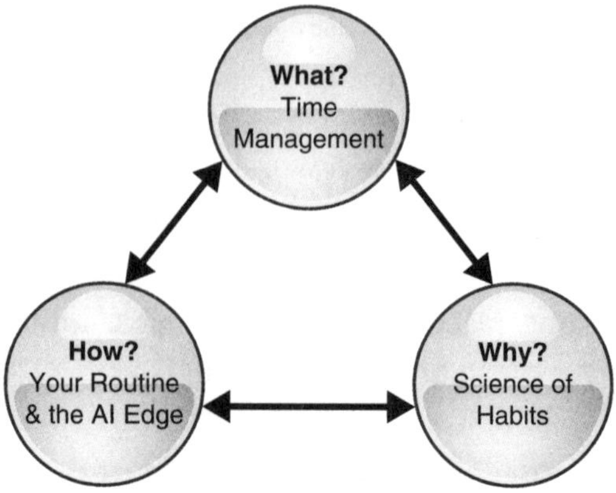

FIGURE 20.1 Three essentials to mastering the routine of success.

growth for the other three branches. Without it, even the most promising strategies can falter. With it, business development becomes not just stronger but scalable and sustainable.

Essential #1: Time Management—Rainmakers' Most Valuable Asset

For rainmakers, time isn't just a resource; it's capital. How they spend it is a direct reflection of what they value, and ultimately, a predictor of the results they generate.

> **Key Insight:** Across our research and experience, we've observed a pattern in how rainmakers structure their weeks. Their calendars aren't just filled; they're designed.

Each category of activity they invest in serves a distinct purpose: to deliver results today, build opportunity for tomorrow, and elevate the firm's overall performance. Let's break down how this plays out.

Direct Project Delivery to Clients (40% of Time/~30% of Firm Value)

Rainmakers don't build success by stepping away from the work. They stay involved. Roughly 40% of their time goes into delivery, not because they must do client delivery, but because it matters to relationships. Delivering client assignments is where trust is reinforced, relationships grow, and credibility holds up over time. It's not about control. It's a choice.

Rainmakers know their value comes from being close enough to see what's changing—and to shape it. When senior clients no longer see them as active or original, the relationship starts to slip.

In long engagements, there's a risk: Clients begin to wonder if their advisor has anything new to offer. Once that doubt sets in, confidence is hard to recover.

Rainmakers manage this risk proactively. They bring fresh thinking to the table, regularly introduce new subject matter experts, and keep their teams energized. They're deliberate about refreshing the consulting bench, not as a reactive reshuffle but as a planned rotation that signals strength. Consultants working on long-term projects can lose motivation or request transfers. Rainmakers anticipate this and create developmental pathways, so team members take on greater responsibility and feel they're growing, not stagnating.

This approach is a delicate balancing act with clients. Some may begin to treat rainmakers as default providers for every minor need, from strategic issues to staffing a junior analyst. Accepting low-value work might keep revenue ticking, but it erodes your brand and burns out your best people. Rainmakers hold the line. They tactfully decline requests that don't align with their value model and, where appropriate, redirect them to internal client resources or labor hire firms.

This commitment to delivery doesn't limit a rainmaker's impact; it amplifies it. Being in the field is what keeps them sharp, relevant, and able to spot the next big opportunity.

Pursuing New Work with Existing or New Clients (20% of Time/~30% of Firm Value)

Business development is essential, but rainmakers approach it with precision, not volume. Around 20% of their time is allocated to generating new work. Much of this has already been explored in previous chapters, particularly about the principles of *hunting with precision*. Rather than rehash those insights here, this time is where new mandates begin, pipelines are built, and strategic relationships are activated.

Key Insight: Building a sales pipeline is not about chasing new leads; it's about converting existing momentum.

Maintaining Relationships and Market Knowledge (15% of Time/0% Direct Value, High Strategic Importance)

The category of maintaining relationships and market knowledge is the most misunderstood. It contributes no immediate revenue, but its strategic value is enormous because it underpins everything else.

Approximately 15% of a rainmaker's week is dedicated to maintaining what we refer to as *base relationships*. These aren't always people rainmakers know well or ones they'd naturally connect with. Rainmakers may barely know some of these people at all but they have one thing in common: They're able to become future buyers of the rainmaker's work.

These relationships usually fall into a few groups:

- Trusted collaborators from past successful projects, akin to teammates who've won a championship together. There's a shared memory of success and a lasting sense of loyalty.
- Former clients who've moved to new roles or companies (often these clients become the rainmaker's best future clients).

- Professional acquaintances in adjacent spheres, private equity leaders, bankers, technologists, lawyers, and search firm leaders, people who may not hire rainmakers directly but can refer or recommend them.
- Internal firm specialists, those with deep networks or niche expertise who can bring rainmakers into opportunities.
- Alumni, past colleagues who know a rainmaker's work and may now be in buying roles or on their way there.

Rainmakers maintain these connections with intention and efficiency. They don't overinvest time, but they also don't neglect it. They utilize tools ranging from smart customer relationship management processes (CRMs) to quarterly check-ins and curated article sharing to stay on the radar in a no-intrusive, value-adding way.

This 15% is also the time rainmakers spend tending to the soil and keeping their knowledge sharp. They monitor trends in their industry, new developments in their service offerings, and broader transformation themes. They follow signals that indicate future demand, often before the market recognizes it. It's quiet work, but it makes them the first call when the moment arrives.

Firm Collaboration and Specialist Support (25% of Time/~40% of Firm Value)

The final 25% of rainmakers' time may not appear on a profit and loss sheet, but it multiplies their impact across the firm. This is where rainmakers support colleagues in other industries, geographies, or service lines, extending the reach of their expertise beyond the borders of a single engagement.

This work takes many forms:

- Roadshow presentations sharing insights from successful projects
- Development of intellectual property, such as methodologies, processes, tools, and playbooks

- Writing thought pieces or contributing to client publications
- Acting as a subject matter expert in pitches or client meetings
- Helping other partners develop winning strategies for large bids
- Coaching younger consultants in the art of selling and delivery
- Coordinating references, testimonials, or case studies

This work is catalytic. One successful project, when shared and amplified throughout the firm, can generate 10 times its initial value. For every $10 million earned in the initial engagement, a rainmaker's structured collaboration can unlock $100 million in related revenue across the firm globally.

Rainmakers understand this leverage instinctively. They don't just think about *their* book of business. They consider how their success can benefit the firm.

A Designed Week

This breakdown isn't just a calendar; it's a deliberate structure. Meetings, calls, and focus blocks all serve a purpose, whether that's building relationships, driving revenue, or making space to think.

Key Insight: Rainmakers don't drift through their weeks. They shape them, using time with intent.

Having a structured week isn't just about winning work. It's about using time well and doing it week after week.

We share more on the practical habits and routines of rainmakers shortly, including the role of AI platforms, engines, or models. However, let's take a step back and ground ourselves in the crucial behavioral science behind habit formation and how to make good habits stick.

Essential #2: The Science Behind Habits and Routine: Why Routines Matter More than Talent

In consulting, sustained success doesn't come from flashes of brilliance. It comes from rhythm, from the things you do repeatedly, even when no one's watching. Yet consulting education rarely teaches this. We focus on how to analyze markets, manage clients, or deliver strategies. However, we seldom teach how to build a system to accomplish these tasks every week at a high level.

Top performers know excellence is not an act. It's a habit.

How Habits Are Formed in the Brain

The brain craves efficiency. That's why it defaults to habit wherever possible to conserve energy and attention. At the core of this mechanism is the basal ganglia, the part of the brain that turns repeated actions into automatic behaviors.[1] It's what allows people to drive home without remembering each turn or to brush their teeth without thinking.

In consulting, having great client related habits is powerful. When rainmakers build muscle memory around business development, like following up with clients or blocking time for deep work, they remove resistance. Those actions become second nature.

A 2010 study found that, on average, it takes about 66 days for a new behavior to become automatic.[2] The process is faster and the habit is more likely to stick when it connects to something meaningful or feels rewarding.

Key Insight: Start small. What matters most is doing a small BD habit regularly. Ten quiet minutes a day gets you further than a perfect plan that never happens.

Systems Beat Willpower: The Behavioral Design Advantage

B. J. Fogg, from Stanford's Behavior Design Lab, offers a powerful framework: Prompt → Behavior → Reward

- **Prompt:** Your first coffee of the day.
- **Behavior:** Send two short prospecting notes.
- **Reward:** Tick them off your list (or better, see them lead to conversations).

Fogg champions "habit stacking"—attaching new habits to existing routines.[3]

Examples from rainmakers:

- After the stand-up meeting → Send a check-in email.
- Friday, 4 p.m. → Pipeline review and priority setting.
- End of day → Prep tomorrow's client insights.

Rainmakers don't always call what they do habit stacking. But they live it. Their calendars, environments, and rhythms are full of embedded cues that reduce friction and increase follow-through.

Small Wins Compound Into Big Results

James Clear makes a simple point in his book *Atomic Habits*[4]:

You don't succeed because of your goals. You succeed because of the systems you follow each day.

Rainmakers succeed because their systems are strong and consistent. One client check-in. One prospect call. One protected hour of strategic thinking. Done daily, these small actions don't just add up; they multiply.

The compounding effect of 1% improvement every day is exponential. This compounding effect is the invisible engine behind big pipelines, deep client trust, and million-dollar practices.

Mason Currey's Creative Case for Routine

Mason Currey's *Daily Rituals: How Artists Work* offers a striking parallel from the creative world that reinforces what science reveals about habit and high performance.[5]

Through his profiles of 161 accomplished artists, writers, and thinkers, Currey shows that sustained creative output rarely comes from divine inspiration or chaotic bursts of brilliance. Instead, it comes from intentional routines, often mundane, sometimes rigid, but always consistent. Beethoven composed after his precise coffee ritual. Maya Angelou wrote in the same sparse hotel room, away from distraction. These routines weren't glamorous; they were grounding. They gave structure to uncertainty and built reliability into inherently unpredictable work.

What Currey's work confirms, and what consulting often overlooks, is that excellence across disciplines isn't about motivation. It's about rhythm. Like top consultants, top creatives didn't wait for ideal conditions. They designed systems that made starting automatic and momentum inevitable. Their routines acted as cues, a way to get into the work. Different setting, same idea. Like a rainmaker's calendar or quiet follow-up after a meeting, this approach wasn't about habit for its own sake.

This discipline was about making it easier to start and to do the work well, again and again.

The Environment as a Catalyst

More than 40% of our actions, according to research by Wendy Wood and David Neal, are shaped not by decision making but by the environment.[6]

Alex's Monday routine worked because the space worked. That café helped him focus. It gave him a clear start, kept him close to his clients, and marked a shift in pace from the rest of the week. None of that was accidental.

> **Key Insight:** If you want better routines, start by looking at your surroundings. Where you work affects how you work.

A whiteboard in view. A blocked-out hour that doesn't move. A space you go to for a specific kind of thinking. Simple changes like these can make a routine stick. Many rainmakers we've spoken to are using AI-powered tools, such as:

- Calendar assistants that automatically block time for high-focus work.
- Knowledge tools that surface forgotten client insights when needed.
- Meeting transcription services that capture conversations and highlight follow-up items.

These tools don't replace routines. They protect them.

That's the quiet power of rainmakers. They don't decide whether to work on their pipeline. The decision was already made last month when they built the system.

Myth Busting: "I'll Do It When I Have Time"

In consulting, you never "have time"; your calendar devours it. Rainmakers don't wait for free space. They create it. Business development is like a client meeting: the same discipline, the same respect. Not as an afterthought. As a foundation.

The real benefit? Peace of mind. Yes, routine delivers results. But it also provides stability. You don't panic when a project comes to an end. You don't panic when the pipeline slows because you've kept showing up, even when things were busy.

Routine doesn't just drive results. It creates stability.

Essential #3: The Rainmaker's Routine and the AI Edge: The Tasks and Activities of Rainmakers

Every rainmaker has their rhythm, but their routines share common DNA:

- **Daily client moments:** Insightful check-ins, thoughtful thank-you notes, or tailored article shares
- **Weekly pipeline reviews:** Friday afternoon or Monday morning ritualized time to assess, prioritize, and act
- **Strategic thinking blocks:** Time protected for proposal design, shaping pursuits, or exploring new industries
- **Monthly growth cadence:** Coffee with dormant clients, reconnecting with industry connectors, revisiting old proposals

But these routines aren't habits by accident. They're engineered. Rainmakers treat these rituals as nonnegotiables, and often protect them with the same seriousness as a boardroom presentation. They know sales isn't the work that follows the work. It is the work.

Where AI Gives Rainmakers an Edge—Right Now

AI is rapidly becoming a copilot for the modern rainmaker, especially in the areas of prospecting, creating value, and trust building.

Prospecting

- **AI-driven list building:** Platforms that draw on firmographic and demographic data to identify and prioritize high-fit targets.
- **AI-assisted networking:** Tools that help generate tailored outreach messages for each connection.
- **AI research assistants:** Systems that quickly scan public or proprietary data to prepare for outreach and client conversations.

In Part I of this book, we explored the *soil of a rainmaker*, the ground where every opportunity begins. That soil is shaped by context: the market, the industry, the company, and the individual decision makers you serve. Today, AI can help us read that soil faster, deeper, and with more precision.

In our research, we've seen many examples of consultants using AI to prepare for high-stakes client meetings. But one example has stayed with us.

It's early morning in Singapore. The air is heavy. The city is already moving. John steps off a long-haul flight from Los Angeles—tie in place, shoes clean, fully switched on.

He works in merger and acquisitions integration and has been flown in for a critical meeting. The client is important, the opportunity significant. His team has spent months laying the groundwork. But this is John's first time in the room.

In the hotel lounge, coffee in hand, he opens his tablet. The night before, his AI assistant had gone to work, scanning investor briefings, media coverage, Glassdoor reviews, LinkedIn activity, and even podcast transcripts. But it didn't stop at business. The AI surfaced that the CEO's daughter had just started university in Boston. He recently spoke at a conference on sustainability, saying he's a Manchester United fan who vacations in Bhutan.

That morning, John didn't just walk into a meeting with market insights. He walked in with context, warmth, and relevance. He didn't pitch. He connected. And that changed everything.

The key habit illustrated in this story is to prepare for connection, not just content. John's routine wasn't just about reviewing the company's strategy deck or latest earnings. It involved using AI deliberately and consistently to create relational content before the meeting. You can embed this practice into your weekly rhythm as a repeatable, high-impact habit before any vital client or prospect meeting. And the result? Much higher rapport, deeper engagement.

Creating Value

- **Proposal accelerators:** Rainmakers are using AI writing platforms to generate first drafts of thought pieces or concept documents, allowing them to refine instead of starting from scratch.
- **Custom AI assistants:** Trained on firm-specific knowledge, these systems instantly surface relevant case studies, thought leadership, or client impact stories.

In our research, we've seen a quiet arms race unfolding, not in delivery but in how firms *create value before the sale*. And what stood out most wasn't just what individuals were doing but how entire firms are moving to institutionalize it.

One global investment bank has publicly stated that it has started building its own AI tools, trained on internal deal history, past pitches, and sector insights. The goal is to help teams create client proposals and analysis faster, in hours instead of days.

Microsoft enables this approach in Dynamics 365, where sales teams can use Copilot to draft value propositions and access firmwide knowledge via simple prompts.[7]

Google isn't far behind, equipping its sales teams with Gemini to co-create strategic proposals, map solution architectures, and even suggest use-case bundles based on client industry data.[8]

They're not alone. McKinsey is training bespoke GPTs on internal playbooks. Salesforce is embedding generative AI across its global growth team. Accenture has 40,000 consultants using AI-powered content generators for pursuits.

This isn't about automation. It's about amplification. And the firms that get there first? They're not just speeding up proposals. They're accelerating trust.

The key habit from this evolution is to systematize value creation before the first meeting. Leading firms are not waiting until the client is "ready to talk." They've built a routine discipline of preparing, shaping, and tailoring value early, with speed, relevance, and precision. You can adopt this rainmaker habit with a repeatable prepursuit ritual as soon as a qualified opportunity emerges or a primary pursuit begins.

Trust Building

- **Meeting assistants:** AI-powered services that transcribe discussions, generate summaries, identify action items, and even suggest follow-ups.
- **AI memory tools:** Systems that automatically surface relevant past notes before a client call, helping rainmakers reenter the relationship with context and care.

Among the many high performers we've spoken to, one senior partner at a global consulting firm put this principle simply: Trust doesn't come from what you say. It comes from *how you act given what you know, and what you should know*.

That's why his team has adopted a new rhythm that blends AI into the art of relationship management.

Every Monday, before their client check-in calls, team members receive a brief autogenerated summary from their AI agent. It draws from past meeting transcripts, old proposals, and even internal email exchanges, surfacing key themes, personal preferences, recent decisions, and action items from months earlier. One note reminds them that the CFO prefers visuals over bullet points. Another flag is that the head of transformation recently returned from maternity leave.

Then, during the call, their AI agent listens silently in the background, transcribing in real time, identifying follow-ups, and syncing outcomes directly into their CRM. No scribbled notes. No "What did we promise?" moments.

The result? Every client interaction starts from context. It feels personal. This isn't a tech trick. It's a habit. And it's making these rainmakers not just remembered but relied on.

Where AI Is Heading—Tomorrow's Consulting Edge

We're only at the beginning of the AI-enabled world. The next wave will further enhance rainmakers' ability to build trust and scale relevance:

- **Emotion-aware AI:** Voice analysis detecting client hesitation or sentiment, flagging follow-up opportunities

- **Contextual client models:** Persistent "client copilots" trained on your interactions, preferences, and business model, helping prep every meeting
- **AI-powered whitespace mapping:** Algorithms identifying unmet client needs based on industry movements, public filings, and behavioral cues

These scenarios are not science fiction. They're early stage, already in pilot at some leading firms.

But here's the key: AI is not replacing rainmakers. It's freeing them to be more human. More present. More thoughtful. More precise.

Practical Tip: Your AI-Augmented Weekly Routine

- Monday: AI-powered pipeline analysis and weekly targeting.
- Tuesday: Use AI platform to personalize insights for five key prospects.
- Wednesday: Deep work on pursuit design, AI cowriting deck narratives.
- Thursday: Client meetings recorded and summarized via AI.
- Friday: Review wins and misses—prompt AI to suggest three improvements.

Over time, this routine becomes a rhythm. Not "digital busywork" but augmentation with purpose.

Conclusion: Rhythm Is the Hidden Engine

Rainmakers don't just rely on ambition or charisma. They rely on systems. On rhythm. On a routine that compounds. And now, with the right AI tools, they scale their strengths further than ever before. Because in the end, it's not who works hardest that wins. It's those who work intelligently. Repeatedly. Relentlessly. Systematically.

Next: Bringing It All Together

By now you'll have a long list of ideas and actions to consider. Chapter 21 will help you build an actionable guide to embedding everything you've learned into your rhythm, your relationships, and your results. This is where you take the next step in your career.

Let's take that step.

PART

IV

SUMMARY

The Branches

Over the last five chapters, we've examined the four outward-facing strategies that rainmakers rely on to grow their impact, much like branches extending from a strong trunk. These strategies aren't standalone moves; they're interconnected, flexible, and often reinforce one another in practice.

Together, they reveal eight enduring truths:

1. **Rainmakers don't rely on luck; they build systems.** What sets top performers apart isn't chance or charm. It's a deliberate, repeatable system that drives consistent results.
2. **Precision beats volume in high-value consulting.** Rainmakers don't chase everything. They focus on the right clients, at the right time, with the right message, and win more by doing less, better.
3. **Rainmaker value creation is proactive, not reactive.** Rainmakers don't wait to be asked. They deliver sharp, relevant insights that solve unseen problems and shift how clients think.
4. **Trust isn't a by-product; it's a strategy.** Long-term success is built on reliability, integrity, and presence. Rainmakers cultivate trust deliberately, and it compounds into influence and opportunity.

5. **Every rainmaker has a rhythm.** They don't operate on inspiration alone. They follow disciplined, elite routines that sustain momentum, even when energy or motivation dips.
6. **Rainmakers execute all four strategies, not just their areas of strength.** Excellence comes from integration. Hunting, value creation, trust-building, and routine are not optional; they are mutually reinforcing.
7. **Rainmakers are strategic with their time and intentional with their actions.** Their calendars reflect their priorities. Their habits shape their outcomes. They don't "find time" for growth; they make it.
8. **The difference between good and great is consistency.** Rainmakers win because they show up with clarity, value, and follow-through again and again. Consistency builds a compounding advantage.

Review Questions for Potential Rainmakers

1. What is my recent win-loss record, and how do I rate my hunting with precision performance? Do I need to adjust my qualification model?
2. What is my assessment of recent client activity against the six levels of unmatched value?
3. How many of the 12 key sources of opportunity am I currently using? Do I need to adjust?
4. What was my value generated in completed engagements?
5. How do I assess my key client relationships in terms of the trust framework?
6. Are my routines working? Am I utilizing them all the time?
7. What does my total time allocation look like? Do I need to adjust?

Where to Go from Here

You've been immersed in the soil, seen the roots, and climbed the trunk. Stretched into the branches. Now we turn our gaze upward. This is where the results start to show.

The canopy and the fruit are what others finally see. They reflect the work done beneath the surface, the trust earned, the value created, the results delivered. And they don't go unnoticed. They draw people in. They create movement. They lead to new conversations. This is what a rainmaker builds over time: a strong practice, deep client partnerships, and a reputation for results.

But here's the twist: This isn't the end. It's just the beginning of a new cycle.

Like a healthy forest, the rainmaker's success doesn't just grow upward; it feeds everything below. The fruit of your efforts seeds new opportunities. The shade you've earned gives others space to grow. And the insights you generate replenish your foundation, making you even stronger the next season.

So, where to go from here? Next, we step into action.

We show you how to bring everything together—mindset, attributes, strategies, habits, and systems—into a blueprint you can live and lead by. One that sustains growth. Sharpens focus. And helps you show up, every day, like a rainmaker.

Let's build your canopy. Let's share your fruit. Let's keep growing.

PART

V

The Canopy and Fruit

Visible Outcomes

CHAPTER

21

The Rainmaker Blueprint: Bringing It All Together

How to Build a Way of Working That Delivers Fulfillment Across Your Career

It's one thing to be inspired.

It's another to be equipped.

Across this book, we've climbed the full height of the rainmaker's tree, step by step, layer by layer, understanding not just what rainmakers do but why they do it and how they hold it together under pressure.

We began in the soil. The shifting environment. The forces shaping the profession and the market for professional services. Rainmakers don't ignore this context; they read it, adapt to it, and position themselves within it. They identify more opportunities and bigger opportunities than average consultants.

We then moved into the roots—identity, purpose, resilience, and ethics. The deeper forces that anchor performance and give it meaning over time.

From there, we built the trunk—the 12 attributes that allow a rainmaker to stand tall when expectations are high and the stakes are real.

And finally, we stepped out along the branches, exploring the four key strategies that rainmakers use to turn potential into winning—how rainmakers convert opportunities, create value, earn trust, and sustain momentum through disciplined routines.

Now we reach the canopy. This is where it all comes together. Where effort becomes visible. Where ideas turn into outcomes.

Where relationships deepen into connection and connection converts into meaningful work.

But this is not an endpoint.

A canopy does more than display growth; it sustains it. The energy it captures feeds the entire system beneath it. In the same way, the outcomes you create as a rainmaker don't just sit on the surface; they reinforce your foundations, expand your reach, and shape the next phase of your journey.

And the fruit? It represents something far more meaningful than success in the conventional sense. Not deliverables. Not presentations. Not plans. Those are inputs.

The fruit is impact. It is momentum inside the client organization. It is capability that remains long after you've stepped away. It is confidence in leadership, clarity in direction, and performance that endures.

It is the visible difference between where a client once stood and where they now stand because of the work you helped shape.

That is the work of a rainmaker.

This chapter is the start of your blueprint—a practical system for embedding everything you've learned into how you operate: your rhythm, your relationships, your decision making, and, ultimately, your results.

Because inspiration, on its own, fades. What matters is integration. What matters is what you do next.

Just like a tree exposed to changing seasons, shifting climates, and unexpected storms, the work of a rainmaker is never finished. It evolves, it adapts, and it renews.

So, let's move from insight to action—and from action to lasting impact.

What Rainmakers Actually Change

Rainmakers don't just win work.

They change the trajectory of organizations, often in ways that are both immediate and enduring. Their impact shows up across four dimensions—direction, momentum, growth, and strength.

Direction—Where the Business Is Going

- Rainmakers bring strategic clarity to complexity, reframing challenges in a way that opens new paths forward, paths that leadership teams often sense but haven't yet articulated.
- Rainmakers give clients the confidence to make critical decisions grounded in evidence, insight, and alignment across stakeholders.

Momentum—How Fast the Organization Moves

- Rainmakers accelerate execution, helping organizations move faster on what matters most, with sharper focus and greater cohesion.
- Rainmakers also shift mindset, moving cultures from cautious to confident, from reactive to proactive, and from incremental thinking to transformative action.

Growth—How the Organization Expands

- Rainmakers unlock new avenues for growth like new markets, new partnerships, new capabilities.
- Rainmakers elevate the customer experience in ways that build trust, loyalty, and advocacy, turning clients and customers into long-term champions.

Strength—How the Organization Endures

- Rainmakers drive sustained improvements in financial performance (e.g., revenue, productivity, margin).
- Rainmakers strengthen the balance sheet through smarter capital allocation and strategic choices.
- Rainmakers anticipate and neutralize risk, and, in some cases, help convert it into opportunity.
- Critically, rainmakers leave behind stronger, more capable teams who can continue the work without them.

These are not short-term wins. They are outcomes that last.

They are the true markers of rainmaking: the visible, measurable impact that proves the work mattered.

And they sit at the heart of a rainmaker's higher purpose.

Success, From the Inside Out

This work is not only external. At a deeper level, these outcomes contribute to something more enduring: legacy. The change you leave behind in your clients. The contribution you make to your firm. The influence you have on the profession itself.

And none of this happens without a commitment to excellence. Not perfectionism. Not performance for recognition.

But a quiet, consistent pursuit of high standards especially when no one is watching.

At a personal level, success takes on a broader meaning. It is not just about winning work or building a reputation. It is about fulfillment, living your purpose through what you do.

It shows up in four ways:

1. **Meaning:** A career that matters. Work that is grounded in values and contribution, where you can see the difference you are making.
2. **Pipeline:** A sustainable engine of opportunity, built on trust, relationships, and your ability to create value in any market conditions.
3. **Longevity:** Continued relevance in a competitive profession, driven by adaptability, insight, and long-term contribution.
4. **Reputation:** Trust earned over time. Clients seek you out. Colleagues respect and rely on you.

This is the real scorecard.

A Quick Recap

By now, the patterns are clear.

Rainmakers:

- Don't just respond to demand; they shape it, guiding conversations toward bigger, more meaningful opportunities.
- Care about more than targets; they are driven by purpose and the desire to create lasting impact.
- Show up consistently, not with noise but with focus, discipline, and intent.
- Bring a set of attributes that hold under pressure and become visible in how they think, act, and engage.
- Operate with discipline across four strategies: finding the right opportunities, creating value, building trust, and sustaining momentum through habit.

You've seen the pieces. Now the question becomes practical:

How will you put them to work?

The Rainmaker Blueprint

The canopy is the point where everything you've cultivated begins to bear fruit.

You've moved from context to capability, from foundation to execution. Now you are in the phase where results begin to show, where systems start to settle, and where your impact becomes visible to others.

But this is not the finish line.

Just as a canopy feeds the roots beneath it, the outcomes you create today strengthen the foundation for tomorrow. The fruit you produce—client transformation, firm reputation, personal growth—becomes the seed for what comes next.

The Rainmaker Blueprint is designed to help you make this system repeatable. It is a practical system for building sustained growth as an individual consultant, focused specifically on your role as a business developer.

Not as the leader of an account or a practice. But as a practitioner, someone who builds relationships, develops a distinctive position in the market, and cultivates a personal pipeline of opportunity.

Often in collaboration with others.

Sometimes leading from the front.

But always with a clear sense of ownership.

At its core, this approach is about originating and closing meaningful work consistently, deliberately, and over time.

It's not a quick fix. It's a way of working.

The blueprint is built on three steps:

1. **Assess** your current position.
2. **Advance** your ambition and practical next steps.
3. **Adjust** your review and reset cycle.

Simple in structure. Powerful in application.

Step 1—Assess My Current Position

Before growth becomes visible, roots go deep. This step is about clarity. Not judgment. Not comparison. Just a clear, honest view of where you stand today. Your baseline.

Capture it in a document across five areas:

1. Identity
2. Relationships
3. Opportunities
4. Attributes
5. Business development habits

Each area matters. Together, they form the foundation for everything that follows.

Your Identity What are you known for? What do you stand for? How do others see you? Your identity includes your brand, your purpose, your resilience, your ethics.

> **Tip:** Be honest. Revisit Part II Summary and answer the review questions. Don't overthink things; get down what comes to mind first and know that you will come back to parts of this work soon. And if you are unsure, take the view of what your colleagues or clients might think about you.

My Relationships Who matters to you in a professional sense? What relationships do you have that contribute to your professional success and standing? Do you have too few relationships? What people would you like to target and build a connection with?

Your relationships are a personal asset that encompasses:

- **Clients:** Sponsors, advocates, project directors, teams
- **Internal colleagues:** Those who help you win
- **External allies:** Partners, advisors, experts

The quality of your relationships determines the value of this asset. Be honest in your assessment.

> **Tip:** Rate the strength of each key client relationship you have or are targeting against the Five-Level Client Trust Model discussed in Chapter 19. Rate internal relationships with colleagues and external allies on a scale of strong, medium, and low.

My Client Opportunities What client projects are you working on?

Look at your pipeline:

- What opportunities have you identified in the short and medium term?
- Where did these opportunities come from?
- What is the probability of success?
- Does your pipeline give you line of sight to achieving your targets?
- What were your best projects in the past two years, and what made them work?
- Are you creating opportunities or responding to them?
- What is moving? What is stuck?

> **Tip:** Revisit Chapters 1 to 5 and 17 and answer the review questions at the end of the chapters. Categorize your opportunities by soil type and by source of opportunity, and identify if and where there might be opportunities to expand and strengthen your sales pipeline. Soon we will work on a plan to capture and work on those ideas.

My Attributes Where are you already strong? Where do you need to grow?

What skill do you need to develop?

Be specific.

You will recall in Chapter 11 we defined an *attribute* as an observable strength that meaningfully supports rainmaker performance and contributes to sustained success in high-stakes, client-facing environments.

Now is your opportunity to self-assess what sets you apart now and where there might be opportunities for growth and development. It is important to rate yourself against elite performers, not just good ones.

> **Tip:** Revisit the self assessment questions in the Part III Summary.

My Business Development Habits What do you actually do, consistently each day or week, to build relationships and win work? Not admin. Not process. Not irregular activity when it's quiet. Real habits. Real routines. Applied consistently.

If nothing comes to mind, then that's a signal for an action to work on.

If you've got some great habits, brilliant; share them with your colleagues.

> **Tip:** Habits are the small, specific things you do daily or weekly that contribute to building client relationships, originating deals, moving things your sales pipeline, and closing and winning work. Think of them like putting on your seatbelt when you get in a car, like brushing your teeth each morning, like sending a thank-you note in the immediate hours after every client meeting.

Step 2—**Advance** My Ambition and Practical Next Steps

Your self-assessment has provided you with a statement of your personal business development assets and provides the platform for your future growth.

If you are an experienced professional with a strong success record, your self-assessment may reveal a trigger for action with a client or a relationship or an opportunity to consider a reset of your career path. It can provide a refresher of what great looks like and remind you of the joy of consulting.

If you are an aspiring or new partner or managing director, your self-assessment may reveal many gaps and opportunities for development. This is understandable, as the evaluation is against the best in class. Your relationships may be at middle management level, your personal brand may not be strongly established, and your business development skills may be underdeveloped. Your challenge will be to find a structured and manageable way to progress, prioritizing the aspects that are most important to you.

The first step is to define what you want to achieve over the next two to three years.

Not abstract. Not vague. Grounded in reality. Built on your current position.

Then recognize this: Your progress will depend on two choices:

1. How much time you invest
2. How much support you accept

Rainmakers don't drift into growth.
They commit to it.

Make Space Rainmakers don't grow by chance. They invest consistently and deliberately, and they draw on the wisdom, expertise, capacity, and challenge of others.

Think about:

- **How much time you're willing to invest**

  How many extra hours can you realistically commit to your development, and where will those hours come from? Moving from a good-high performer to a rainmaker typically will require an additional four to six hours per week. Think of this as seasonal watering: a blend of structured learning and real-world application, spread across both personal and work time, including time spent strengthening and expanding relationships through delivery.

- **Auditing your calendar**

  How much of your time is currently spent on low-value activity rather than value-creating activity? Can some of it be automated using digital tools or AI agents, or delegated to others in your firm? Revisit the discussion on time management in Chapter 20 to recalibrate how you invest your time and energy.

- **Building your A Team support network**

  Surround yourself with the right people—for example, internal colleagues, external coaches and mentors, alumni, and others who will support your growth and challenge your thinking along the way.

  These activities are designed to create ongoing space for growth, not as a one-time exercise but as a consistent part of your weekly rhythm.

Work in 100-Day Sprints So, now that you have a realistic ambition, have allocated the time you need to take the next step, and put in place your A Team of support, it is time to capture your practical next-step actions.

We do this in 100-day sprints, so they become clear, focused, and achievable. And repeatable.

Follow the same structure as in Part I and aim for one to two actions in each of the five areas per 100-day sprint. Do just the ones that matter, not the nice-to-do actions.

Think of this step like pruning a tree to help it grow stronger and straighter. It is about making intentional choices about where you're headed and how you'll get there.

Prompts for Your First Sprint

Identity

- Would you buy from yourself? What makes you distinctive and sets you apart from your competitors? Capture this clearly in an updated articulation of your personal brand.
- Is your higher purpose deep and compelling, and do your clients know it? Do you feel proud sharing it? If not, refine what you developed earlier.
- Do you have a personal ethics statement (i.e., your clear red lines on what you will and won't do)? If not, consider documenting a short, thoughtful statement aligned with your firm's approach.

Relationships

- Be clear on which relationships you are accountable for growing and strengthening and which you are supporting alongside colleagues. If this is unclear, start here: Document them, and align with your team.
- Step back and assess both quality and quantity. How many relationships sit at Level 4 or 5 of the Five-Level Client Trust Model? Which need attention over the next 100 days? How many relationships could realistically become clients or sponsors within the next 12 months? Is that sufficient, on a weighted probability basis, to support your pipeline and revenue goals? If not, revisit the Consulting Opportunity Matrix in Chapter 17 to identify where to expand.
- Growth is faster and stronger in a forest than in a field. Seek out someone with experience, a rainmaker who can offer guidance, perspective, and challenge. The person can be someone inside your firm or outside it, local or global.
- From this review, identify three to four specific relationship actions to take over the next 100 days.

Client Opportunities

- Be clear on which opportunities you are accountable for progressing and closing and which you are supporting others on. Rainmaking is a team sport, but it works best when accountability is clear. If it isn't clear, document roles and responsibilities and align them with your colleagues.
- As with relationships, step back and assess your pipeline honestly. Assign a probability of winning and an expected conversion timeframe to each opportunity. What does this tell you? Is there a gap to your targets? If not, can you invest time now in building next year's pipeline or supporting colleagues?
- For your current opportunities, ask: Can they be strengthened to increase your probability of winning? Revisit Chapters 16 to 20 and, in particular, Chapter 18: "Creating Unmatched Value," and identify two to three ideas to elevate your highest-value pursuits.
- If your pipeline feels too thin—or too cluttered—return to the Part I Summary. Develop one bold idea to take to a client: a transformation that will leave a mark. This could become your flagship fruit, a pursuit worth focused attention. It will be a team effort, but one where your fingerprints are clear, from relationship building and deep client understanding through to origination, shaping, and proposal development.

Attributes

- Choose one attribute to focus on and elevate to an elite level over the next 100 days: for example, *Leveraging Firm Strengths for Growth*.
- Make your improvement action practical. Each week, connect with a new internal colleague who could support your next opportunity or deepen an existing relationship to explore a joint pursuit.

Habits Habits are built through small, consistent actions. Revisit Chapter 20 and decide what you can introduce—permanently—into your day or week to improve your performance.

Examples might include:

- **Monday:** During my morning coffee, I will send three messages to clients to set up meetings.
- **Tuesday:** Before regular hours, I will meet a colleague to progress a bold client idea.
- **Wednesday:** Before closing my laptop, I will send two relevant insights to clients or prospects.
- **Thursday:** In team stand-ups, I will introduce a 10-minute discussion to capture client issues, challenges, and emerging opportunities.
- **Friday:** Over coffee, I will review my pipeline, define next actions, and create space in my diary next week for thinking and relationship building.

Keep it simple. Keep it consistent.

Step 3—**Adjust** My Review and Reset Cycle

Growth is not constant. Even the strongest trees move through seasons, periods of expansion, consolidation, and renewal. Each phase plays a role in long-term strength.

Rainmakers understand this.

They don't just push forward relentlessly. They pause. They reflect. They learn.

Every 100 days, three times a year, take stock:

- What has shifted?
- What have you done, and what came from it?
- Where did you stretch or improve?

- Where did momentum build?
- Where did you fall short and why?
- What surprised you?
- What needs to change?
- Are you living your higher purpose?

Write it down. Talk it through with someone you trust. Use the review not as a critique but as a tool for alignment and growth.

Then reset. Refocus your energy. Refine your actions. Recommit to what matters.

This is the rhythm.

Final Thoughts

Following the three steps of the Rainmaker Blueprint is how you work now. Not in bursts of effort. Not by chance.

But with intent. With structure. With rhythm.

The canopy is not the destination. It is the beginning of regeneration. The fruit is not the reward. It is the fuel for what comes next.

And the rainmaker, like the tree, continues to grow, adapt, and flourish.

Season after season.

Let's begin again.

Conclusion

Becoming a Rainmaker: Your Journey Begins

It starts with a spark.

A conversation that lingers. A project that stretches you. A passing comment from a client or colleague that makes you pause and wonder, "*Could I do more?*"

Something shifted. Subtly, dramatically. But something inside you stirred. That's why you're here.

You didn't pick up this book for entertainment. You picked it up to grow. To unlock the next version of yourself: sharper, bolder, more intentional.

That's what rainmaking is all about.

A Journey of Depth and Discovery

This book has been a journey, not just through the world of consulting but through the inner world of growth, identity, and influence.

We began in the soil, beneath the rainmaker's tree, exploring the world we operate in: a fast-moving, high-stakes, trust-dependent one, where opportunities germinate quickly, compete fiercely for attention, and take root only when nurtured with insight, discipline, care, and, increasingly, intelligent use of data and technology.

We reached down into the roots of your mindset, purpose, and motivation. The unseen forces that anchor you when things get uncertain.

Then we built the trunk, the 12 core attributes that give a rainmaker strength, shape, and resilience. Attributes you can strengthen, shape, and stretch over time.

From there, we extended the branches, the four strategies that reach out into the world to build relationships, grow pipeline, and win the work that matters:

1. Hunting with precision
2. Creating unmatched value
3. Forging unshakeable trust
4. Mastering the routine of success

And finally we looked up to the canopy. Where opportunity blossoms. Where the fruit is found. Where identity becomes action.

Where habit becomes momentum. Where everything you've built starts to deliver returns for your clients, your firm, and your future.

This book is about what rainmakers do. But more than that, it's been a book about belief.

The belief that *you* can do this.

The Rainmaker Mindset

Before we part, let's return to the most crucial idea in this book.

Rainmakers believe they can shape the future.

That's the core mindset. They don't wait for work to arrive. They don't let the calendar dictate their value. They don't accept "busy" as a strategy.

They believe they can initiate. Influence. Open doors. Change the game. And so they do.

- They lead conversations, not just projects.
- They offer perspective, not just capability.
- They anticipate needs before they're spoken.
- They build connection *before* the transaction.
- They move when others hesitate.
- They follow up when others forget.
- They do the small things that add up to a significant impact.

Rainmakers don't hope for success. They build for it.

You Don't Need to Be Someone Else

Here's what most people misunderstand: Becoming a rainmaker isn't about becoming someone different. It's about becoming more of who you already are, but with purpose.

You don't need to shout louder, network harder, or "sell" in a way that makes you cringe.

- You need to act with more clarity.
- You need to show up more consistently.
- You need to connect more deeply.
- You need to be more selective with your time and more generous with your insights.

You already have the raw materials: intelligence, empathy, and drive. What this book gives you is structure. A frame to grow through. A model to return to when things get busy, noisy, or uncertain.

And, most important, a mindset to hold, especially when the results don't come immediately.

Because they *will* come.

The Patterns That Matter Most

If we strip it all back, what do rainmakers do differently?

They. . .

- Think bigger than the immediate task.
- Connect deeper than the transactional.
- Show up earlier in the buying cycle.
- Ask bolder questions.
- Prepare better.
- Follow up faster.
- Stay with relationships longer.
- Reflect often.
- Keep learning.
- Keep showing up.

These are not magic tricks. They're habits. Tiny, visible expressions of an invisible belief: *I have something valuable to offer. And I'm willing to put it to work.*

What Comes Next?

You've absorbed the thinking. You've reflected.

Now comes the real work. Not doing everything, just doing something. One thing. Repeatedly. Intentionally. Consistently.

So, revisit Chapter 21 and make the Rainmaker Blueprint your program.

Start small. Start soon. And stay with it. Over time, your system will take root. Your confidence will grow. Your reputation will compound.

And one day you'll look around and realize: Your pipeline is healthy. Your name is being mentioned. Your clients are calling *you*. Your work aligns with your ambitions.

You're not chasing. You're shaping. You're not surviving. You're leading. You're not hoping. You're making it happen.

Because you are a rainmaker.

A Final Invitation

Rainmaking isn't about being the loudest voice in the room. It's about being the clearest. It's not about closing deals. It's about creating possibilities.

It's not about charisma. It's about consistency. And it's not about where you start. It's about the choice you make next.

So, choose.

- Choose to focus.
- Choose to commit.
- Choose to show up for your clients, your practice, and yourself.
- Choose to lead.

You don't need permission. The blueprint is yours. The tree has taken shape.

Now it's time to grow upward, outward, and onward.

Go make rain.

Appendix

RFPs: Playing a Game Most Get Wrong

In most industries, the request for proposal (RFP) has become the default method for hiring consultants. What started in government and heavily regulated sectors has steadily moved into banks, utilities, retailers, tech companies, and more. Boards and executives want transparency. Procurement teams want comparability and defensible decisions.

The machinery around RFPs has become far more sophisticated. Documents are tightly structured. Timelines are rigid. Submissions are scored, ranked, and sometimes reviewed by software before anyone on the client team has even read a word. It's not unusual for AI tools to scan responses for gaps, verify claims, and check alignment with a long list of criteria before a panel sits down to discuss them.

On the surface, the process can look like highly rational: clear rules, set questions, formal scoring. Underneath, the familiar human realities remain: relationships, trust, risk appetite, and the stories people tell themselves about who they are hiring and why.

Most consultants treat an RFP as an exam: Read the questions carefully, fill in all the boxes, attach the CVs, and hope that the correct answer equals a win.

That's not how rainmakers think about it. They know you rarely win merely by responding. You win by shaping.

Should We Even Play?

Before rainmakers write a single line, they pause and ask a different set of questions. They are not admiring the size of the opportunity or the impressiveness of the client logo on their slide deck. They are asking, almost bluntly:

- Have we actually shaped the thinking behind this opportunity, or are we being invited in late to decorate someone else's design?
- Is there something we can bring that genuinely changes the outcome for this client, not just another version of what others will say?
- Do we really have the people, time, and headspace to produce our best work here, or would we be forcing it?
- Does this piece of work strengthen the story we want to be known for in the market, or does it drag us sideways?
- If we win, will this feel like a good decision for both us and the client six months in, or will it turn into a grind?

If too many of those answers feel like a "no" or even a nervous "maybe," rainmakers don't chase the opportunity. They move on and free up energy for work that fits.

Walking away from an RFP is hard for many consultants. It feels like saying no to revenue. Rainmakers see it differently. They are saying yes to focus.

When the answers line up, when they know the client, have shaped the conversation, can bring something distinctive, and have the capacity to do the job properly, then rainmakers lean in. And when they lean in, they treat the RFP as a stage on which to lead, not a form to complete.

Understanding What's Really Going On

Rainmakers don't start with the client's RFP document. They begin with the client's world. They look beyond the document to understand why this RFP exists at all. What has changed? Who is under pressure?

What's happening in the boardroom? What's the bigger story around this piece of work?

Research usually involves a mix of things: reviewing public information, listening to earnings calls, talking to people in their network, and reading between the lines of past conversations. Increasingly, it also involves modern tools that can pull together external data in ways that were not possible a few years ago. But the point isn't the technology; it's the curiosity.

One highly successful partner responding to a global logistics RFP didn't just skim the questions. She spoke to former executives, analyzed analyst commentary, and reached out to a handful of employees she knew within the organization. By the time she sat down to draft the proposal, she had a much clearer view of what the leadership team actually cared about and how this project fit into the bigger picture.

Her proposal opened with three insights that were nowhere in the RFP. She reframed the work as a growth opportunity, not just a cost or efficiency exercise. The client noticed immediately and said, "You seem to understand our world better than the others."

Another consultant, reading the same document, followed the structure and restated the requirements. The client described that response as "fine, but generic."

Both had access to the same RFP. Only one made the effort to understand what was really going on behind it.

Qualifying with a Cooler Head

Many firms still have a culture where every RFP feels like an opportunity to be chased. That's how teams end up exhausted, writing late-night proposals for work they never had a realistic chance of winning.

Rainmakers qualify differently. They look at relationship strength, strategic fit, risk, likely margin, and whether they can genuinely be distinctive. Increasingly, they also draw on better data from their own firm: win–loss history, where they have performed strongly and where they have not, and the typical conditions under which they do best.

One senior partner, Priya, used this approach when her firm was invited to pitch for a significant government engagement. On paper, the work was attractive and the agency prestigious. A more traditional mindset would have said, "We must go for this."

The analysis told a different story. Her firm had limited experience in that specific niche. There was a strong incumbent. The panel composition suggested the competitor would have the edge. Rather than pretend otherwise, Priya declined to bid. Instead, she offered the client a small, focused piece of work in an adjacent area where her team had deep experience. That project led to a longer-term relationship, outside the RFP channel.

Another consultant, Carl, never stopped to ask these questions. He put his hand up for almost every RFP—12 proposals in one quarter, one small win, and an exhausted team.

One approach looks like unproductive and random hustle. The other looks like strategic judgment.

Writing to Lead, Not to Comply

Once rainmakers commit to an RFP, the proposal is not treated as a "response pack." It is seen as an opportunity to demonstrate how they think and how they will work with the client.

This approach shows up in a few ways:

- The opening pages discuss the client's world before turning to their own firm.
- The problem is described in language that feels familiar to the client, but with added clarity.
- There is a straightforward, simple narrative: where the client is now, where they could get to, and the path between the two.

The tone is confident but not arrogant. The writing is plain, direct, and free of jargon. The structure makes it easy for a time-poor executive to see what matters without wading through unnecessary detail.

One rainmaker responding to an extensive RFP from a government investment authority noticed the brief focused almost entirely on financial optimization. The question behind the question was *"How do we tidy up these distressed assets?"*

Rather than align with that framing, he included a short section titled "An Alternative View." In it, he suggested another way of thinking: What if these assets were treated as long-term strategic platforms, supported through different forms of collaboration and funding? He drew on relevant examples and kept the tone respectful, signaling that he was not dismissing the original brief but building on it.

It was a risk, but a considered one. When the evaluation panel discussed the proposals, this section became a focal point. It didn't just answer the question; it widened the conversation. His firm won the work.

Showing Credibility Without Dumping Everything You've Ever Done

Clients do need reassurance that you can deliver. But they do not need every case study your firm has produced in the past 15 years.

Rainmakers choose proof carefully. They select examples that mirror the client's situation: a similar sector, a related problem, or a comparable level of complexity. They focus on what changed: how the client was better off at the end, not just on the activities completed. When possible, they include work done for that same organization, written in the client's own language.

They present a small number of strong examples with precise results rather than a long list of loosely related projects. That's often more convincing.

Lisa added three brief case studies to her proposal, each one trimmed to the essentials and tied directly to the RFP's goals. One drew on an earlier project with the same organization and used the client's own language and success measures. Later the client mentioned that those few pages were what convinced them that her team genuinely understood their needs.

By contrast, Michael attached a generic, lengthy capability document that wandered across service lines and geographies. Most of it had nothing to do with the problem at hand. The client admitted they stopped reading.

Making It Easy to Understand and Easy to Say Yes

A surprising number of proposals fail not because the ideas are weak but because they are hard to follow. Rainmakers pay attention to the experience of reading the document. They assume that the panel may be tired, under time pressure, or flicking between multiple submissions on a screen.

So, they ask themselves:

- Can someone get the main story in a few minutes?
- Are the key choices and trade-offs clear?
- Is the language simple enough for nonspecialists to follow?

They also look for small ways to add value beyond what is requested. This might be a simple framework to help the client think about the issue differently, a short diagnostic, or a low-risk, low-cost starting point that lets the client test the relationship.

When Helena turned in a proposal of roughly 15 pages—lean, visual, and written in plain language—the evaluation panel remarked that it was the only one they could grasp right away and genuinely enjoy reading. It stood out because it wasn't trying to win points through sheer length.

Proposals Are a Team Sport

Despite the myth of the heroic rainmaker working alone, the reality is that strong proposals usually come from a team effort.

Rainmakers pull in delivery leads, commercial people, subject matter experts, and sometimes designers or communications specialists. They explain the client's context, not just the mechanics of the RFP. They make sure everyone understands why the client cares about this work and how it fits into a bigger agenda.

They also put some gentle structure around the collaboration: who is writing which parts, who is reviewing, and how it will all be brought together so that the final document reads as one voice, not a patchwork.

Naomi, who was running a key pursuit, started by holding two working sessions with her team. In the first, she laid out what she understood about the client, the people involved, and the real pressures behind the request. In the second, the group hashed out the storyline they wanted to put forward. Once those conversations were out of the way, the writing moved faster, and the proposal came together with a clear through-line.

Ben handled his bid very differently. He gathered bits from five colleagues and patched them together a couple of nights before the deadline. The client noticed the mixed tone and asked in the clarification meeting, "Who would actually be leading this?" The answer didn't do much to reassure them.

Pricing as Part of the Story, Not the Last Page

Price matters. It always will. But the way price is framed can either support the message or undermine it.

Rainmakers don't treat the pricing table as an administrative afterthought. They treat it as part of the value story.

They explain how the price links to scope, outcomes, and risk. They use structures that make sense from the client's point of view:

phases, options, or tiers that make trade-offs visible. They are transparent where they can be and clear about where they have flex and where they do not.

In one bid, Robert put forward three price options: a tightly defined version of the work, a bigger and more exploratory version, and a third that added capability building for the client's team. Each option reflected a different level of value and risk sharing. The client's questions shifted from "Can we afford this?" to "How bold do we want to be?"

Charlotte, by contrast, offered a single figure and described it simply as the panel rate. That line of discussion more or less stopped there.

Facing Concerns Before They Become Objections

Every meaningful project carries risk. Timelines slip. Data isn't ready when you need it. Sponsors change.

Rainmakers know these realities and assume their clients do too. Rather than pretending otherwise, they put potential issues on the table early and show how they will manage them. That might mean calling out dependencies, describing contingency plans, or using experience to illustrate how they respond when things don't go exactly as planned.

One partner, Anthony, considered what could reasonably worry the client: whether they had enough internal capacity to support the work, whether key stakeholders would engage, and whether the ambitious timeline was realistic. He addressed each concern directly in a short section on risks and mitigations, using examples from prior projects to show how he had handled similar situations.

The client later remarked that this approach gave them more confidence than the optimistic tone of some of the other proposals.

Working Smarter on the Mechanics

There is a large amount of repeatable work in every RFP: maintaining consistent bios, keeping service descriptions up to date, formatting, and ensuring compliance with all the minor, easily overlooked requirements.

Rainmakers don't spend heroic amounts of time redoing this from scratch. They encourage their firms to invest in robust internal systems so that much of this information can be reused, refined, and improved over time.

The goal is not to make the whole process mechanical. It is to clear away as much low-value strain as possible so the team can concentrate on the thinking, shaping, and writing that actually influences the client.

When Tanya led a pursuit using a well-organized internal library and standard templates, her team spent far more time tailoring and less time hunting for old documents. They submitted early and with less stress.

Gary, managing his proposal using a combination of shared drives and team emails, struggled with conflicting edits, broken formatting, and last-minute panic.

What Happens After You Hit "Submit"

Many consultants treat the moment a proposal is lodged as the end of the process. For rainmakers, it is only the end of one chapter.

They follow up thoughtfully: a short message of thanks, an offer to walk through the proposal, a willingness to clarify anything that might not have been clear in writing. They stay present without being pushy.

If they lose, they still ask for feedback. If they win, they look for early ways to deliver some quick value and confirm that the client made a good choice. Either way, they are investing in a relationship, not just a win-loss record.

Andre, after submitting his proposal, wrote a short note to each key stakeholder acknowledging their time and connecting back to specific points they had raised in conversations. He also offered a brief, no-fee follow-up session to explore a future issue that had come up in passing. The client took up the offer and later commented that this professionalism and initiative made a strong impression.

Sophie, by contrast, submitted her response and waited. Two weeks later, she assumed the opportunity was lost and moved on.

Another firm, which stayed engaged and continued to bring small, relevant ideas, ended up winning the work.

Shape the Game or Step Away

RFPs are not going away. In many organizations, they are now tightly embedded in governance and procurement processes.

They can be seen as a bureaucratic burden or as a structured moment when clients are actively seeking someone they can trust to help them solve real problems.

Rainmakers choose the latter. They decide carefully which games are worth playing. When they do play, they treat the RFP as a tool to lead, not a hoop to jump through. They bring perspective, clarity, and a sense of partnership into a process that can easily feel mechanical and transactional.

They know that a proposal is never just a document. It is a demonstration of how they think, how they communicate, and how they will show up when the work begins.

If you have to work in a world of RFPs, you could play the game well. Decide where you can be truly distinctive. Shape the brief whenever you can. Write in a way that makes life easier for the people on the other side. Be honest about risks and price with a straight face. And don't disappear once you've pressed send.

That is how you turn a formal process into an opening, not a cage. And that is how you give yourself a far better chance of making it rain.

Acknowledgments

This book rests on the shoulders of thousands of people we've had the privilege to work with over the decades. Every insight, story, and lesson shared in these pages has its roots in the experiences we've had alongside remarkable clients, colleagues, mentors, and sometimes even competitors across every corner of the world. To all those we've learned from, coached, served, and sparred with, our heartfelt thanks. You've shaped not only this book but the careers and characters of its authors.

Second, our gratitude extends to the many people who generously contributed their time, reflections, and stories during the writing process. We reached out to dozens of former colleagues, clients, and competitors, asking them to share their stories and what they had seen and learned from the best in our profession. Without exception, they responded openly and honestly. Some of their stories are captured here while many more live on through our workshops, coaching programs, and conversations with consulting leaders around the world.

Many people pushed our thinking. They questioned our ideas, picked at our assumptions, and brought in viewpoints we hadn't thought about. A few of those conversations were tough, but they sharpened our arguments and helped the book land in a more practical, readable, and better place. Several also offered excellent insights and lessons into the writing and publishing processes, which have kept us motivated throughout each stage of the book's development. We are deeply grateful for those conversations.

Third, we owe enormous respect to the researchers, academics, and authors whose pioneering work underpins much of modern consulting and behavioral science. Their insights have informed and inspired us for years. We hope we have done justice to their ideas by interpreting and applying them here. Readers seeking to explore further will find a list of sources and references in the Notes section at the end of the book.

Fourth, we would like to thank the team at Wiley for their support, professionalism, and belief in this project, which made it possible. From the first conversation through to publication, the team's guidance has helped us turn an idea into something tangible and enduring. We are especially grateful to Richard Narramore, Michael Joseph Das, Kezia Endsley, Debra Manette, Trinity Crompton, Raven Buckler, and the Wiley Graphics team, whose editorial insight, patience, and encouragement made this journey smoother and often more enjoyable than we could have hoped.

Finally, to our families. To our amazing partners, Kristy and Sue, and to our children, you have been the quiet strength behind everything we do. Your love, patience, and belief have sustained us through long days, late nights, and countless drafts. At the height of our executive and consulting careers, we traveled and were away from home more than any family should be asked to endure. Yet you never stopped cheering us on. This book, in so many ways, is dedicated to you.

About the Authors

Neil Plumridge has spent more than 30 years helping leaders and organizations find clarity, growth, and purpose in complex, changing environments. His consulting career has taken him to more than 20 countries, working with some of the world's largest corporations and public institutions to deliver transformation and results that last.

A former senior partner at Kearney, EY, and PwC, Neil served on both local and global leadership teams, helping to shape firm strategy, build high-performing teams, and coach hundreds of partners and directors to operate at the highest levels. Across boardrooms, client sites, and long flights between them, he learned that enduring consulting success is built not just on ideas but on the daily habits that sustain trust, growth, and client relationships over time.

Neil studied in Australia at Swinburne University of Technology and in the United States at Emory University and Harvard Business School, where his curiosity for leadership, behavioral science, and performance first began to intersect.

Today he divides his time between advising executives and running professional development programs for consulting firms around the world. Known for his grounded storytelling and practical wisdom, Neil's work blends strategy with reality, helping consultants and leaders alike create bigger impact, one deliberate habit at a time.

He lives in Melbourne, Australia, with his family, continues to travel frequently, and reminds others that great consulting starts not with answers or your capability but with client context and understanding.

Robert Nason's career spans 25 years in management consulting and 16 years in senior corporate roles. He has worked as a chairman, board member, CEO, and executive in the United States, Southeast Asia, and Australia. Robert's global consulting career includes national, international, and global leadership roles at KPMG, PwC, and Kearney.

After leaving school at the age of 16, Robert achieved academic and business success through a commitment to lifelong learning. Along the way he built successful consulting practices and became a trusted advisor to industry leaders on how to meet the challenges of disruption, technological change, and global competition. Robert has a particular fascination for identifying the most effective leadership behaviors and actions during "moments that matter"—the key action and decision points that impact strategic direction and transformational change.

Robert is a passionate believer in the skills and processes of management consulting and the techniques that provide value to clients seeking results. He remains actively involved in business affairs and the professional development of consulting staff. Robert has six children and five grandchildren and currently lives with his family in Sydney, Australia.

Notes

Introduction

1. ConsultingPoint. "McKinsey & Company Launches Internal Generative AI Tool Lilli." August 28, 2023. https://www.consultingpoint.com/news/2023/8/31/mckinsey-amp-company-launches-internal-generative-ai-tool-lilli.
2. Marr, Bernard. "How BCG Is Revolutionizing Consulting with AI: A Case Study." *Forbes*, July 10, 2024. https://www.forbes.com/sites/bernardmarr/2024/07/10/how-bcg-is-revolutionizing-consulting-with-ai-a-case-study/.
3. Fox Business. "Goldman Sachs Announces Firmwide Launch of AI Assistant." June 23, 2025. https://www.foxbusiness.com/markets/goldman-sachs-announces-firmwide-launch-ai-assistant.

Chapter 1

1. Joe O'Mahoney, *Management Consultancy* (Oxford: Oxford University Press, 2010).

Chapter 2

1. John S. Mbiti, *African Religions and Philosophy*, 2nd ed. (Portsmouth, NH: Heinemann, 1990).
2. George A. Steiner and Arthur D. Little, *The Business of Innovation* (Boston: Harvard Business School Press, 1997).

3. Pauline Graham, ed., *Mary Parker Follett: Prophet of Management—A Celebration of Writings from the 1920s* (Boston: Harvard Business School Press, 1995).
4. Mary P. Follett, *Dynamic Administration: The Collected Papers of Mary Parker Follett*. Edited by Henry C. Metcalf and Lyndall Urwick (New York: Harper & Brothers, 1942).

Chapter 3

1. Accenture alone employed 730,000 people of as 2024. Accenture, *Quarterly Market Release Statement (Fact Sheet)*, Q2 2025. www.statista.com/topics/8112/global-consulting-services-industry/. IBIS World. *Global Management Consultants—Market Size (2005–2031)*. November 2024.

Chapter 5

1. Kurt T. Dirks and Bart de Jong, "Trust Within the Workplace: A Review of Two Waves of Research and a Glimpse of the Third," *Annual Review of Organizational Psychology and Organizational Behavior* 9 (2022): 247–276. doi.org/10.1146/annurev-orgpsych-012420-083025
2. Daniel Kahneman and Amos Tversky. "Prospect Theory: An Analysis of Decision Under Risk," *Econometrica* 47, no. 2 (1979): 263–291. 10.2307/1914185
3. Dan Ariely, *Predictably Irrational: The Hidden Forces That Shape Our Decisions* (New York: HarperCollins, 2008).
4. Donald C. Hambrick and Phyllis A. Mason, "Upper Echelons: The Organization as a Reflection of Its Top Managers," *Academy of Management Review* 9, no. 2 (1984): 193–206. 10.2307/258434
5. Kahneman and Tversky, "Prospect Theory."
6. Rachel Botsman, *Who Can You Trust? How Technology Brought Us Together and Why It Could Drive Us Apart* (New York: PublicAffairs, 2017).
7. Greg Kelly, Lisa Harkness, and Steve Reis, "Agents for Growth: Turning AI Promise into Impact," McKinsey & Company, November 3, 2025. www.mckinsey.com/capabilities/growth-marketing-and-sales/our-insights/agents-for-growth-turning-ai-promise-into-impact
8. Richard H. Thaler and Cass R. Sunstein, *Nudge: Improving Decisions About Health, Wealth, and Happiness* (New Haven, CT: Yale University Press, 2008).

Chapter 7

1. Daniel Morales, Elizabeth Ledet, and Lauren Rebagliati. 2024. Measuring Leadership: Inspiration and Accountability," McKinsey & Company, September 17, 2024. www.mckinsey.com/featured-insights/people-in-progress/measuring-leadership-inspiration-and-accountability
2. Tasha Eurich, *Insight: The Surprising Truth About How Others See Us, How We See Ourselves, and Why the Answers Matter More than We Think* (New York: Currency, 2018).
3. David Zes and Dana Landis, *A Better Return on Self-Awareness* (Los Angeles: Korn Ferry Institute, 2013).
4. Matt Gavin, "Leadership Self-Assessment: How Effective Are You?" Harvard Business School Online, November 21, 2019. https://online.hbs.edu/blog/post/leadership-self-assessment. Alan Zeller, Anil Gaba, and Ludo Van der Heyden, "Intelligent Boards Know Their Limits," INSEAD Knowledge, February 24, 2017. https://knowledge.insead.edu/leadership-organisations/intelligent-boards-know-their-limits
5. Sonia K. Kang, Jacob B. Hirsh, and Alison L. Chasteen, "Your Mistakes Are Mine: Self-Other Overlap Predicts Neural Response to Observed Errors," *Journal of Experimental Social Psychology* 46, no. 1 (2010): 229–232. doi.org/10.1016/j.jesp.2009.09.012
6. Niklas K. Steffens, Nicholas Wolniec, Tyler G. Okimoto, Frank Mols, S. Slexander Haslam, and Adam A. Kay, "Knowing Me, Knowing Us: Personal and Collective Self-Awareness as Predictors of Perceived Authentic Leadership and Leader Endorsement," *Leadership Quarterly* 32, no. 6 (2021). www.sciencedirect.com/science/article/abs/pii/S1048984321000047

Chapter 8

1. Alex Liu, 2022 *Joy Works: Empowering Teams in the New Era of Work* (Hoboken, NJ: John Wiley & Sons, 2022).
2. William Damon, *The Path to Purpose: Helping Our Children Find Their Calling in Life* (New York: Free Press, 2008).
3. Felipe A. Csaszar, Harsh Ketkar, and Hyunjin Kim, "Artificial Intelligence and Strategic Decision-Making: Evidence from Entrepreneurs and Investors," *Strategy Science* 10, no. 3 (2024): 345–367. https://d30i16bbj53pdg.cloudfront.net/wp-content/uploads/2024/08/Artificial-Intelligence-and-Strategic-Decision-Making.pdf

4. Amy Wrzesniewski, Clark McCauley, Paul Rozin, and Barry Schwartz, "Jobs, Careers, and Callings: People's Relations to Their Work." *Journal of Research in Personality* 31, no. 1 (1997): 21–33. doi.org/10.1006/jrpe.1997.2162

Chapter 9

1. Edward L. Deci, Richard J. Vallerand, Louise G. Pelletier, and Richard M. Ryan, "Motivation and Education: The Self-Determination Perspective." *Educational Psychologist* 26, no. 3–4 (1991): 325–346. https://selfdeterminationtheory.org/SDT/documents/1991_DeciVallerandPelletierRyan_EP.pdf
2. Ann S. Masten and Mary-Gabrielle J. Reed, "Resilience in Development." In *Handbook of Positive Psychology*, edited by C. R. Snyder and Shane J. Lopez, 74–88 (Oxford: Oxford University Press, 2002).

Chapter 10

1. Dale T. Miller and Daniel A. Effron. "Psychological License: When It Is Needed and How It Functions," *Advances in Experimental Social Psychology* 43 (2010): 115–155.
2. Frederieke Scheenstra, "Foundations and Challenges: Ethics in Consulting," *Management Consulting Journal* 7, no. 2 (2024): 74–79. doi.org/10.2478/mcj-2024-0008.

Chapter 11

1. Daniel Goleman, *Working with Emotional Intelligence* (New York: Bantam Books, 1998).
2. Kevin Cashman, "On Becoming a Warren Bennis Leader," *Briefings21: In Review* (2025): 68. www.scribd.com/document/400088404/Briefings21-InReview-p68
3. Michael H. Kernis, "Self-Esteem and Authenticity: Implications for Well-Being and Interpersonal Functioning." In *Advances in Experimental Social Psychology*, Vol. 35, edited by Mark P. Zanna, 1–62 (San Diego: Academic Press, 2003).

Chapter 12

1. Andris A. Zoltners, Prabhakant Sinha, and Sally E. Lorimer, *Building a Winning Sales Force: Powerful Strategies for Driving High Performance* (New York: AMACOM, 2009).

Chapter 13

1. John Sweller, "Cognitive Load During Problem Solving: Effects on Learning," *Cognitive Science* 12, no. 2 (1988): 257–285. doi.org/10.1207/s15516709cog1202_4

Chapter 15

1. Carol S. Dweck, *Mindset: The New Psychology of Success* (New York: Random House, 2006).

Chapter 17

1. Igor H. Ansoff, *Corporate Strategy*, rev. ed. (London: Penguin Books, 1987).
2. Rachana Pallikaraki, "B2B Sales Statistics 2026: Benchmarks & What's Actually Working," Martal Group, February 5, 2026. https://martal.ca/b2b-sales-benchmarks/
3. Alyssa Merwin, "B2B Selling Is in Trouble. Deep Sales Is the Answer," *Harvard Business Review*, September 20, 2022. Sponsor content from LinkedIn. https://hbr.org/sponsored/2022/09/b2b-selling-is-in-trouble-deep-sales-is-the-answer
4. Neil Rackham and John DeVincentis, *Rethinking the Sales Force: Redefining Selling to Create and Capture Customer Value* (New York: McGraw-Hill, 1999).
5. Johan Arndt, "Role of Product-Related Conversations in the Diffusion of a New Product," *Journal of Marketing Research* 4, no. 3 (1967): 291–295. doi.org/10.2307/3149462
6. Gabie Caballero, "What is BANT? The Way to Qualify Better Leads and Close More Deals," Salesforce: The 360 Blog, September 3, 2024. www.salesforce.com/blog/what-is-bant-lead-generation/

7. Erin Hueffner, "An Essential Guide to Using the MEDDIC Sales Framework." Salesforce: The 360 Blog, October 22, 2024. www.salesforce.com/blog/meddic-sales/
8. Neil Rackham, *SPIN Selling* (New York: McGraw-Hill, 1988).
9. WeFlow, "CHAMP Sales Methodology: 23 Qualification Questions and Examples," updated May 4, 2026. www.getweflow.com/blog/champ-sales

Chapter 18

1. Anantharanthan Parasuraman, Valarie A. Zeithaml, and Leonard L. Berry. "A Conceptual Model of Service Quality and Its Implications for Future Research," *Journal of Marketing* 49, no. 4 (1985): 41–50. doi.org/10.2307/1251430
2. Allan R. Cohen and David L. Bradford, *Influence Without Authority*, 2nd ed. (New York: John Wiley & Sons, 2005).
3. Donald R. Lichtenstein, Nancy M. Ridgway, and Richard G. Netemeyer, "The Role of Perceived Value in the Relationship Between Trust and Performance in Business Relationships," *Journal of Business Research* 69, no. 10 (2016): 4565–4572.
4. Berend Wierenga, Ralf van der Lans, Ingrid Geyskens, and Peter C. Verhoef, "Customer Engagement as a Multidimensional Construct: Empirical Generalizations from Three Data Sets," *Journal of Marketing Research* 57, no. 4 (2020): 659–674.
5. V. Kumar, Zameeruddin Rahman, and Abdul A. Kazmi. "The Impact of Customer Engagement and Customer Value on Customer Loyalty: Evidence from the Telecom Industry." *Industrial Marketing Management* 82 (2019): 86–97.
6. Wierenga et al., "Customer Insight Generation in Data-Rich Environments: Managerial and Organizational Challenges."
7. Kent Grayson and Radan Martinec, "Consumer Perceptions of Iconicity and Indexicality and Their Influence on Assessments of Authentic Market Offerings," *Journal of Consumer Research* 31, no. 2 (2004): 296–312. doi.org/10.1086/422109
8. Parasuraman et al., "A Conceptual Model of Service Quality and Its Implications for Future Research."
9. Katherine N. Lemon, Roland T. Rust, and Valarie A. Zeithaml, "What Drives Customer Equity?" *Marketing Management* 10, no. 1 (2001): 20–25. www.researchgate.net/publication/284404248_What_drives_customer_equity

10. James C. Anderson, James A. Narus, and Wouter van Rossum, "Customer Value Propositions in Business Markets," *Harvard Business Review* 84, no. 3 (2006): 90–99. https://hbr.org/2006/03/customer-value-propositions-in-business-markets
11. Joseph P. Cannon and William D. Perreault Jr., "Buyer–Seller Relationships in Business Markets," *Journal of Marketing Research* 36, no. 4 (1999): 439–460. DOI:10.2307/3151999
12. Sarah Schnitker. "7 Strategies to Make Decisions with Clarity and Confidence," *Psychology Today*, September 22, 2021. www.psychologytoday.com/au/blog/the-path-to-passionate-happiness/202109/7-strategies-to-make-decisions-with-clarity-and

Chapter 19

1. Roger C. Mayer, James H. Davis, and F. David Schoorman, "An Integrative Model of Organizational Trust," *Academy of Management Review* 20, no. 3 (1995): 709–734. doi.org/10.2307/258792
2. David H. Maister, Charles H. Green, and Robert M. Galford, *The Trusted Advisor* (New York: Free Press, 2000), p. 712.
3. Zaheer, Akbar, Bernard Campbell, and Deanne N. Den Hartog. "Trusting as a 'Leap of Faith': Trust-Building Practices in Client–Consultant Relationships," *Industrial Marketing Management* 47 (2015): 92–105.
4. Mayer et al., "An Integrative Model of Organizational Trust."
5. Kurt T. Dirks and Donald L. Ferrin, "The Role of Trust in Organizational Settings," *Organization Science* 12, no. 4 (2001): 450–467.
6. Elayne M. Whitener, Sue E. Brodt, Ann L. Korsgaard, and John M. Werner. "Managers as Initiators of Trust: An Exchange Relationship Framework for Understanding Managerial Trustworthiness," *Academy of Management Review* 23, no. 3 (1998): 513–530.
7. Geert Hofstede, *Culture's Consequences: International Differences in Work-Related Values* (Beverly Hills, CA: Sage, 1980).
8. Francis Fukuyama, *Trust: The Social Virtues and the Creation of Prosperity* (New York: Free Press, 1995).
9. Fons Trompenaars and Charles Hampden-Turner, *Riding the Waves of Culture: Understanding Diversity in Global Business*, 2nd ed. (New York: McGraw-Hill, 1998).

Chapter 20

1. Ann M. Graybiel and Scott T. Grafton, "The Striatum: Where Skills and Habits Meet," *Cold Spring Harbor Perspectives in Biology* 7 (2015), a021691. https://cshperspectives.cshlp.org/content/7/8/a021691.full cshperspect
2. Phillippa Lally, Cornelia H. M. Van Jaarsveld, Henry W. W. Potts, and Jane Wardle, "How Are Habits Formed: Modelling Habit Formation in the Real World," *European Journal of Social Psychology* 40, no. 6 (2009): 998–1009. doi.org/10.1002/ejsp.674
3. B. J. Fogg, *Tiny Habits: The Small Changes That Change Everything* (New York: HarperCollins, 2020).
4. James Clear, *Atomic Habits: An Easy & Proven Way to Build Good Habits & Break Bad Ones* (New York: Avery, 2018).
5. Mason Currey, *Daily Rituals: How Artists Work* (New York: Alfred A. Knopf, 2013).
6. Wendy Wood and David T. Neal, "A New Look at Habits and the Habit–Goal Interface," *Psychological Review* 114, no. 4 (2007): 843–863. doi.org/10.1037/0033-295X.114.4.843
7. Microsoft Build 2026, *Copilot in Dynamics 365 Sales Overview*, updated April 8, 2026. https://learn.microsoft.com/en-us/dynamics365/sales/copilot-overview
8. Google, *Google AI for Sales Teams*, n.d. https://workspace.google.com/solutions/ai/sales

Index

S